Maryland Trout Fishing

The Stocked and Wild Rivers, Streams, Lakes and Ponds

By Steve Moore

Dedication

To the Maryland Department of Natural Resources for answering a thousand questions patiently and thoroughly.

To the members of the Maryland, Potomac-Patuxent and Northern Virginia Chapters of Trout Unlimited, Potomac Valley Fly Fishers, and the Annapolis Chapter of the Free State Fly Fishers who reviewed the book and provided targeted comments to improve it.

Special thanks to Denis E. LaCroix and Tom Starrs for their thorough review and suggestions that made the book a better reference.

Published by Calibrated Consulting, Inc
ISBN: 978-09823962-8-5 (0982396287)
Feedback: feedback@catchguide.com

Cover photo of Middle Fork by Chris Moore

Other CatchGuide books by Steve Moore:

Wade Fishing the Rappahannock River of Virginia
Smallmouth Bass and Shad

Wade Fishing the Rapidan River of Virginia
From Smallmouth Bass to Trout
The Confluence to Skyline Drive

Wade and Shoreline Fishing the Potomac River for Smallmouth Bass
Chain Bridge to Harpers Ferry

Trout and Smallmouth Fishing on the North Branch of the Potomac
A Western Maryland River

Steve Moore gets lucky.

Steve is an avid, hard-core, terminally addicted fisherman. He was ruined for life when his father introduced him to the sport at the age of 7 while living in Norway as a result of military duty. Chasing trout on mountain streams left an enduring imprint and drive to find new water... something that tortures Steve to this day.

Of course, this was preordained since Steve's father was fishing in a local bass tournament on the morning Steve was born. His father claims to have had permission to go, but Steve's mother does not remember the actual facts matching that story. The point that he won a nice Shakespeare reel did nothing to mitigate the trouble he was in upon his return.

Table of Contents

Introduction

To catch fish, you need to know where to fish.

When I committed to writing this book, I did not fully appreciate the challenge. Having fished in Maryland extensively, I assumed that I had been to most places and could bang this out in no time. Boy, was I wrong! As I did my research, I realized that my years of fishing had merely scratched the surface given the extensive opportunities available across the State. In the process of visiting 100% of the stocked trout water as well as the well-known wild streams, I discovered Maryland is an even more fantastic trout fishing destination than I had imagined. While the western counties, Garrett and Allegany, have the monopoly on traditional big trout water, a Trout Unlimited Top 100 fishing destination, the Gunpowder Falls River (aka "the Gunpowder"), stretches its 7.32 productive miles within an easy drive of Baltimore. Additional jewels sparkle throughout the State, polished by the surrounding protective buffer of State or local parks.

In Maryland, the trout season kicks off with the stocking activity in early October and concludes in June when the water in most places warms to the point of trout mortality. Despite that, tailwaters and high mountain streams provide cold water for a trout fix in the middle of the hottest summer for those who become bored chasing bass. Much of the credit for the success of the trout program must be laid at the doorstep of the Maryland Department of Natural Resources (DNR). Their long-term view created a vibrant fishery supported by an aggressive hatchery program that grows thousands of fish to feed the trout addiction of Maryland's anglers. Even though the weather and the terrain are optimum in the far west, the DNR does not exclude any part of the State from the trout program. This means that even the Eastern Shore receives a healthy dose of trout with over 3,400 stocked. Farther north and east, Deer Creek, near the Delaware border and over 150 miles from the pristine western mountains, was the second most heavily stocked location in the Spring of 2011, receiving 8,675 fish.

Not every setting is scenic or offers ideal trout habitat. In the eastern end of the State, most streams run wide and flat across a nondescript sandy bottom. Farther west, Garrett County jealously hosts the North Branch of the Potomac, the Savage and the Youghiogheny River, all tailwaters with a mix of wild and stocked trout in spectacular mountain settings. Wild brookies are harder to find given the dearth of cold water, but pockets exist wherever there are higher elevations and shaded creeks.

Like the other CatchGuides, this book augments the written descriptions with 551 pictures. Regardless of level of experience, each angler has a vision in his/her mind's eye of what constitutes an attractive destination. Every location discussed has at least one picture to facilitate the translation of mental vision to on-stream reality. If something doesn't look right, regardless of what the words say, you can go someplace else.

While writing was invented in ancient times and photography in the 18th century, we live in the 21st, so shouldn't the book incorporate modern technology to bring you additional value?

The ubiquitous availability of portable electronic devices with constant pervasive connections to the Internet as well as GPS enabled navigation systems, can and should be leveraged to increase your enjoyment of the sport. The common denominator becomes a set of GPS coordinates. A few mouse clicks can reveal high resolution satellite photography allowing you to plan your attack and, with a few more clicks, produce exceptionally detailed driving directions. Even better, plug the GPS coordinates directly into the device and have it figure out the most efficient route. This book includes 902 GPS coordinates, most of them for stream access points.

Do not place absolute reliance on the GPS coordinates of the stocked boundaries. They are approximate. Where available, I quote the written DNR guidance that describes the extent of the fishable area. A few things to note:
- The written description of the fishable area may exceed the extent of the stocked area shown on Google™ maps. According to the DNR, this is on purpose to keep us from wasting time pursuing trout outside of the stocked section, so use the approximate boundaries instead of the description to collapse your focus.
- Even though a section of a stream falls within the stocked area, it does not necessarily mean that it is open to the public. Given so much fishable water across the state, the DNR cannot keep up with the vagaries of individual landowner desires. Rest assured that when private property restrictions become excessive, that location will drop from the stocking plan. Therefore, anything stocked should have reasonable public access. Pay close attention to the posted signs and respect private property; do not trespass.

I show the GPS coordinates in a format compatible with Google™. Depending on your GPS, you may have to remove the "minus" sign in front of the second number. Finally, when you open Google™ Maps using the coordinates, you may have to zoom out until you see the **_green_** arrow. The green arrow is the actual location. Google™ tends to jump a known feature shown using a **_red_** arrow.

Since the vast majority of trout fishing locations in Maryland are stocked, this book necessarily must consider where the DNR plants fish. I have no inside information and base my conclusions on the fact that the transport vehicle is a big truck that has to get within a reasonable distance of the stream to unload. Since the list of access points is as comprehensive as I could make it, it should, by default, include every feasible stocking location.

eBook: There is an eBook version available from _www.CatchGuide.com_ that includes color versions of the pictures. **_Every GPS coordinate is a clickable link to the Google™ satellite view._** The eBook includes links to many of the State and local parks that host the streams, creeks, lakes and ponds, allowing you to do additional research regarding the surrounding environment and the activities that may or may not be available.

Prior to reading this book, some final cautions:

- Please put safety first when fishing. Major rivers and streams are all exceedingly dangerous after heavy rains. If it looks too high to fish, it is. Even ponds and lakes can be treacherous if the banks are slippery. You should wear a personal floatation device (aka PFD or life vest) whenever you step away from the shoreline. The self inflating brands provide an additional level of security in case you whack your head when falling.

- Along those lines, please reread the disclaimer and warning at the front of the book. You are ultimately accountable for what you do or fail to do when fishing. I, the author, as well as the publisher and anyone else involved in the creation of this book, disclaim all liability from actions you take. As stated in the disclaimer, by reading this book you agree to an unrestricted release from liability. If you cannot agree to that, then put the book down right now and read something else.

After discovering didymo, an invasive alga, in Maryland waters, the DNR took aggressive action to prevent its further spread. Didymo coats the bottom of streams with "rock snot"- a yellow-brown slime that can wipe out the food source for trout. Studies confirmed that felt sole waders are the ideal transport mechanism and are probably to blame for the world-wide spread of the alga as anglers move from place to place.

In 2011, Maryland banned felt sole waders and is enforcing the ban with hefty fines of $1,000 for the first offense and $2,000 for the second.

Didymo can attach to other materials and the DNR placed Wader Wash stations at key fishing locations to allow anglers to scrub their boots and waders prior to entering the watershed. Please take advantage of the stations and do your part to control the problem!

I do not know who said this the first time, but if you follow this anonymous guidance, you will have a good day as you pursue Maryland's abundant trout:

If fishing is slow, move fast. If the fishing is fast, move slow.

Stocked Trout Behavior

Stream just stocked? Skunked again? Blamed it on the "locals?" Or is something more sinister at work? A gang of rowdy blue herons?

Stockers have been driving fisheries professionals insane for years with their core questions being the same as ours, "What happened to all the fish? Were they caught? Did they die? Did they leave?" Understanding the answers is crucial to the fisheries mission to provide a good angling experience that, in turn, stimulates license sales supporting wildlife programs. The problem was succinctly stated in a Wyoming Fish and Game presentation on tailwater trout survival as "*How do you lose 250,000 trout?*"[1] The good news is that there are many studies done with full academic rigor focused on answering these compelling questions. Once we understand the results and apply the lessons learned, our day on the stream will improve. It's even better since the studies all reach the same general set of conclusions, an academic event as rare as a teenager offering to take out the garbage or putting gas in the tank.

You may think your stream is cleaned out, but unless the locals fish with hand grenades, the fish are there and probably laughing at you. A comprehensive British study discovered that only 40% of the stockers planted were reported caught by fishermen.[2] Of that 40%, 65% were caught within five weeks of stocking with only 1% able to holdover to the following year in water that supported a year round wild population.[3] Even factoring the 40% number upwards for poaching and the heron gang, there are plenty of fish in the water after the localized, shoulder to shoulder frenzy that follows the publication of the daily stocking report. So, if there are so many uncaught fish, why do you get skunked?

When taken off a diet of pellets, a freshly stocked trout needs time to learn what to eat. Understanding the timeline of the switch is especially critical to flyrodders since they rely on fooling trout with replicas of natural food. Brown trout present the worst case scenario, taking up to 50 days before completely adapting to natural foods.[4] The good news is that rainbow trout, a hatchery favorite, begin their adaptation to wild food in about a week, but, even their

---

[1] Wayne Hubert, Dave Zafft, Darin Simpkins, Lance Hebdon, and Christiana Barrineau, "Winter Survival, Movement, and Bio-energetics of Trout in Tailwater Habitat" (presentation , Wyoming Game and Fish Department, http://seo.state.wy.us/Forum/2007/Annear_winterhabitat_Mar07.ppt, March 2007), 16.
[2] R.C. Cresswell, G.S. Harris and R. Williams, "Factors Influencing the Movements, Recapture and survival of Hatchery Reared Trout Released into Flowing Waters and their Management Implications", Food and Agriculture Organization of the UN, http://www.fao.org/docrep/009/ae996b/AE996B13.htm.
[3] Ibid.
[4] Ibid.

learning curve can be slow.[5] The Oklahoma Department of Wildlife Conservation confirmed this in April 2005 when they examined the stomach contents of rainbow trout stocked in January.[6] In Oklahoma study-speak, "Non-food items were the dominate prey item."[7] However, after being in the water three months, non-food items composed a smaller portion of the fish's intake, dropping from 27% in April to 11% by June.[8] While the actual food items in the Oklahoma trout diet were primarily snails and invertebrates[9], do not extrapolate that mix directly to local water since your environment is probably different.

The implication is that the game slowly tips in favor of the flyrodder. If they put faith in the fact that 60% of stocked trout were unaccounted for, they can afford to wait for the fish to adapt to the wild. The longer a stocker is resident in a stream, the more it will learn what to eat. Interest in attacking dry flies and nymphs, common fly fishing lures, picks up in direct proportion to the length of time in the stream as trout adapt and learn through trial and error. On the flip side, if you are one of the anglers who remain convinced of the need to hit the stream soon after stocking to have a shot at catching anything, focus on spinners, bait or brightly colored streamer flies to provoke reaction strikes rather than using delicate natural imitations. If you really get desperate, you can employ a trick revealed to me by a wildlife professional that works regardless of how you fish. At the hatcheries in his State, automatic feeders scatter pellets at 7:30 AM and 4:30 PM. Over time, the trout become attuned to the schedule and wait anxiously for the patter of pellets on the water's surface to know it is time for chow. If you find that nothing is working on the stream, pick up a handful of small gravel and throw it into the middle of the pool followed quickly by your lure. The gravel mimics pellets, attracts the fish to the noise where they see your lure and you end up having a good time.

The transition to natural food is not the end of the story. By waiting for a stocker to develop a taste for stream fare, you also give them time to disappear. Where do they go? Answering this question is exactly what motivated the Pennsylvania Fish and Boat Commission to do a series of studies between 2003 and 2006 in reaction to complaints from anglers asserting that the fish were gone by opening day.[10] It turns out the anglers were right. The Pennsylvania studies

[5] T. A. Lasenby and S. J. Kerr , "Brown Trout Stocking: An Annotated Bibliography and Literature Review", Ontario Scholars Portal, https://ozone.scholarsportal.info/bitstream/1873/8502/1/10293909.pdf, 17

[6] Randy Hyler and Paul Blakenbush, "Assessment of Impacts to Spring Creek from Introductions or Rainbow Trout in 2004 and 2005", Spring Creek Coalition and Spring Creek Conservation Coalition, http://www.springcreekok.org/docs/reports/report_ODWC_2004-2005.pdf, 4
[7] Ibid.
[8] Ibid.,13-14
[9] Ibid.
[10] PFBC Staff Report, "Factors Influencing the Post-Stocking Movement of Hatchery Trout in Streams", Pennsylvania Fish and Boat Commission, http://www.fish.state.pa.us/images/fisheries/info_sheets/trout_movement.pdf, 1

concluded that rainbow trout will hold where stocked for three days, browns for seven and brookies for ten.[11]

Once fish adapt, they move. They move downstream. Some even take giant steps. The Pennsylvania study reported one radio-tagged rainbow was found a staggering 123 miles from its stocking location while the most adventurous brown moved six miles and comparable brookie almost 8 miles.[12] Although a South Dakota study of Rapid Creek was silent on how far a stocker typically moves since it limited recapture efforts to an arbitrary 300 yards, it pegged the average distance at 224 yards.[13] The British Study reinforced this by discovering that 90% of fish recaptured by electro-fishing were within 656 yards of the stocking site five to thirteen days later.[14] South Dakota was the outlier to the downstream imperative and reported some upstream movement during periods of lower flow.[15] While the actual distance moved depends on the specific characteristics of the particular streams studied, the point is that the fish "get out of Dodge" and most board the downstream train. Not surprisingly, their favorite destination was a pool or run area.[16]

There was no statistical significance related to the presence or absence of environmental factors. While stockers hang around longer in the presence of good structure – logs, boulders, stable banks – they still eventually migrate.[17] In total, Pennsylvania considered 20 different variables to determine if any was the prime motivator spurring movement. For those who watch the environment of their local waters closely, an instant assumption might be that water chemistry and temperature should be key drivers. After all, if the water is too acid or too warm, trout should move immediately to seek out better habitat. In terms of temperature, the 2006 Pennsylvania study did not see this behavior since there was no significant difference between the water temperature of the hatchery, the stock truck or the destination streams.[18] Pennsylvania did discover a weak correlation with pH since more trout were recaptured in the 300 yard footprint of interest in less acidic areas.[19] In general, fish moved at the same rate regardless of the characteristics of the water they found themselves in.[20]

---

[11] Ibid., 2

[12] Ibid.

[13] Greg Simpson, "Rainbow Trout Movement after Stocking in Rapid Creek", South Dakota State Government, http://e.library.sd.gov/SodakLIVE-Docs/content/GFP/GFPdoc067.pdf, 13

[14] Cresswell et al," Factors Influencing"

[15] Simpson, "Rainbow Trout Movement", 11

[16] Ibid., 12

[17] PFBC Staff. "Factors Influencing", 3

[18] Daryl Pierce, Michael Kaufman, Russell Green, Robert Wunk, "2006 Preseason Stocked Trout Residency Study", PA State Government, http://www.fish.state.pa.us/images/fisheries/trout_residency.pdf, 10

[19] Ibid., 10

[20] PFBC Staff. "Factors Influencing", 3

What about flow? The Rapid Creek study discovered stockers placed into water flowing in excess of 100 cubic feet per minute immediately migrated downstream until they found pools.[21] You might think that a flood would influence the downstream dispersion as in "all the fish were washed downstream by the big storm," but that is not the case. Radio-tagged trout held in position during two Pennsylvania floods in 2005.[22] This makes sense. A stocked fish may not be accustomed to strong flows and go with the current when deposited in a stream running at high volume. Once acclimated and comfortable, fish find protected holding positions where they can weather high water conditions. So, the common assumption that fish wash downstream after a storm is incorrect.

This is the last piece of the puzzle. While spin and bait fishermen can avoid being skunked within hours of stocking, fly anglers must wait a week or more for the fish to recognize the standard fly patterns that mimic natural food. By that time, the stockers will no longer be lying next to those easy spots by the road. Knowing the trend is for trout to migrate downstream, anglers, regardless of how they fish, can lay in a simple strategy for success. Start as far downstream of the stocking access points as possible and work up, targeting the pools and runs that form the optimum holding locations. Since the most intense pressure on the stocking points is in the several days immediately after stocking, anglers who wait will probably have the stream to themselves as everybody else chases the stock truck to the next location. After all, many will make the assumption that the stream is cleaned out when, in fact, the trout have just moved out. To catch fish, fish where the fish are. Pretty simple advice.

---

[21] Simpson, "Rainbow Trout Movement", 11
[22] PFBC Staff, "Factors Influencing", 3

Blue Lining

To diehard trout addicts, a good blue line is better than a vein of gold. "Blue line" refers to the standard way a topographical map shows a body of water - in this case, a thin blue line denoting a stream. A thin blue line wandering down the mountainside gives the wild trout purist the optimistic hope of pitting his skill against a wild and wary brook or brown trout.

This book concentrates on stocked trout water simply because there is more of it. I do cover some of the well-known wild streams that are spread around the State with most of my coverage devoted to the Savage River watershed; no secrets revealed. There are several reasons for not expanding the book to include a larger chunk of wild water. As you heft this book and feel its weight, the first reason is obvious. The book would just get too big. The second recognizes that wild streams discussed in any printed media will immediately attract more attention even though the ancient ethic of keeping wild water secret is outdated.

Outdated? Absolutely. If a stream is secret, there is no constituency ready to rise up and vigorously argue to control the development that would destroy it. Need proof? Look what happened with the Paint Branch. It was protected only because people knew about it and their energy created the conservation organization, *Eyes of Paint Branch* (www.eopb.org), to watch over it. The Eastern Brook Trout Joint Venture, under the auspices of the National Fish Habitat Action Plan, is doing this for the eastern seaboard. A key part of their mission is to document every stream that could possibly support brook trout so that fact can be considered in any future environmental or development decision. To that end, anyone can download data and maps from their website documenting every stream capable of sustaining brook trout on the east coast. You can even upload the data into Google Earth™ and display it, along with an almost infinite number of data overlays, to create your own "trout command center." The website, wildtroutstreams.com, has detailed instructions on how to do this. *In short, there are no secrets.* Before you panic, recognize that giving people choices distributes a finite number of anglers over an almost infinite number of stream-miles, resulting in even lower pressure on all - not just the popular, well-known few.

If you are still concerned, recognize that most wild streams do not run along the side of the road. Fishing wild water requires some level of physical fitness and the investment of sweat, the ultimate and very effective filter to pressure. Another protection is that just knowing that the characteristics of a stream can support trout does not mean that it is robust enough to actually do so. To hold wild trout, the stream must be large enough to support their growth to a decent catchable size. Finding that blue line takes research. Randomly following any ribbon of water up the mountainside will certainly give you a good workout, but no guarantee of anything more. The purpose of this chapter is to give you the step-by-step rules to follow to identify the best blue lines to fish.

To start, get a topographical map for the region based on the Eastern Brook Trout Joint Venture data that confirms the area has the correct water characteristics to hold brook trout. You can "cheat" and avoid doing all the primary research by either visiting wildtroutstreams.com and following the links to Maryland Streams or searching on Google for the "2006 Brook Trout Management Plan" from the DNR. Wildtroutstreams.com has a good list of **named** wild trout streams with the latitude and longitude along with the type of trout (brook, brown, cutthroat or rainbow) confirmed to be indigenous. The DNR study is more comprehensive and has far more choices, providing the watershed, county, stream name, coordinates as well as the estimated stream miles inhabited. The DNR list also tells you whether the stream runs over public or private property. *Important! Neither list is exhaustive.* Some of the best wild trout water flows through **unnamed** streams down unnamed mountains and ridges.

You need a topographical map for two reasons; (1) Identify the boundaries of public property; (2) Find blue lines that represent streams. If you have access to the Internet, the government provides free topographical maps for instant download. Visit http://store.usgs.gov and follow the links to find the map locator and downloader. Alternatively, visit the USGS site that hosts the national map viewer at http://viewer.nationalmap.gov/viewer/. This website allows you to build and download a topographical map for any place in the US with overlays of your choice.

Once you have your map, follow the next steps to analyze the terrain.

Rule 1: Look for a waterfall.

Waterfalls are usually not marked on the map unless there is year-round flow. In the example to the right, this stream has two waterfalls (actually three, just two marked), indicating robust flow and promising water. In addition, there are usually a good, deep fishable pool at the base of every waterfall.

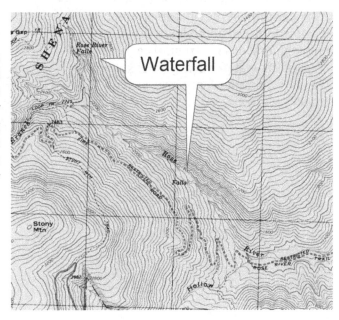

Rule 2: Avoid intermittent streams

An intermittent stream does not have full-time water. Without a constant flow, year to year survival is limited. There may be a few trout able to survive in deep community pools, but a full-time stream is always a better choice.

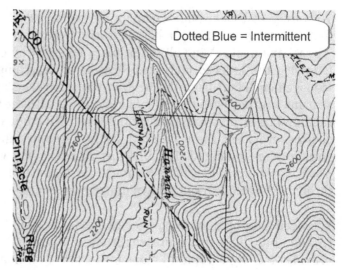

Rule 3: Look for a long, steep incline

Steep inclines lead to pocket water. As water tumbles down a steep slope, it pools in dips and hollows, creating holding positions for trout. The same amount of water on a gentle slope typically indicates a very shallow creek.

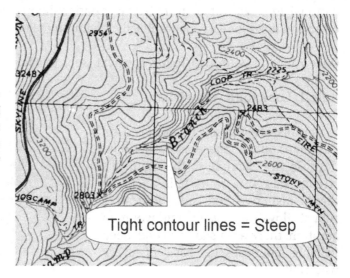

Rule 4: Look for multiple tributaries.

This rule is the opposite of avoiding intermittent streams. Find a blue line that is fed by many other blue lines. The larger the main stream, the better the possibility of year-round survival. In addition, some tributaries are strong, fishable streams in their own right.

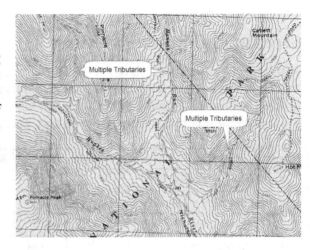

Rule 5: Look for a blue line with no trail directly adjacent to it or a hard hike.

Once you find a good, strong stream, look for the places where the trail veers away or, even better, there is no trail at all. The harder the stream is to reach, the fewer people will visit. If there is a trail, assess the difficulty of the hike to reach the stream. Fishing pressure is directly proportional to the challenge. A hard hike always translates to exceptionally low pressure.

Now that you found a good looking blue line, be sure to let people know where you are going before you go. GPS-based satellite emergency warning beacons are cheap and should be mandatory for anyone who ventures off the beaten track; especially trout hikers who will climb over dangerous, slippery rocks on steep hillsides.

Stream and Pond Rankings

Want to know the best places to fish? Easy. Just look at the number of trout stocked. The numbers in the tables below came from the Maryland Spring 2011 stocking plan. The definition of "best water" is regional. Deer Creek is a far cry from being as good as the Casselman River, but it is the best public stream in the eastern part of the State. Hence, it gets a high dose of fish.

Rank	Location	Trout	Rank	Location	Trout
1	Casselman River	9195	26	Friends Creek	5050
2	Deer Creek	8675	27	N. Br. Potomac River (DH)	5000
3	Bear Creek	8185	28	Deep Creek Lake	4805
4	Savage River	8185	29	Antietam Creek	4775
5	Evitts Creek	7225	30	N. Br. Potomac River, Westernport	4650
6	Wills Creek	7225	31	Town Creek	4500
7	Big Elk Creek	6735	32	Youghiogheny River (C&R)	4450
8	Jennings Run	6255	33	Little Falls Mainstem	4335
9	Gunpowder Falls, Lower	6020	34	Little Gunpowder Falls	4325
10	Gunpowder Falls, Upper	6020	35	Cunningham Falls Lake	4085
11	N. Br. Potomac River, Barnum	5935	36	Savage River Reservoir	3850
12	South Branch Patapsco River	5795	37	Lake Habeeb (Rocky Gap Lake)	3840
13	Little Patuxent River	5770	38	Patuxent River (State Park)	3700
14	Owens Creek Mainstem	5770	39	N. Br. Potomac River, Kitzmiller	3405
15	Patapsco River, Daniels	5750	40	Little Youghiogheny River	2885
16	Great Seneca Creek	5540	41	Battie Mixon Ponds	2880
17	Patapsco River, Avalon	5540	42	Flintstone Creek	2880
18	Greenbrier Lake	5535	43	New Germany Lake	2880
19	Middle Creek Mainstem	5330	44	Piney Reservoir	2880
20	Northwest Branch	5300	45	Fishing Creek	2640
21	Beaver Creek	5295	46	Morgan Run	2500
22	Fifteen Mile Creek	5295	47	Centennial Lake	2405
23	Sideling Hill Creek	5295	48	Licking Creek Mainstem	2395
24	Blairs Valley Lake	5290	49	Lake Needwood	2165
25	Youghiogheny River, Oakland	5285	50	Cosca Lake	2155

Use these tables to guide your fishing priorities. Many locations get stocked on the same day or within the same week. You will have a better experience on the higher quality water - denoted by the greater number of fish planted.

Rank	Location	Trout	Rank	Location	Trout
51	Elkhorn Lake	1920	76	Carroll Creek	1395
52	Georges Creek	1920	77	Howards Pond	1350
53	Muddy Creek	1920	78	Hutchins Pond	1255
54	Severn Run	1920	79	Israel Creek	1200
55	Wheatley Lake	1920	80	Beaverdam Creek	1195
56	Farm Museum Pond	1915	81	Frank Bentz Pond	1195
57	Myrtle Grove Ponds	1915	82	Melwood Pond	1195
58	Rainbow Lake	1910	83	Izaak Walton Pond	955
59	Youghiogheny River, Friendsville	1910	84	Mill Run	955
60	Greenbelt Lake	1675	85	Orchard Pond	955
61	Lake Artemesia	1675	86	Tucker Pond	955
62	Stansbury Park Pond	1675	87	White Sulfur Pond	955
63	Middle Patuxent River	1500	88	Lt. Tonoloway Creek Upper Section	865
64	Piney Run Reservoir	1445	89	Lt. Antietam Creek	820
65	Tuckahoe Lake/Creek	1445	90	Shad Landing Pond	820
66	Evitts Creek Ponds	1440	91	Whiskey Springs Pond	815
67	Patuxent River, Laurel	1440	92	Hughesville Pond	795
68	Accident Pond	1435	93	Lions Park Pond	770
69	Broadford Lake	1435	94	Jones Falls Mainstem	765
70	Gwynns Falls	1435	95	Brunswick Pond	725
71	Herrington Lake	1435	96	Forest Hill Pond	720
72	N. Br. Potomac River, Gorman	1435	97	Indian Springs Pond	720
73	Piney Run Mainstem	1435	98	Laurel Lake	720
74	Principio Creek	1435	99	Lt. Tonoloway Creek (YB)	720
75	Snowy Creek	1435	100	Martin Luther King Jr Pond	720

The small ponds bring up the back of the pack, but do not write them off. The size of most ponds average one acre on a good day. In terms of fish per acre, the opportunity to catch something out of small water is pretty good with Rising Sun Pond, a youth fishing area, being the best.

Community ponds are where families with lawn chairs show up on the same evening as the stocking. Folks will be chattering, joking, and having a great time trying to hook up with some of the freshly inserted fish that were all grown specifically to provide some fun in route to the dinner table. The water in the ponds is terminally warm for trout once summer kicks into high gear, so do not feel guilty keeping these fish since that is precisely why they were grown and stocked. The small ponds are great for kids for that same reason. High numbers of fish in a compressed place raises the chance that a small child can haul in a nice fat trout ... and be ruined for life as the fishing obsession takes hold!

Since many small ponds have special regulations (blind, youth, senior), check the guidebook prior to driving to them to ensure that you qualify.

Rank	Location	Trout	Rank	Location	Trout
101	Rising Sun Pond	720	108	Glade Park Pond	480
102	Urbana Lake	720	109	Avalon Pond	480
103	Hamburg Pond	675	110	Calvert Cliffs	480
104	Woodsboro Community Pond	675	111	Herrington Creek	480
105	Cotton Cove Pond	580	112	Parkview Pond, Grantsville	480
106	Laurel Run	580	113	Sharpsburg Pond	480
107	Catoctin River	500	114	Pangborn Pond	240

To make it easy to keep score, I will indicate whether a place is one of the top 25 locations as part of the discussion.

Note: Where I could find an official position on the size of lakes and ponds, I used it. Otherwise, I calculated an estimate.

Allegany County

Battie Mixon Ponds

Approximate Boundary: 39.541304,-78.617331 to 39.539964,-78.607675 (33 acres)

Type: Put and Take

Directions:
East: From I-81 south of Winchester, VA take exit 310 onto VA 37N. Merge onto US 522N towards Berkeley Springs. Turn left onto VA 127W/Bloomery Pike. Turn right onto WV 29N. WV 29 eventually becomes WV 9 south of Woodrow. Continue on WV 9 to the Maryland border north of Paw Paw. WV 9 becomes MD 51. Continue on MD 51N/Oldtown Road SE. Turn left on Oldtown Road followed by an immediate right on Opessa Street. Turn left onto Green Spring Road and follow it to the parking area on the right.

West: From I-68 in Cumberland, MD take exit 43 for MD 51S/S Mechanic Street. Turn right on Oldtown Road followed by an immediate right on Opessa Street. Turn left onto Green Spring Road and follow it to the parking area on the right.

Access Point: Parking lot on the north side of the canal (39.540344,-78.612524)

The DNR created the Battie Mixon fishing ponds by flooding the Chesapeake and Ohio Canal between locks 69 and 70. Both are inside the C&O National Historic Park with the C&O towpath running along the southern edge. We owe a debt of gratitude to Battie Mixon, the Allegany County Game Warden, who conceived of the idea to restore this section of the canal, re-water it and open it for fishing. Volunteers implemented the idea in 1945, and now we can enjoy a mile of hot action adjacent to Oldtown, Maryland.

There is plenty of parking on the north edge of the canal with portable toilets if you need them. Do not drive across the canal because the road leads to the tollbooth and the Potomac River. In addition to the trout stocked during the season, cranky smallmouth bass cruise the ponds looking for a fight. The northern side of the canal is muddy and full of silt with no "fish holding" depth within 15 feet of the shore. The western pond, near the building, has a fishing ramp that extends approximately 20 feet along the edge of the canal and overlooks a deep spot. It is accessible to wheelchairs and is a good place to sit and fish. Above the pier, farther to the west, the trail along the northern bank becomes less obvious and eventually disappears. Fishing from the towpath on the other side is the best approach.

Looking west. Fishing pier on the right   Looking east. Towpath on the right.

Cotton Cove Pond

Approximate Boundary: 39.673334,-78.933702 to 39.672795,-78.933657 (1 acre)

Type: Put and Take

Directions:
East: From I-68, take exit 34 onto MD 36/New Georges Creek Road SW toward Frostburg. Turn left onto MD 36. Turn right onto Shaw Street followed by a right on Rynex Avenue. Drive past the baseball field. The pond is at the end of the road.

West: From I-68, take exit 29 for MD 546. Turn left onto MD 546/Beall School Road. Take the US 40W exit toward Morgantown (you will backtrack) followed by a right onto Piney Run Road. Turn right onto US 40E. Turn left onto Shaw Street followed by a left on Rynex Avenue. Drive past the baseball field. The pond is at the end of the road.

Access Point: Parking area adjacent to soccer field 7 (39.673334,-78.933702)

The bowl shaped Cotton Cove Pond is not much to look at. It's basically a large puddle below soccer field 7 inside the Lions Community Park. Although muddy after a rain, the small footprint of the pond makes every inch accessible to anglers. The bottom drops off quickly from the shore to the deeper middle. There is a wide, gravel path, supported by vertical banks, running around three quarters of the perimeter.

There are no benches; anglers must sit on the ground to fish. The best place to do that is on the northern and southern banks where the steep pitch creates natural chairs.

Dans Mountain Pond

Approximate Boundary: 39.563541,-78.950743 to 39.56311,-78.949954 (1 acre)

Type: Put and Take

Directions:
North: From I-68, take exit 34 onto MD 36S/New Georges Creek Road SW. Turn left onto Rockville Street SW. Rockville Street turns into Water Station Run Road SW. Do not turn left on Bluebaugh Road. Stay to the right. Take the next fork to the left to continue on Water Station Run Road and follow it to the pond.

South: Follow MD 36N from Westernport to Lonaconing. Turn right onto Rockville Street SW. Rockville Street turns into Water Station Run Road SW. Do not turn left on Bluebaugh Road. Stay to the right. Take the next fork to the left to continue on Water Station Run Road and follow it to the pond.

Access Point: Parking lot next to the pond on Water Station Run (39.562734,-78.950222)

This pond is seemingly an afterthought tucked into a corner of a steep hillside off the main road leading into the 481 acre Dans Mountain State Park. The facade of remote wilderness falls away with a quick turn 500 feet to the east of the pond onto Recreation Area Road SW that leads to the bustling Olympic size swimming pool, bathhouse and concession area.

A cold stream dribbling in from the north feeds the pond, creating a muddy shoreline at the entry point. The remainder of the pond is accessible via a level, beaten path on the southern perimeter that merges into a rough fisherman's trail on the north side. Pavilions and picnic tables complement the idyllic setting. While the center of the pond retains some depth, the bank is shallow with the bottom gently sloping away from the shoreline. The majority of the shade hovers over the southern bank as a result of densely packed tall trees. However, there is enough setback, with perfectly placed gaps, to allow fly anglers to unload a full backcast.

Evitts Creek

Approximate Boundary: 39.673806,-78.724451 to 39.722808,-78.688231 (4.86 miles)
DNR Guidance: Mainstem upstream of Interstate Route 68.

Directions:
From I-68, take exit 46 onto MD 807/Naves Crossroads NE. Turn north at the bottom of the ramp and follow Naves Crossroads until it merges with Mason Road.

Access Point:
- Various turnouts along Mason Road (39.67677,-78.72042, 39.68029,-78.71683, 39.698976,-78.702087)
- Mason Road and Old Mt Pleasant Road NE (39.696178,-78.702934)
- Mason Road and Ferguson Lane NE (39.705322,-78.698079,
- Smouses Mill Road NE bridge (39.709913,-78.696622)

Although the stocked section extends down to I-68, the first possible access point is not until Mason Road begins to run parallel to the creek approximately 1,500 feet after it turns north away from the Interstate (39.67677,-78.72042). Even then, the road runs high above the creek with thick brush and trees blocking access to all but the most ardent bushwhacker. Of course, one can debate whether fish stocked upstream would migrate into this lightly pressured section and, if they do, then the bushwhacking becomes worthwhile. However, the road begins to run down the side of the ridgeline to rejoin the stream at 39.68029,-78.71683 where there is severely restricted roadside parking. At that point, you get your first good look at the water. The creek runs 20 to 30 feet wide across a freestone bottom that is a mix of small rocks interspersed with sand. Once the road leaves this spot, it veers away from the creek for the next mile, refusing access until reaching the intersection with Old Mt Pleasant Road.

Upstream from Old Mt Pleasant Road

Reinforced rock bank, downstream

The creek hugs the road for the next 1,500 feet with enough room for several turnouts. Since the property on the downstream side of the bridge is posted, focus on fishing upstream. The streambed is a mixture of small boulders and rocks spread across a bed that is now approximately 30 to 40 feet wide. The water runs shallow, so fish the deep channels and holes where you can find them. As the road leaves the straight glide to move around the corner to the left, the right-hand bank takes a steep pitch upward. There is a good pool sheltered by a tree with a reinforced rock bank supporting the road. The creek drops down a short gradient break, gathers steam and compresses as it turns the corner into the tree. The packed, beaten trail to the creek's edge proves that this is a popular place.

Continue north towards Pennsylvania and stop at Ferguson Lane. There is good parking on both sides of the bridge, with the fisherman's trail leading to the creek from the western side. As it moves under the bridge, the water deepens and the creek broadens, becoming almost 50 feet wide with a nice set of riffles and a fallen tree providing structure at the upstream bend.

After having to park on the side of the road at the southern access points, you will be relieved to discover the first formal parking area adjacent to the bridge where the creek runs under Smouses Mill Road. Gentle open fields provide the western boundary while thick brush protects the upstream eastern side. The upstream west bank is posted, so fish up the eastern side. Use the lightly traveled trail to negotiate through the thick vegetation to reach the stream. Sadly, the trail peters out close to the bend. Downstream, fishing is easier since the bank is initially open with streamside vegetation only presenting a minor obstacle that can be overcome by wading.

Smouses Mill Road Upstream

Smouses Mill Road Downstream

Even though the stocked section extends up to the Pennsylvania border, Smouses Mill is where you should end your day since the next access point is at the Mason Road bridge crossing on the Pennsylvania side of the border. There is no place to park and no DNR signage indicating that they actually stock this far north or that you have permission to cross private property. Given that the bridge is actually in Pennsylvania, I doubt the DNR inserts fish in Pennsylvania water even though Maryland is 50 feet downstream. Besides, if stopped by conservation police officer at that bridge, you would be asked for a Pennsylvania license.

Evitts Creek is the fifth most heavily stocked stream in the State.

Evitts Creek Ponds

Approximate Boundary: 39.662298,-78.717075 to 39.66183,-78.720585 (4 acres)

Type: Put and Take

Directions:
From I-68, take exit 46 for Naves Cross Road. Turn south at the bottom of the ramp, followed by another turn to the south to MD 807/Christie Road. Follow Christie Road to the ponds (on the right).

Access Point: Parking lot on the south side of Christie Road NE (39.662298,-78.717075)

The ponds occupy the lion's share of the 6 acre Evitts Creek Ponds Fish Management Area that sits to the west of Cumberland. Evitts Creek, stocked above I-68, creates the northern border of the three separate ponds that make up the fishing complex and provides a constant stream of cool water into the ponds.

A manicured path, punctuated by a few scattered picnic tables, runs along the northern boundary of all three ponds. The westernmost pond is the only one approachable from the south as a result of the steep cliff that forms the southern boundary of the first two. The ponds are shallow along the accessible edges with a dark green tint denoting deeper water running consistently along the cliff. Cold water from the creek feeds in at the eastern terminus and fish huddle near the output pipe, searching for relief from the hotter water at the center of the pond. The banks slope at a moderate pitch and do not present a challenge to movement from the path to the water's edge. Likewise, the bottom of the lake extends away from the shoreline at a gentle angle that allows for the rapid growth of underwater vegetation. The middle lake matches the first and the only advantage of the western lake is that there is more shade along the southern and western border, providing a welcome relief to anglers on a hot day. On a clear, sunny day, you can see the larger fish cruising the perimeter of the shallow shelf where it breaks into the deep water.

View from parking lot   Third pond and the shaded bank

Fifteen Mile Creek

Approximate Boundary: 39.624486,-78.384976 to 39.712304,-78.446767 (12 miles)

Type: Put and Take

Directions:
Upper Section: From I-68, take exit 62 north on 40. After 100 yards, turn left on Fifteen Mile Creek Road. Drive over the bridge and look for Campsite 2. Start fishing anywhere after that spot.

Middle Section: From I-68, take exit 64 south. Follow the hardball past the turn to the Park Headquarters. The road transitions from asphalt to dirt. Follow it to the stream.

Lower Section: From I-68, take exit 68/Orleans Road south. Follow it to the stream.

Access Point:
- Numerous turnouts along Fifteen Mile Creek Road near I-68 (examples: 39.706170,-78.451750, 39.669654,-78.459259, 39.67849,-78.457435, 39.68664,-78.454614)
- Mountain Road intersection with the creek (39.656226,-78.396599)
- Southern end of Yonkers Bottom Road (39.639174,-78.389822)
- Intersection of Appel Road and Orleans Road SE (39.628005,-78.389449)

Fully enclosed within the 46,000 acre Green Ridge State Forest, the dramatic scenery amplifies the joy of fishing. For those who want to stretch their fishing trip over a weekend, the State Forest offers 100 designated primitive campsites with permits available from the Green Ridge State Forest headquarters. According to the DNR, campsites 24-49, 100 as well as group sites one and two are adjacent to the stocked fishing area. Fifteen Mile Creek starts in the north as a low gradient freestone stream running through a level valley and, a short distance below I-68, after several tributaries contribute additional water, transitions into a rapidly flowing river running through a narrow canyon. Regardless of whether you fish in the north or the south, look for fish around deadfalls, undercut banks and in the deep pools that provide respite from the shallow glides that connect them.

The section above I-68 is the easiest to fish. The road runs within spitting distance of the creek and numerous turnouts make approaching the water trouble-free. The banks are low and the vegetation sparse during the Spring season. The creek runs 15 to 20 feet wide, mostly shallow, with deep pools at the bends or in the few places it narrows and gouges a channel. Small rocks and cobble dominate as the subsurface structure. Fishing from the bank is uncomplicated and the small rocks do not present an obstacle to those who want to wade. Most of the action occurs at the multiple bridge crossings where construction created deep spots with easy stocking access. In the far northern portion of the stocked area, the amount of water in the creek is minimal. The best looking water is available much farther south after the numerous tributaries have had the opportunity to add volume to the flow. However, that does not discourage the DNR from inserting stocked fish throughout the entire extent.

Above I-68

Above I-68

Below I-68, the river briefly changes character with sand predominating and the water becoming shallower. There continue to be plenty of turnoffs and, during the season, most of these will be heavily populated with anglers. Even though the "stocked trout water" line on the map extends the entire distance between I-68 and the town of Little Orleans miles downstream, "posted" signs predominate after turning left onto Dug Hill Road. It does not really matter since the topography prevents access. Once the road makes its initial turn to the west away from the stream, it charges up a steep mountainside and runs along a ridgeline that is almost 1,000 feet above the stream. Therefore, do not drive farther than the last easy turnout on Fifteen Mile Creek Road.

To reach the Mountain Road access point, bump over the rutted, dirt road that runs down a steep ridgeline to a broad parking lot adjacent to the river. Unless the road has been graded, consider using a high clearance vehicle. Upstream from the parking lot, Fifteen Mile Creek runs through a narrow valley with dramatic scenery that includes the popular hiking and swimming destination called "Long Pond," but no trout. It is impossible for the stocking truck to unload above the intersection with the river. While some fish run upstream, most of the trout will be in the pool adjacent to the parking lot or wander a short distance downstream.

Long Pond

Upstream from Mountain Run

Near Mountain Run parking

Deep gorge, pretty water at Mountain Run

The Yonkers Bottom Road access is also at the end of a dirt road, but does not require a high clearance vehicle. The road dead ends at a large turnout adjacent to several nice campsites. Fifteen Mile Creek runs in a loop around the bottom of the parking area and a short walk through the gated path puts you on the creek. It runs clean and clear, about one foot deep, across a rock covered bottom at normal water levels. The deep channel is adjacent to the southern bank and at the turns. The best approach is to move south from the parking lot and begin fishing at the steep rock cliff. You will have to bushwhack through some dense underbrush on the southern shore to move farther downstream, so be prepared to wade. The creek is "trouty" looking as a result of the quick drop in elevation that creates fast water with pools below each line of rocks.

Upstream from Yonkers Bottom   Downstream from Yonkers Bottom

The final access point is at the New Orleans bridge crossing. There is a wide turnout on the south side of the bridge with parking for six or seven vehicles. At the bridge, an island divides the creek with the best access being on the left-hand side. The creek remains true to its rocky character at the southern end with the water running clean and clear. The thick vegetation on each bank forces anglers to wade into the slow-moving stream.

Well maintained campsites   Upstream from New Orleans

Fifteen Mile Creek is the 22nd most heavily stocked streams in the State.

Flintstone Creek

Approximate Boundary: 39.702112,-78.566802 to 39.722679,-78.591177 (2.49 miles)

Type: Put and Take

Directions:
East: From I-68, take exit 56 toward MD 144. Turn right onto Flintstone Drive NE. The road at the next intersection is Flintstone Creek Road with the creek directly to the front.

West: From I-68, take exit 56 toward MD 144. Turn left onto MD 144/National Pike NE. The road at the intersection is Flintstone Creek Road. The creek is across the road.

Access Point:
- School on National Pike NE (MD 144) (39.700624,-78.565937)
- MD 144 and Black Valley Road Veterans Memorial (39.7006,-78.565861)
- Lot under the I-68 bridge (39.704484,-78.567141)
- All of the following are turns off of Flintstone Creek Road:
  - Intersection with Flintstone Drive NE (39.707825,-78.566764)
  - Intersection with Shale Barren Trail (39.71149,-78.56825)
  - Intersection with Laurel Branch Trail (39.71782,-78.57808)

The Pennsylvania border is at 39.72257,-78.59023.

Flintstone is a pretty freestone stream that winds its way north towards the Pennsylvania border. The stocked section starts at the northern boundary of the school on the south side of National Pike NE (MD 144) where anglers have their first opportunity to reach the water. There is a Veterans Memorial at the intersection of Black Valley Road and National Pike adjacent to the creek surrounded by thick, almost impenetrable brush. Rather than bushwhack through, drive 200 feet north towards the Interstate to pull into the expansive parking lot shaded by the highway overpass. The creek runs 25 feet wide, clean and shallow across a rocky bottom with the immediate deep channel on the eastern side snuggled up to the cliff. To fish, you must wade. There is no easy path next to the bank and the thick vegetation defeats any thought of not getting wet.

Thick brush at the Veterans Memorial   Upstream from I-68 bridge

Continuing north on Black Valley Road, the parking areas surrounding the Glendale Church of the Brethren is the next opportunity to jump in the water. Black Valley Road makes a hard right across the bridge over the creek. Flintstone Creek Road continues directly north with the water on the right. While the manicured lawn of the church makes for easy walking on the western shore, the eastern bank features a flat, slick rock face that rises vertically from the edge of the water. In fact, from here to the end of the stocked section, count on the eastern bank being steep, forbidding and inaccessible since it is the southern boundary of Tussey Mountain and Buck Ridge. As a general rule, the deep channel runs along the cliff side.

Church looking upstream - note steep bank   Good water on side of road

After passing the intersection with Shale Barren Trail, the road runs directly adjacent to the creek for approximately 1,000 feet with few turnouts. Other than the challenge associated with parking, access is easy since the banks are low without a protective wall of thick brush. From Tussy Hollow Road all the way up to Laurel Branch Trail, there is a dirt road that runs parallel to Flintstone Creek Road closer to the water. As long as it has not been posted, the road provides the easiest access to the majority of the creek. There are plenty of deep stretches that supply an idyllic setting and perfect holding structure. Throughout its length, the streambed is covered in rocks with plenty of riffles to provide scenic interest and back up deeper water on the upstream side.

Near Tussey Hollow   Near Shale Barren Way

Although the theoretical northern boundary of the stocked section lies at the Pennsylvania border, do not be tempted to park in the small turnout at the northern end. The turnout is actually in Pennsylvania and may trigger a request for a Pennsylvania fishing license.

Georges Creek

Put and Take Section

Approximate Boundary: 39.495606,-79.045436 to 39.591541,-78.949434 (10.9 miles)
DNR Guidance: Mainstem from the upper extent of Town Park in Westernport upstream to Neff Run.

Type: Put and Take

Directions:
MD 36 runs from I-68 to Westernport. All of the access points are either on MD 36 or on side roads adjacent to it.

North: From I-68, take exit 34 onto MD 36S/New Georges Creek Road SW. The first access point is in the small town of Midland.

South: Follow MD 135 from Keyser, WV or Bloomington, MD. Turn north on MD 36.

Access Point:
- Baseball field on Church Street (39.592038,-78.948623)
- Baseball field near the intersection of Railroad Street and Chestnut Street (39.588162,-78.953258)
- Conservation park east of Brodie Road SW (39.577921,-78.959776)
- Roadside at bridge crossing on MD 36 near Brodie Road SW (39.57962,-78.967229)
- Side of the road on Rockville Street near the bridge (39.57207,-78.97445)
- Park on east side of W Main Street north of Detmold Street (39.563971,-78.983832)
- First Assembly of God Church south of Lonaconing (39.556016,-78.988835)
- Turnoff south of bridge on MD 935 south of Pekin Street (39.548375,-79.00214)
- MD 939 and Laurel Run Road (39.540799,-79.006658)
- Parking at Meadow ball field on Takoma Drive SW (39.536506,-79.014166)
- Parking at Bartlett Street and Hyde Road SW(39.533488,-79.015582)
- Parking at small walking trail/park on Lower Georges Creek Road SW and Berrys Lane SW (39.523541,-79.018748)
- Turnout on Lower Georges Creek Road SW and Kyle Hill Road SW (39.520868,-79.019533)*
- Southern end of Lower Georges Creek Road SW (39.51032,-79.02748)*
- Turnout on MD 36 south of Autumn Breeze Lane (39.506916,-79.042853)*

* Dead zone caused by the McDonald Mine seep upstream.

The stocked area of Georges Creek begins in a small public park in Midland. From there, the creek winds its way almost 11 miles down to the junction with the North Branch of the Potomac. Between the start and the confluence, the creek runs consistently across a rocky bed, typically 20 feet wide. Although there are many places where the creek touches various roads, exercise extreme care selecting parking and how you reach the stream to avoid trespassing.

In the upper reaches near Midland, the stream is tight with overhanging vegetation and trees anxious to play mind games with inexperienced casters. Not having the advantage of the numerous tributaries that join the creek farther south, the water is shallow and force the trout into scattered pools. Elk Lick Run merges into the creek south of Midland and provides needed additional water just in time for the access points that begin at Brodie Road.

Near Midland

Chestnut Street

Continuing south on MD 36, be grateful for the deeply cut mountain valley with starkly steep hills on either side that pushes the creek next to this main transportation artery. Although it also collapses all human habitation into the narrow band of level ground surrounding the creek, it makes the access points easier to locate. The challenge, of course, is to respect private property with "posted" signs speckling the landscape near some likely entry points. Most of the bridge crossings feature a small amount of parking with fisherman's trails providing both a beaten path to the water's edge and marginal, *unreliable* confirmation that access is permitted since DNR signage is not present at most places.

The small parking lot on the south side of MD 36 at the stream bank restoration project is the best opportunity to get into the water without having an issue with private property. There is a small fisherman's trail on the north side of the parking area leading to the water. At normal water levels, the creek runs shallow and flat, creating the need to tramp up or downstream to find the best fishing. The orange hue prevalent upstream as a result of runoff is gone and the creek exhibits a healthy green sheen with large rocks and boulders dominating the landscape.

Detmold Street

Near Detmold Street

The next public park downstream near Detmold Street supplies another worry free access location with a good pool located upstream at the bend in the creek. In Moscow, there is a small turnoff just past the junction of Laurel Run. There is a large pool just upstream of the bridge that provides the punctuation for a scenic high gradient stretch with water careening around boulders strewn randomly across the streambed. The stream ranges between 20 and 30 feet wide.

Near Meadow ball field

Upstream from Meadow

Lower Georges Creek Road provides an additional set of access points where you can find more turnouts and easier parking than on the busy MD 36. However, most of the road below Barton runs next to dead water as a result of the 2005 McDonald Mine seep. Apparently, an old mine collapsed and squirted a surge of highly acid water into the creek. This wiped out all life downstream with the ooze continuing to this day. Do not bother to fish the lower creek until you see the youth and blind area reappear on the stocking plan. Once it comes back, that is confirmation from the DNR that the acid issue has been remediated and the stream is healthy enough to hold fish.

Youth and Blind Section

Approximate Boundary: 39.485084,-79.045774 to 39.495359,-79.045452 (4,408 feet)
DNR Guidance: From upper extent of Town Park in Westernport downstream approximately one mile to Washington Street Bridge near the confluence of Georges Creek with the North Branch of the Potomac.

Type: Youth and Blind

Directions:
North: From I-68, take exit 34 onto MD 36S/New Georges Creek Road SW. Continue to the town of Westernport. Turn left on MD 937/Creek Side Drive. Make a slight left onto Main Street. Follow it to the parking lot on the east side of the park.

South: Follow MD 135 from Keyser, WV or Bloomington, MD. Turn north on MD 36. Turn right on Clayton Street. Turn left onto Main Street. Follow it to the parking lot on the east side of the park.

Access Point: Parking lot north of the intersection of Main Street and Ross Street (39.490461,-79.042291)*

Will not be stocked until the McDonald Mine seep problem is fixed.

The lower end of the youth and blind area is easy to find since it lies adjacent to a manicured public park. By the time the creek reaches Westernport, the mountains pull back and the valley floor flattens. This causes the creek to widen to 40 feet with plenty of boulders providing scattered scenery. Unfortunately, thick vegetation lines the bank along the park with the exception of one wide area where there is direct access. At normal flows during the season, there is plenty of water pushing through this short stretch. Therefore, since it is reserved for children and the blind, exercise caution and pay close attention to the danger presented by high flows. Although there is a wide empty lot at the upper end of the section, walking to the river requires crossing the tracks and negotiating a very steep, congested bank that is not appropriate for kids. If aggressive and physically capable, fish upstream to reach the good pools and stair-stepped gradient breaks above the park.

Upstream in park   Upper end - not appropriate for kids

Jennings Run

Approximate Boundary: 39.695168,-78.786664 to 39.70131,-78.843827 (3.43 miles)
DNR Guidance: Mainstem downstream of the confluence of North Jennings Run.

Directions:
From I-68, take exit 44 for Baltimore Avenue. Turn left onto Willowbrook Road (name changes to Baltimore Avenue). Turn right on Henderson Avenue to remain on US 40 Alt W. Make a right onto MD 36S/Mt Savage Road. The stream parallels Mt Savage Road.

Access Point:
- Intersection with Proenty Road (39.691618,-78.80343)
- Intersection with Windy Ridge Drive (39.697199,-78.813902)
- 500 feet west of Portertown Road (39.698049,-78.823998)
- Intersection with Barrelville Road (39.700612,-78.843133)
- Miscellaneous turnoffs along Mt Savage Road NW to include 39.69251,-78.792872, 39.691767,-78.797915, 39.694718,-78.810385, 39.700926,-78.831814, 39.700492,-78.838643

Jennings Run is an impressive stream. Not only does it feature almost universal access since Mt Savage Road closely parallels the entire stocked length, but the rocky bottom and cool water provide the perfect setting for trout fishing. A quick look at the Spring stocking plan confirms that the Maryland DNR shares this perspective since Jennings Run is one of the most heavily stocked streams in the state.

Sadly, there are issues with the Jennings Run/Wills Creek sewer service operated by the Allegany County Utilities Division that impact the stream. As of 2011, the transmission pipes are in a state of disrepair and the sanitary commission is anxious to use American Reinvestment and Recovery Act funding to fix the problem. The basic issue is that the system overflows and raw sewage ends up in the stream. Therefore, you probably should not fish within a mile of Barrelville Road after a hard rain.

Pollution warning   At junction with North Jennings Run

That said, on a good day, the scenery is pristine and you will appreciate the fact that the stream is rarely over 20 yards from the shoulder of the road, minimizing hiking and maximizing fishing. In addition to the places listed above, there are additional random wide spots that can hold a single vehicle close to the water. Unlike many stocked streams in the State, there are numerous DNR signs confirming that the water is both stocked and access permitted. There are only a few places where blue blazes speckle the trees, indicating posted property. Trees line both banks and, in many areas, are dense enough to block the view of the road. With that, you can enjoy the tranquility of a remote setting with the dream temporarily interrupted by the recurring buzz of vehicles on the nearby highway.

Plenty of rocks to add interest

Decent depth... right off the road

The only pool obvious from the road is where North Jennings Run joins Jennings Run from the north. After churning together, the water moves downstream and smashes into a stark rock cliff that guards perfectly deep water for the trout dumped unceremoniously into the creek at the confluence. Downstream, the good spots are not obvious and require exercise and sweat to discover the deep channels and holding pools. With Piney Mountain looming 1,435 feet above the streambed on the southern side, the easiest movement will be between the road and the creek. Among fly anglers, Jennings Run has a reputation for being a good nymphing stream. Spin fishermen need to focus on pools large enough to allow the action of the lure to begin.

Open, easy casting

Road to the left

Jennings Run is the eighth most heavily stocked stream in the State.

Lake Habeeb (Rocky Gap Lake)

Approximate Boundary: 39.697357,-78.663104 to 39.715417,-78.641303 (243 acres)

Type: Put and Take

Directions:
From I-68, take exit 50 toward Rocky Gap Street. Turn right onto Pleasant Valley Road NE. The road parallels the eastern side of the lake. Turn left to pick a parking lot. If you have a boat, go to the northern access point to use the boat launch. There is another launch directly across the lake off of Campers Hill Drive.

Access Point:
- Various off of Pleasant Valley Road NE (39.699503,-78.658383, 39.709166,-78.642691, 39.711694,-78.641801)
- Various from the camp areas off of Campers Hill Drive (39.711305,-78.644773, 39.709518,-78.65025)
- Dam off of Old Hancock Road NE (39.697388,-78.662755)

Sitting in the shadow of Evitts Mountain and fully enclosed within Rocky Gap State Park, Lake Habeeb is a massive body of water fed by Rocky Gap Run. As you would expect on a lake this size, it features a public boat ramp at the north end (39.711759,-78.641784) but, surprisingly, only allows electric motors. If you do not have your own boat, you can rent boats, canoes or kayaks at either the day use beach area or at the campground beach.

In addition to trout stocked during the season, anglers can catch catfish and bass. Shoreline anglers should find the 4.5 mile Lakeside Loop Trail encircling the lake their ticket to fishing without a boat. In fact, as it runs along the west side of the lake, it offers up a remote experience. For those not interested in walking, the park management strategically placed fishing docks near the campsites and at the dam.

As a modern park, fishing is not the only thing to do. Hiking, golf, nature activities, swimming and a host of other diversions await your visit with the opportunity to stay in either a primitive campsite or a world-class lodge.

Big lake... big water   Golf course borders the lake

Laurel Run

Approximate Boundary: 39.545154,-79.006984 to 39.558854,-79.017155 (1.3 miles)

Type: Youth, Senior or Blind

Directions:
North: From I-68, take exit 34 for MD 36. Head south and drive through the town of Lonaconing. Turn right on MD 935S/Lower Georges Creek Road. Turn left at the "T" intersection to remain on MD 935. Make a sharp right onto Laurel Run Road SW. Laurel Run begins at the bridge.

South: From Westernport, drive north on MD 36. Turn left on MD 935S/Lower Georges Creek Road. Turn left at the "T" intersection to remain on MD 935. Make a sharp right onto Laurel Run Road SW. Laurel Run begins at the bridge.

Access Point:
- Intersection of Laurel Run Road and Pike Road (39.54567,-79.00845)
- Intersection of Laurel Run Road and Laurel Valley Drive (39.55098,-79.01455)
- Bridge crossing on Laurel Run Road (39.56007,-79.01803)
- Bridge crossing on Laurel Run Road (39.56327,-79.01781)
- Intersection of Laurel Run Road and Willow Crest Road (39.56653,-79.01776)

Laurel Run is a small freestone stream that weaves back and forth across Laurel Run Road. The road runs through a narrow canyon that compresses the stream, at times, to an width of two to three feet. It flows clear and cold across a rocky bottom throughout the entire stocked section. While it is stocked with a small number of fish compared to other streams in the area, pulling them out becomes a job limited to children or blind who are accomplished casters. At times, the stream is a mere trickle dribbling down the mountainside, forcing all the attention onto a rare deep pool. While the stream is initially free from obstructions, it is more constricted higher up the mountain, requiring technical fishing skills until reaching the bridge crossing at 39.56327,-79.01781. Prior to this spot, dense forests line both banks with numerous overhanging bushes and trees perfectly designed to interfere with casting – no matter whether you fish with fly or spin gear.

Tight vegetation   High gradient... shallow

The best place to fish for those who are not experts is in the upper section from Willow Crest Road downstream. It is the only place where there are defined turnoffs. While the western bank is overgrown, anglers can negotiate it with care. The east bank is a stone encrusted cliff that prevents movement. The best fishing will be in the pools formed by the several gradient breaks and near large boulders. Since this is a mountain trout stream, flow is minimal, causing most of the stream to be shallow except where the topography creates pools.

Without a doubt, Laurel Run is difficult to fish. Since there is no room for a long cast from the bank, the angler must be in the creek and able to negotiate the slippery streambed to get into position. Given the shallow water, the best fishing will be in the two weeks immediately after stocking. Note that the stocking schedule plants fish early in the season when the water levels are likely to be higher and the fish can circulate. In addition to stocked trout, Laurel Run supports a small number of wild trout with approximately 100 adult fish per 3,200 feet according to a 2003 survey.

Upper section   Hard fishing for a kid

Lions Park Pond

Approximate Boundary: 39.669814,-78.934098 to 39.669706,-78.934763 (1 acre)

Type: Youth, Senior or Blind

Directions:
East: From I-68, take exit 34 onto MD 36/New Georges Creek Road SW toward Frostburg. Turn left onto MD 36. Turn right onto Shaw Street followed by a right on Rynex Avenue. Turn left to go south on Laurel Avenue. The parking area for the pond is on the right.

West: From I-68, take exit 29 for MD 546. Turn left onto MD 546/Beall School Road. Take the US 40W exit toward Morgantown (you will backtrack) followed by a right onto Piney Run Road. Turn right onto US 40E. Turn left onto Shaw Street followed by a left on Rynex Avenue. Turn left to go south on Laurel Avenue. The parking area for the pond is on the right.

Access Point: Parking area adjacent to the pond (39.669764,-78.933701)

A short distance away from Cotton Cove Pond, inside the same Lions Community Park, is the similarly sized Lions Park Pond. However, it is positioned in a more scenic area than its sibling to the north. Tall trees surround three sides of the pond and the asphalt trail makes it universally accessible. The only potential obstacle for a disabled or blind person is the small wooden bridge spanning the creek that enters from the north. There is a wheelchair accessible fishing pier adjacent to the parking lot on the east side of the pond.

Although I did not measure it with the depth finder, this pond appears to be deeper than Cotton Cove. The bottom does not drop off as quickly and underwater vegetation hugs the bank except on the southwest side. The banks are not steep and access to the pond is easy. Several picnic tables and large rocks provide places to sit and supervise activity.

Right half of pond - parking to right   Left half of pond

North Jennings Run

Approximate Boundary: 39.70131,-78.843827 to 39.722174,-78.845801 (1.62 miles)

Type: Put and Take

Directions:
From I-68, take exit 44 for Baltimore Avenue. Turn left onto Willowbrook Road (name changes to Baltimore Avenue). Turn right on Henderson Avenue to remain on US 40 Alt W. Make a right onto MD 36S/Mt Savage Road. Turn right onto MD 47N/Barrelville Road. The stream parallels Barrelville Road.

Access Point:
- Intersection of Barrelville Road NW with Abucevicz Road (39.703778,-78.843814)
- Intersection of Barrelville Road NW with Old Spring Road (39.713212,-78.839624)
- Turnout 1,000 feet north of the intersection of Belle Star Road (39.717545,-78.842215)

North Jennings Run is a sparkling small stream that must be fished early in the season when water levels are high. Boulders and gravel fill the 10 to 15 foot narrow course of the creek, with the water getting a good push of velocity as it runs down the 180 foot drop in elevation between the Pennsylvania border and the junction with Jennings Run adjacent to MD 36. Thankfully, in many places, the banks are not overloaded with vegetation and movement is easy in either direction. Of course, the best places will be protected by obstacles that place a premium on the ability to deliver accurate, short casts. Piles of rocks and small boulders line both shorelines and call for caution when sneaking to the next deep channel or pool.

Although the boundary extends all the way up to the Pennsylvania border, scattered residential development and associated private property makes fishing above the turnout north of Belle Star Road NW problematic. Be careful in that area and look for "posted" signage. Frankly, it is no great loss since the water becomes less attractive, getting smaller and smaller closer to the border.

First bridge crossing

Top end near border

Orchard Pond

Approximate Boundary: 39.555343,-78.514369 to 39.556216,-78.513205 (2 acres)

Type: Put and Take

Directions:
North: From I-68, take exit 68. Turn left onto Orleans Road NE. Follow it until it dead ends. Turn right on Oldtown Orleans Road SE. It will fork after passing Malcolm Road. Take the left fork (David Thomas Road) and follow it until it dead ends on MD 51/Oldtown Road SE and turn right. Turn right onto Gorman Road. Follow it until it dead ends and turn right on Dailey Road SE. The lake is approximately one mile north on the left side.

South: From US 522 heading west from Winchester, turn left on VA 127/Bloomery Pike. Turn Right on WV 29. Continue onto WV 9W. It merges with MD 51 on the north side of Paw Paw. Continue west on MD 51. Turn right onto Gorman Road. Follow it until it dead ends and turn right on Dailey Road SE. The lake is approximately one mile north on the left side.

Access Point: Parking area off Dailey Road SE (39.555592,-78.513146)

Like its neighbor to the north, White Sulfur Pond, Orchard Pond was added to the stocking schedule in 1991 and is a small jewel at the southern end of the Green Ridge State Forest. Although there is only one bench adjacent to the parking area, it sits under several shade trees that turn fishing on a hot day into a pleasant experience.

Unfortunately, most of this jewel does not get polished as a result of the thick band of cattails growing thickly around most of the shoreline. On the eastern side, there are only a few spots where anglers can edge their way to the bank. A path runs around most of the pond, but it dead ends when the pond merges with a wetland at its northern extremity.

Most anglers fish from the southern end where there are gaps in the vegetation. These spots are within close proximity to a fallen tree that creates a both a landmark and good structure. The pond water has a unique rust color and remains relatively clear after rainfall. There seems to be a reasonable amount of depth in the pond and the bottom drops off quickly from the shoreline.

Town Creek

Approximate Boundary:
Upper Section: 39.59073,-78.548924 to 39.595724,-78.558902 (1.41 miles)
DNR Guidance: That portion of Town Creek lying within Green Ridge State Forest from a red post located approximately 0.75 mile downstream of the upper ford on Lower Town Creek Road, just south of the Wagner Road intersection, downstream to a red post located just upstream of the lower ford on Lower Town Creek Road (Mallory Place).

Lower Section: 39.56225,-78.551091 to 39.572572,-78.550318 (4,147 feet)
DNR Guidance: From a red post located approximately 0.5 mile downstream of Maniford Road to a red post located approximately 1.75 miles downstream (Bull Ring Ranch).

Type: Delayed Harvest

Directions:
North: From I-68, take exit 68/Orleans Road. Go south on Orleans Road NE. Turn right onto Oldtown Orleans Road SE. The road becomes David Thomas Road SE. Turn right onto MD 51N/Oldtown Road SE. Turn right on Lower Town Creek Road.

South: From I-81, take exit 310 onto VA 37 toward US 11. Exit onto US 522N/N Frederick Pike. Turn left onto VA 127W/Bloomery Pike. Continue onto WV 127W. Turn right on County 45/7/Gaston Road. Turn right onto WV 29N and continue onto WV 9W. Once across the river, the road becomes MD 51N/Oldtown Road SE. Turn right on Lower Town Creek Road.

Town Creek is one of the main fishing draws of the Green Ridge State Forest. It is low gradient, dropping a mere 12 feet per mile as it drifts lazily from Pennsylvania into Maryland with a stream bottom consisting primarily of small gravel, cobble, sand and bedrock. It is a wide stream by Maryland standards, sometimes exceeding 50 feet in width. Even though the banks are forested, the water warms in the summer, resulting in no trout survival between seasons. Even ardent catch and releasers should keep what they catch following the end of the delayed harvest season. In addition to the trout stocked in both the Spring and the Fall, there is a robust population of smallmouth bass and associated warm water species to provide summer fishing action.

The stocked section of Town Creek is divided into an upper and lower section with no access to the broad expanse of river dividing the two. The upper section receives the least amount of pressure as a result of the limited parking and deep water. If you fish in the Fall during hunting season, be sure and wear blaze orange.

Upper Section

Directions:
Town Creek Access: To fish the upper section, continue past the turn for Maniford Road and follow Lower Town Creek Road to the creek. Do not take the fork to the right on Peckenbuck Road.

Wagner Road: Instead of turning north on Lower Town Creek Road, continue west on Oldtown Road SE. Turn right on Wagner Road just east of Oldtown. Drive approximately 4.5 miles until you begin to see yellow blazes on the trees marking the boundary of public property and park near the old barn. There is a path that leads 800 feet east to the stream.

Access Point:
- Lower Town Creek Road where it crosses the creek (39.590595,-78.548782)
- Wagner Road parking lot near an old barn (39.590238,-78.563817)

Follow the Town Creek Road directions to bump into the tight parking lot at the edge of the river. "Parking lot" is an aggressive term to apply to a small turnoff at the end of the road. There is a ford where the adventurous drive across, but I do not recommend it. During the high water in early Spring, precisely when you would be here to fish for trout, the water level probably exceeds the capability of most vehicles to make the voyage safely. Instead, wade across the river along the ridgeline that extends perpendicular to the shoreline near the parking area. The terrain is tight on the southern bank with steep cliffs preventing any significant upstream progress. Beyond the obstacle presented by steep terrain, the creek is unwadeable along the southern bank and that fact makes it the initial target of your day's expedition. Attack the deep water from a northern perspective all the way up to the cliff face. At that point, the river shallows out a bit.

The ford you should not drive across

Wade across on the ridge

At the corner, the river deepens again and stays that way through the upstream section to the end of the stocked water with the shallow side lying to the east. If you need to move quickly from place to place, leverage the northern bank. Stay near the bank, close to the water, since the bushes form a dense buffer extending to an open field approximately 25 yards from the stream. If you park at Wagner Road, the path leads to the corner without the challenge of wading across a high creek.

Upstream from the ford

West into the bend

Lower Section

Directions:
Once on Lower Town Creek Road, continue north, turning right on Maniford Road SE to reach the lower section. The parking lot is on the right. Follow the trail to the river (1,600 feet from the parking lot).

Access Point: Parking lot adjacent to Maniford Road (39.57639,-78.547173)

The lower section is easier to fish than the upper with the first indication being the well-developed parking area next to the trail. The path starts at the west end of the lot and, after going through the gate, it is a nice, level road all the way to the river. The road parallels the creek for approximately 1,600 feet until it veers west. Since the level road runs along the high bank above the creek, it provides a highway to move quickly away from the pressure that naturally builds close to the trailhead. Lower Town Creek is the perfect place to use a bike since the stocked area continues for 2,500 feet downstream beyond the end of the road. A bike gets you to that spot quickly. Fishing the lower section is like fishing in a park. The vegetation on the west bank throws calming shade across the surface of the water and, once you negotiate the steep bank to find a good spot to wade, the fishing is easy and comfortable on the uncomplicated streambed. Fly anglers will discover that there is nothing to tangle a backcast and spin fishing is equally simple. While anglers need to be alert for the deep spots, the river is typically between two and four feet deep with a moderate current.

Upper end near parking lot

Lower end

The shade evaporates once the road breaks west and that is where the water will be warmest. Therefore, if fishing for trout at the end of the delayed harvest season, avoid going all the way downstream and stay close to the parking lot where the water will be coolest. Since the trout are stocked, fly anglers should initially use brightly colored streamers. Spin fishermen can use the normal assortment of trout spinners, matching the color of the flash to the brightness of the sky. Once the stocked trout become accustomed to eating insects, fly anglers can take advantage of that to improve their success rate. The Maryland DNR comments that the aquatic insect hatches are "very prolific." Once the trout adapt, stoneflies are the best early-season pattern followed by caddis in April.

White Sulfur Pond

Approximate Boundary: 39.651567,-78.478561 to 39.651154,-78.477124 (1 acre)

Type: Put and Take

Directions:
From I-68, take exit 64 for US 40/15 Mile Creek Road. Turn left onto MD 144/National Pike. Turn left onto Old Williams Road followed by a quick left onto Black Sulphur Road. Follow it to the dead end and turn left on Wallizer Road. The pond is on the left approximately 1.5 miles from the turn.

Access Point: 39.651567,-78.478561 (parking area off Wallizer Road)

Added to the stocking plan in 1991, White Sulfur Pond has been a reliable producer, not only holding trout during the season, but for bass as well. In fact, the prevalence of bass will cause you to flip priorities many times during the day as one or the other species "turns on."

The pond is tucked into the northwest corner of the Green Ridge State Forest with a well-maintained dirt road leading to it. The eastern shoreline of the lake is easily accessible via a grassy bank with a smooth path leading between benches strategically placed along the perimeter. The western side is harder to negotiate using a small fisherman's trail hanging on the bottom edge of the sharply pitched hill that creates a narrow barrier between the lake and the road where it climbs laboriously up the ridgeline. There is no room for a fly angler's backcast from the western side. As the season progresses, a mat of moderate density underwater vegetation grows from the shoreline and is thickest at the entry point near the parking area. There are no abrupt drops into deep water from the bank since the bottom slopes gradually away from the shoreline.

Wills Creek

Approximate Boundary: 39.691676,-78.780594 to 39.663559,-78.780688 (5.2 miles)
DNR Guidance: Mainstem upstream of the US Army Corps of Engineers Flood Control Project at The Narrows above Cumberland.

Type: Put and Take

Directions:
From I-68, take exit 44 for Baltimore Avenue. Turn left onto Willowbrook Road (name changes to Baltimore Avenue). Turn right on Henderson Avenue to remain on US 40 Alt W to reach the first three access points that are all right turns.

Beach View Drive: Make a right onto MD 36S/Mt Savage Road. Turn right on MD 831C/Kreighbaum Road NW on the east side of Corriganville. Turn right on Beach View Drive. The parking area is at the end of the road.

Forest Grove: Turn right off of MD 36/Mt Savage Road onto MD 35. Turn right on Forest Grove Road with another left on Kings Grove Road to drive up to the border.

Access Point:
- Parking lot of the Fruit Bowl (39.666561,-78.781871)
- Parking on east side of the bridge on Locust Grove Road NW (39.670695,-78.789335)
- Parking at the end of Wabash Street NW (39.677285,-78.789057)
- Parking lot at the end of Beach View Drive (39.695341,-78.78717)
- Forest Grove Road bridge crossing (39.718428,-78.771375)
- Pennsylvania border (39.723016,-78.769136)

Wills Creek is not really a creek, it is a river. Wills was added to the stocking schedule in 2010 and already has earned a spot as one of the top stocked streams in the State; getting 7,225 fish in the Spring 2011 season. Despite being popular, there is an issue. As of 2011, the sewage transmission pipes in the area are in a state of disrepair and the sanitary commission is anxious to use American Reinvestment and Recovery Act funding to fix the problem. The basic issue is that the system overflows and raw sewage ends in the stream. A sign warning anglers sits at the small one vehicle turnout on the east side of the bridge on Locust Grove Road with an even more aggressive warning posted to the bridge abutment, "*This is a combined storm water sewage outfall.*" Thanks. Please fix it. Given that warning, focus your fishing above the junction of Braddock Run with Wills Creek at the narrows if there has been a heavy rain.

The DNR stocks the river between the Narrows and Braddock Run from the railroad side. Since the rail line hugs Wills Mountain to the east, there is no access from that side. The first potential access point is at the north end of the parking lot of the Fruit Bowl store. At the end of the fence, there is a beaten trail leading to the creek. Ask for permission before parking for an extended time. Failing that, the Locust Grove bridge crossing is only a half mile upstream with parking on both sides of the street as well as along the trail leading back to the railroad tracks.

The nicest place to jump in the river is at the end of Wabash Street near the railroad bridge. Do not block the school bus turnaround at the north end of the street. Park on the east side, close to the railroad tracks, without obstructing the dirt road leading to the tracks. The river is on the other side of the berm and there are several trails leading to the water. At normal levels, the river is wadeable with the streambed being a mix of rocks and boulders spread across a 70 foot width. The deep channel is on the south side of the small island a hundred feet down from the bridge. This is the last access point before reaching Corriganville. Even though you might be tempted to park on the wide shoulder on the east side of the road, there is a 600 foot buffer of private property protecting the stream. Likewise, there are plenty of "no trespassing" signs posted in the commercial complex just north of the railroad bridge.

Using the first access point in Corriganville at the end of Beach View Drive, anglers can take advantage of the deep water created by the confluence of Jennings Run with Wills Creek. A superb spot is on the east side of the railroad bridge. There is a small trail leading upstream from that point providing access to the west bank.

At the bridge, the river runs 100 feet wide over a rocky bottom mixed with sand. Where the river levels out or turns a corner and loses velocity, more sand appears. There are plenty of deep spots, channels and enough large rocks to create varied structure. Heavy vegetation grows on both banks with tall trees throwing plenty of shade over the water. The banks are high and make for a skidding, full contact entry down the muddy slope to the shoreline.

Wabash Street railroad bridge

Upstream from Beach View Drive

The next spot is below the Pennsylvania border at the Forest Grove Road bridge crossing. Go across the bridge and park on Kings Grove Road on the east side of the creek. Follow the fisherman's trail that leads directly downstream from the west bank to reach the river. There is additional easy access on the other side via numerous dirt roads created by dirt biking fanatics whose acrobatic exploits cut wide paths through the trees. Although the creek runs about 50 feet wide and flat over a bottom that is a mix of small rocks and sand, there is a deep cut in the middle that is fishable by moving out onto the shelf above the bridge. The eastern bank slopes gradually up to join the heavily vegetated shoreline. Unlike farther downriver, the shoreline is not congested to the point of preventing movement. The view downstream is favorable. A wide gradient break creates a broad riffle where the river tightens up and narrows.

Forest Grove Road bridge upstream   Forest Grove Road bridge downstream.

The final access point is adjacent to the residential area at the Pennsylvania border. Kings Grove Road runs parallel to the creek and provides several opportunities to turn out, park and walk across the 40 foot protective barrier of vegetation to reach the water between the bridge and the border.

Wills Creek is the sixth most heavily stocked stream in the State.

Anne Arundel County

Lake Waterford

Approximate Boundary: 39.113847,-76.558352 to 39.114838,-76.565261 (11 acres)

Type: Put and Take

Directions:
From I-97, take exit 14 to merge onto MD 100E toward Gibson Island. Take exit 19 and turn south on Catherine Avenue. Turn right on MD 648/Baltimore Annapolis Boulevard (aka Old Annapolis Boulevard). The park and lake are on the left.

Access Point:
- Parking lot on south side of lake off Old Annapolis Boulevard (39.113847,-76.558352)
- Parking lot on north side of lake off Old Annapolis Boulevard (39.114918,-76.559896)

Lake Waterford has not been stocked since the spring of 2010 as a result of "environmental issues." Other than trout, if they are ever stocked again, the lake has a robust population of warm water fish including bass and catfish. Fishing is easy along the eastern dam with three fishing piers permitting disabled access. The best trail runs along the southern shoreline and, if you intend to use it, park in the southern parking lot. While the shoreline is thick with vegetation, the picture shows one of the many openings created by anglers that allow you to reach the bank. The lake stays clean and, except for the southeastern corner, does not have an oppressive growth of shoreline vegetation to make casting problematic.

As a side note, the DNR prohibits fishing for 3,000 feet downstream of the dam between January and the end of April. Outside of that restricted season, there is bushwhacking access off of Old Mill Road to the lower river.

Severn Run

Approximate Boundary: 39.102857,-76.691696 to 39.081973,-76.629481 (7.06 miles)
DNR Guidance: Mainstem upstream of Route 3.

Type: Put and Take

Directions:
From I-97, take exit 12 onto MD 3S. This is New Cut Road and it leads to all of the access points. New Cut takes a fork to the right to dead end into Burns Crossing Road. Turn right at that dead end to reach the Burns access, followed by a left on Old Mill Road to drive to the western end of the stocked section. For Dicus Mill, take the left fork after leaving I-97 (Gambrill Road) and follow it to the intersection with Dicus Mill. Turn left on Dicus Mill to drive to the stream.

Access Point:
- Old Mill Road at 39.102862,-76.691204
- Burns Crossing Road at 39.102862,-76.691204
- New Cut Road at 39.108346,-76.651484
- Dicus Mill Road at 39.085692,-76.632625

Severn Run is an obstacle course. This narrow, five to ten foot wide stream threads through a deeply cut bed protected by a thick, sharp tangle of thorn vines that will trip, snag and poke with a vengeance. There is no place to sit, stand or even move. The overhead vegetation is oppressive and, while bait anglers can fish this water easily, there is no room for spin or fly casting. No kidding about the sandy bed being deeply cut below the level of the surrounding land. At times, this sad little creek runs ten feet below the top of the bank. In most places, the water is inches deep with trout pathetically huddling in what passes for "deep" holes at each bend. The DNR inserts trout when the water is high enough for them to skitter away from the road, but the level can drop quickly, stranding the trout in shallow water. The streambed is as miserable as the bank. It is a messy tangle of logs that provides no room to play a fish. Instead, the technique is "hook and jerk" with heavy line to avoid tangling. My recommendation is that if you have someplace else to fish, go there.

High banks protected by thorns

Streambed is a tangled mess of fallen trees

Baltimore County

Avalon Pond

Approximate Boundary: 39.22971,-76.728983 to 39.230317,-76.729584 (1 acre)

Type: Youth, Senior and Blind

Directions:
From I-95, take exit 47 for I-195E towards the BWI Airport/MD 166/Catonsville. Merge onto I-195. Take exit 3 for Washington Boulevard/US 1 toward Elkridge. Turn right on US 1 (south). Turn right onto South Street. Turn left onto River Road. Turn right onto Gun Road. Turn left onto Glen Artney Road and follow it to the parking lot.

Access Point: Parking lot adjacent to Glen Artney Road (39.230529,-76.729176)

One of the attractions of Avalon Pond is the easy access for disabled anglers facilitated by four fishing piers that overhang the water. The improved walking path connecting them makes movement easy, even for those confined to wheelchairs. Thick vegetation packs the shoreline, especially at the western end. Other than the piers, there are only a few places where anglers have beaten back the shoreline vegetation to create paths to the water's edge. The bottom of the lake falls off quickly from the shoreline and there is no clogging growth of underwater vegetation during the trout season. In short, when combined with the adjacent picnic areas, this is a good place to bring a child.

Beetree Run

Approximate Boundary: 39.677301,-76.666896 to 39.694177,-76.668699 (1.6 miles)

Type: Catch and Return

Directions: From I-83, take exit 33 onto MD 45, York Road. Turn left on Kaufman Road and follow it to the BeeTree Preserve.

Access Point:
- Turnout on Bee Tree Road (39.684346,-76.666329)
- TCB Trail parking on Bentley Road (39.675022,-76.670421)

The 263 acre Beetree Preserve hosts Beetree Run, a small wild trout stream. The Towson Presbyterian Church manages the preserve and establishes the rules for access. According to their literature, "*The preserve is generally open to all responsible individuals and groups during daylight hours. However, large groups should reserve times with the church prior to use. Written authorization is required for all evening and overnight use.*" Assuming you are responsible and not a large group, you can fish here without further coordination.

If you plug the above GPS coordinates into a Garmin vehicular GPS system, the voice may insist you make a right turn onto Bee Tree Road once you pass the large kiosk on the left at the intersection of Kaufmann and Bee Tree. Ignore the course correction and continue straight through the intersection, crossing a small bridge prior to arriving at the second bridge adjacent to the Torrey C Brown Rail (TCB) Trail.

Upstream from parking   Downstream from parking

The tiny stream parallels the TCB trail for most of its length and that is how many calculate the fishable length as being over five miles, especially since the trail runs all the way up to the Pennsylvania border. However, given the vagaries of private property, the only place you are guaranteed access is in the Beetree Preserve. While you can certainly fish outside the preserve, you must ensure that you are not trespassing. Use a bike or hike along the trail to find the best places to access the water. The fishable property lies in the preserve to the east of the trail. Approximately 600 feet to the north of Beetree Road, the stream runs onto private property only to swerve back to the east into the preserve 500 feet later. From the bridge, the preserve extends approximately 0.8 miles south to end just north of Bentley Road and runs almost a mile to the north, giving anglers plenty of skinny water to follow in pursuit of that isolated pool full of wary brown trout. Be prepared to walk or bike to find the best places to fish. Since the TCB trail does not run directly adjacent to the stream, you have to leave that level surface and bushwhack over to the water.

Low gradient

Narrow with pools at bends

The stream bottom is a mix of rocks and sand with plenty of deeply undercut banks providing holding locations for the wild population of small brown trout that happily inhabit this water. The banks run three to four feet high and slope gradually to the stream. Tall grass grows to the water's edge, making this an ideal location to flip terrestrial flies. Look for deep pools at the bends. Trees throw shade on the water, but they are not thick enough to present an obstacle to casting as long as you wade. Likewise, walk along the stream to find the best places to fish since the best spots are not visible from the trail. Since the wild trout are skittish, exercise stealth or resign yourself to sweating without a payoff.

Deep spots with undercut banks

Wide, shallow runs lead to pools

Gunpowder Falls

Prettyboy Reservoir - Downstream Catch and Release

Approximate Boundary: 39.599406,-76.626424 to 39.619243,-76.706557 (7.32 miles)
DNR Guidance: Mainstem from Prettyboy Reservoir Dam downstream to Blue Mount Road.

Type: Catch and Return

Directions:
Points East of I-83: Take exit 27 for MD 137/Mt Carmel Road and head east.
- For Blue Mount Road, turn right on York Road. Turn left on Monkton Road. Turn left on Blue Mount Road at the fork.
- For Big Falls Road, turn right on York Road. Turn left on Monkton Road. Turn left on Big Falls Road at the fork.
- For York Road, turn left on York Road.
- For Bunker Hill Road, turn left on York Road. Turn left on Bunker Hill Road.

Points West of I-83: Take exit 27 for MD 137/Mt Carmel Road and head west.
- For Masemore Road, turn right onto Masemore Road.
- For Falls Road, turn right on Evna Road. Turn right onto Falls Road.

Access Point:
- Bridge crossing at Blue Mount Road (39.599422,-76.626293)
- Bridge crossing at Big Falls Road (39.60941,-76.635331)
- Bridge crossing at York Road (39.61401,-76.659141)
- Dead end at Bunker Hill Road - south side (39.609325,-76.672212)
- Dead end at Bunker Hill Road - north side (39.612813,-76.672191)
- Bridge crossing at Masemore Road (39.611276,-76.682775)
- Parking lot 1 along Falls Road (39.61467,-76.69640)
- Parking lot 2 along Falls Road west of the bridge (39.61751,-76.69292)

There are almost an infinite number of opportunities to fish the Gunpowder Falls River as it winds its way from the Prettyboy Reservoir through almost 20,000 acres of the Gunpowder Falls State Park and other public land with accessibility enhanced by hiking trails that parallel the river. The fact that the park consists of so much land, serving so many different recreational uses, puts anglers in competition with other outdoor enthusiasts. Do not be surprised if clueless non-anglers disrupt your fishing. Kayakers, canoeist and tubers cause the most obvious problems, but I heard a story of anglers fishing when an oblivious passerby threw an object into the middle of their pool followed by the crashing splash of the well-trained Labrador swimming hard to retrieve it. Trout Unlimited rates the Prettyboy Reservoir section as one of the top 100 streams in America. As such, you will find that hundreds of anglers want to visit and test their skill against the over 1,000 trout per mile that live in this beautiful section. The DNR does not stock the catch and release area and relies on the excellent habitat to sustain the wild trout fishery. While the catch and release section is best known for wild trout, the entire Gunpowder Falls River from Prettyboy Dam all the way down to the Loch Raven Reservoir supports wild fish with the most robust population being near the headwaters.

The angling pressure and scenic beauty drops proportionally the farther you move downstream from Prettyboy Dam. Although the section from Falls Road up to the dam is ideal from a trout fishing perspective, there will be an angler standing in the stream every 50 yards, or less, on weekends. Every pool will be occupied and the trout will huddle, trembling in fear, under any available cover. That said, the Falls Road section is ideal to fish during the week when the trout have had the opportunity to settle down. During periods of low pressure, you can wander unconstrained and fish the spectacular pools that dot every twist and turn of this glorious river.

Prettyboy Reservoir

Starting at the dam and working downstream. The river runs tight and narrow through a soaring canyon towering 300 feet above the streambed. The shoreline is overloaded with vegetation with large fallen trees stretching bank to bank, creating confused masses of structure. It seems as if the river bottom felt it needed to match that challenge and composed itself using a jumble of randomly sized boulders and rocks custom-made to trip the unwary angler. Wading can be treacherous if you step carelessly. The trails from either of the Falls Road parking lots moving upstream are tight and narrow as they wind their way up and down the precipitous hillsides. With a thick curtain of vegetation separating the trail from the river, you may surprise other anglers when poking your head out to check out the stream. Given that, approach quietly so as not to destroy someone else's fishing experience. By the time the river reaches the Falls Road bridge crossing, it has widened to run across a rocky bottom that includes a significant amount of gravel. Shallow water comes with the increase in width.

Masemore

Downstream of Falls Road, the river takes a break as it leaves the tight canyons and enters a slightly wider valley upstream of the Masemore bridge. At this point, the tortured twists and turns disappear and the banks become normal for Maryland. Upstream of the bridge crossing, the trail drops down to the river where the bank merges gradually into the water itself. There are no large boulders, just rocks and gravel. Tall trees stretch to the sky on either side and provide plenty of shade. Fishing here is a matter of finding the deep cuts and the undercut banks. The downstream perspective is the same. Some mud begins to appear on the sides where the river deposits silt as it loses velocity, having dropped over 100 feet in elevation from the base of the dam.

Upstream from bridge   Looking back to the bridge from downstream

Bunker Hill Road

In the 1.2 miles between Masemore and Bunker Hill Road, the river drops a paltry 25 feet, something that is obvious when you stand at the bank after walking the 0.3 miles/112 foot vertical from the Bunker Hill Road parking lot. Instead of featuring the rocks and plunge pools of the Prettyboy section, the river adopts the characteristic of a normal central Maryland stream and oozes lazily through the deep cut between high hills, only losing a few feet in elevation between Bunker Hill and Big Falls Road.

Rough road below large parking lot

Upstream from Bunker Hill Road

Big Falls Road

By the time the river reaches Big Falls Road, it has no significant velocity as it winds slowly underneath the tight canopy of overreaching trees and bushes. The river narrows to 30 feet and has dug its way deep into the mud and sand that create the banks. Near the road, the river is essentially a gash with high banks demanding caution as you pick the best place to reach the water's edge. The farther upstream you go, the river widens and the less of a challenge this becomes. The amount of silt on the river bottom should not discourage fishing. Random, capricious storms and floods treated trees like matchsticks, throwing them across the river to create huge woodpiles that strain the water as it heads south. The trout are here, it just takes some work to pull them out.

Banks OK and river wide farther upstream

Typical tangle and associated pool

Blue Mount Road

Blue Mount Road is the downstream boundary of the catch and release section. At this point, there is no defined trail on either side of the bank if you ignore the TCB trail on the ridge high above the river. Enter using the beaten path next to the bridge and fish upstream. There are deep channels running over a gravel bottom that has some silt with undercut banks. Do not be surprised if kayakers or canoeists drift through your fishing hole and accept the fact that more tubers than you will be comfortable seeing use Blue Mount Road to begin their float to Monkton. The river downstream from Blue Mount Road is designated as a wild trout water with a two fish per day limit (not stocked). Frankly, it is not worth fishing. Between Blue Mount and Monkton, the river runs shallow with only a few gradient breaks to create interest. There are some deep pools adjacent to undercut banks on the southern side, but not enough to make it worth the hike.

Upper Gunpowder Falls

Approximate Boundary: 39.510398,-76.624861 to 39.564743,-76.622651 (5.47 miles)
DNR Guidance: Mainstem from a red post located 1.6 miles downstream of Corbett Road downstream to the hiker/biker bridge located approximately one mile downstream of Phoenix Road.

Type: Put and Take

Directions:
From I-83, take exit 20 to merge onto Shawan Road east towards Cockeysville. Turn left onto MD 45N/York Road. Options:
- Turn right onto Phoenix Road
- Turn right onto Sparks Road
- Turn right onto Lower Glencoe Road

For the Glencoe Road bridge crossing, continue on Lower Glencoe Road and turn right onto Glencoe Road.

Access Point:
- Old Monkton Train Station on Monkton Road (39.579178,-76.615418)
- Upper Glencoe Road turnout (39.556595,-76.640422)
- Bridge crossing at Glencoe Road (39.550176,-76.63575)
- Lower Glencoe Road turnout (39.543994,-76.641095)
- Bridge crossing at Sparks Road (39.539619,-76.638185)
- Bridge crossing at Phoenix Road (39.523798,-76.623506)
- Lower take-out on Phoenix Road (39.519188,-76.619292)

The water temperature in the upper section stays cold enough to support year-round trout survival.

Monkton

Even though the old Monkton train station is outside of the nominal stocked area of the upper Gunpowder, it is worth mentioning. This location is the major access point to the Torrey Brown trail. Get familiar with the trail since it extends for 21 miles along the river. It is perfect for hikers, bikers, horseback riders and, most importantly, anglers who want to walk away from the access points intent on making pressure a distant memory. Remember, the entire river supports a wild trout population.

On weekends, the Monkton parking lot will be packed with scores of hikers, bikers and tubers (during the warmer months). There is no immediate access to the river at the train station. Follow the trail upstream for approximately 1600 feet to where it rejoins the river. Fishing upstream from that point puts you into a "wild" area that is not stocked, but the river does support wild fish. Frankly, with a sandy bottom, the shallow depth and languid flow, you have better options. If you really want to catch a trout, this should be your last choice.

Glencoe Road

The Glencoe Road access points are within 4,500 feet of each other and provide the best entry to good fishing on the upper Gunpowder. Parking is limited. At the Glencoe bridge crossing, there are a few parking spaces next to the Torrey Brown trail. Some people park in the open lot adjacent to the bridge. However, that looks suspiciously like private property to me and, besides, you risk being captured and trapped by careless, unthinking people who block other vehicles by parking close to the road without considering how earlier arrivals will exit. Farther south, the lower Glencoe Road access point has room for three or four vehicles at most. Going in the other direction, the upper turnout is similarly congested with a small shoulder where the road bends west.

At normal levels near the bridge, the river runs a foot or two deep. Both shorelines are heavily overgrown with tall trees, bushes and other vegetation that forces anglers into the river. The shaded river has plenty of sand and a few rocks while running 20 to 30 feet wide. The deep areas alternate from bank to bank moving upstream with productive spots near shade. Near the Glencoe Road "elbow," the shoreline begins to break up, featuring more grass instead of trees. Once around the bend, there are a few places with rocks and deep channels. When done fishing, walk east to intersect the trail and use it as a less stressful way to get back to your vehicle.

At the lower turnout, take the faint trail heading downstream to discover the river has a sandy bottom as it tightens to 15 to 20 feet wide. The banks are high, steep and require care to find the right place to slide unceremoniously down to the river. There are deep holes scattered throughout the section, but the average depth is only a foot or two. A point of fishable interest is the rock wall supporting the road on the west side of the river. Expect to see canoeists float by and be prepared for the associated disruption.

Upstream from bridge   Lower turnout upstream - expect canoes

Sparks Road

There is plenty of parking at Sparks Road. This is a major takeout for canoeists as well as a waypoint for hikers and bikers enjoying the trail. From the lot, follow the road towards the bridge and hop onto the narrow trail that parallels it on the southern side. At this point, the river runs, wide and slow, through a level valley. If you want to walk away from the pressure near the parking lot, use the Torrey Brown trail to move in either direction. There are a number of places where you can cut over to the river and hop into the water. Although not heavily vegetated, the banks remain steep with plenty of deep channels along the eastern bank, forcing you to look hard for the right place to get down to the river.

Phoenix Road

At the Phoenix Road bridge crossing, there is a small two car turnout, but it lacks a well-defined, path down the steep hillside to reach the trail below. If you decide to wade fish from this spot, fish upstream since wading is prohibited downstream of the bridge in the watershed property. The river is quite a distance from the trail, so be prepared to bushwhack. The final access point is the canoe take-out approximately a mile downstream. There is plenty of parking with stairs easing entry to the river for canoeists and kayakers. Thick, tangled vegetation, protected by a robust growth of poison ivy, limits shoreline fishing in the immediate vicinity of the takeout. To fish from the shore, walk upriver.

Sparks Road   Phoenix Road

The upper section of Gunpowder Falls is the tenth most heavily stocked stream in the State.

Lower Gunpowder Falls

Approximate Boundary: 39.426647,-76.528902 to 39.415905,-76.409583 (8.61 miles)
DNR Guidance: From Cromwell Bridge Road downstream to the I-95 bridge.

Type: Put and Take

Directions:
- Belair Road: From I-695, take exit 32 for US 1N/Belair Road. Follow it to the bridge. The parking area is on the east side.
- Harford Road: From I-695, take exit 31 onto MD 147N/Harford Road. Follow it to the bridge. Turn left to go to the Notchcliff Road turnoffs, right to go to the Factory Road turnoff.

Access Point:
- Bridge crossing at Belair Road/US 1 (39.427668,-76.443483)
- Bridge crossing at Harford Road (39.422229,-76.502106)
- Turnouts on Factory Road east of bridge (39.421361,-76.498106, 39.42172,-76.499214)
- Wide shoulder along entire Notchcliffe Road from 39.422577,-76.50318 to where the road bends north away from the river.

Even though there are only a few places where the stocking truck can edge close enough to insert its load, anglers can leverage the extensive Gunpowder Falls State Park trail system to fish almost the entire length of the lower Gunpowder. While the trout may not move significant distances from the stocking locations, the river is overrun with warm water species including large and smallmouth bass. With summer water levels supporting wading, the Gunpowder becomes a year-round destination.

Belair Road

The largest parking area in the lower Gunpowder is the one on the north side of the river at Belair Road. Pull off on the east side and be prepared to make a tough decision. Which trail to follow? If you decide to head west, the Stocksdale Trail runs upstream on the north side while the Big Gunpowder Trail parallels the southern bank in both directions. To fish east towards I-95, follow the Lost Pond Trail on the north bank. There is a tunnel underneath US 1 that allows anglers to move east or west along the north bank as well as a pedestrian bridge to the southern bank and the Big Gunpowder Trail. In the immediate vicinity of the parking area, the banks are clogged with vegetation requiring the investment of a small amount of sweat to move along the trail until it drops to the level of the river. Even though the trails are wide and well marked, the DNR prohibits the use of bicycles into the Wildlands to the west. Be prepared to hike to get to the best places.

This is "big water." Not only is the river over 70 feet wide, it carries a huge volume of water that could easily push you all the way to the Chesapeake Bay. Therefore, be especially careful before you step off the bank and wear a PFD. A good rule is that if you cannot see the bottom, the flow is too high.

Downstream   Upstream from trail

Harford Road

Measured using the yardstick of the shortest distance from parking lot to water, the Harford Road bridge crossing sits in the middle of the most accessible area of the lower Gunpowder. There are two access points to the east of the bridge, one at the bridge and the entire Notchcliffe Road is universally accessible as a result of the broad shoulder that parallels the river. Be prepared to enter the river to fish. The banks are replete with bushes and trees whose only purpose is to obstruct movement along the shoreline. If fishing from the shore, look for the small gaps between the large trees and, even then, casting will be restricted. Wait until the river drops to a safe level and wade away from the bank to avoid those obstacles. Although this is only a few miles upstream from Belair Road, the river has already begun to narrow in its final approach to the Loch Raven Reservoir.

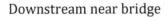

Downstream near bridge   Off Notchcliffe Road

The lower section of Gunpowder Falls is the ninth most heavily stocked area in the State.

Gwynn Oak Pond

Approximate Boundary: 39.325272,-76.720239 to 39.328372,-76.71867 (4 acres)

Type: Put and Take

Directions:
From I-695, take exit 18 for MD 26E/Liberty Road toward Lochearn. Turn right onto Flannery Lane. Turn left onto Gwynndale Avenue, Turn right onto Gwynn Oak Avenue and follow it to the park.

Access Point: Gywnn Oak Park parking lot off of Gwynn Oak Avenue (39.32616,-76.716532)

After parking in the small lot, follow the path past the playground and pavilions to reach the edge of the lake. It looks like a giant used in ax to create a narrow wedge between Woodlawn Cemetery to the west and the remainder of Gwynn Oak Park to the right. This is a shallow pond, with the deep spots in the north near the dam and along the main channel, outside of casting range, in the middle of the pond.

Except for where the asphalt path borders the eastern edge, the remainder of the bank to the south is overgrown with vegetation with a few beaten gaps created by anglers. Movement from gap to gap is easy on the mowed field paralleling the shoreline. The western bank is not fishable as result of the soft mud. Consistent with other area parks, there are plenty of picnic tables, a playground and a pavilion to provide a family friendly environment.

Gwynns Falls

Approximate Boundary: 39.351423,-76.741501 to 39.368312,-76.737272 (1.53 miles)
DNR Guidance: Mainstem below Route 140.

Type: Put and Take

Directions:
From I-695, take exit 18 for MD 26W/Liberty Road. Turn right onto Washington Avenue, Turn right on Milford Mill Road. Turn left onto Silver Creek Road.

Access Point:
- Milford Mill Road east of I-695 (39.359752,-76.744891)
- Street parking along Cloudyfold Drive
- Street parking along Leafydale Terrace
- Cliffedge Road and Templecliff Road (39.36684,-76.737389)

Sadly, the stream does not have much going for it. Although it has a decent amount of velocity, it wanders across a sandy bottom with few rocks or other scenic structure. After a rain, it will be thick and stained a deep chocolate. Bushes clog the low, muddy bank, making it a fight to reach the water. If you fish this water, be prepared to wade. The most scenic place is downstream from the Milford Mill parking area as a result of the higher flow stemming from the additional water contributed by Level Branch. Use the Gwynns Falls Trail along the west side of the stream to move quickly from place to place. Since both the trail and the stream run through the thickly wooded Villa Nova Park, the area has a remote feel despite being just inside the Baltimore Beltway. Upstream from Milford Mill, there is easy access from the roadside parking along the various residential streets on the east side of the park.

Downstream from Milford Mill parking   Adjacent to residential areas

Jones Falls

Upper Section - Baltimore County

Approximate Boundary: 39.375138,-76.65054 to 39.378236,-76.643986 (2,129 feet)
DNR Guidance: That portion of Jones Falls and tributaries above Stevenson Road to their source.

Type: Youth, Blind and Senior

Directions:
From I-695, take exit 21 north onto MD 129/Park Heights Avenue. Proceed to the bridge.

Access Point:
- Intersection of Greenspring Valley Road and Chattolanee Hill Road (39.40852,-76.742819)
- Park Heights Avenue bridge crossing (39.407251,-76.729215)
- Old Valley Road bridge crossing (39.410053,-76.719269)

The stream supports a reproducing population of trout and is not on the stocking plan. Before you get excited about the opportunity to pursue wild trout within minutes of Baltimore, much of the stream is off limits as a result of private property.

At the far western end, the limestone stream originates as a small dribble in the Green Spring Valley Golf Course whose boundaries are peppered with "posted" signs. There is a small turnoff on Greenspring Valley Road outside the golf course where you can walk back to the bridge and theoretically fish the stream to the east. However, given that it is only a few feet wide, shallow and winds through thick, overhanging vegetation, fishing would be a miserable experience for either a child or blind person and not much fun for experienced seniors either.

Park Heights is the most scenic section with the stream unloading to the east through an open farmer's field with tall trees sprinkled along the bank. In addition, as a result of the flow contributed by two tributaries upstream with an additional one downstream, there is more water, resulting in a higher quality fishable environment. However, there is no DNR signage advertising that this is public water, so be careful and obey any new "posted" signs that may appear.

There is no access downstream at Old Valley Road. The landowner erected a 6 foot high iron fence to clearly indicate their preference to keep the stream off limits. If you intend to fish in the other direction, roadside parking is limited and you may end up having to park at the corner and walk back. Frankly, I expect the upstream section to sprout "posted" signs at some point to mirror the downstream restriction. Finally, even though the DNR guidance indicates that the fishable section is everything upstream from Stevenson Road, the high fence at Stevenson Road also sends a clear message - do not even bother to try.

Unfishable at western end

Park Heights area

Lower Section - Robert E Lee Park

Approximate Boundary: 39.375138,-76.65054 to 39.378236,-76.643986 (2,129 feet)
DNR Guidance: Mainstem below Lake Roland.

Type: Put and Take

Directions:
From I-83, take exit 10 for Northern Parkway E. Turn left on MD 25/Falls Road. Turn right onto Lakeside Drive.

Access Point:
- Turnout to the east of Falls Road north of the intersection of Falls Road and Coppermine Terrace (39.388481,-76.658973)
- Roadside at west end of Lakeside Drive (39.37641,-76.64669)
- End of Lakeside Drive (39.379028,-76.641904)

Up until recently, there used to be roadside parking on the long road leading into the 415 acre Robert E Lee Park at the southern boundary of Lake Roland. As a result of new construction, large 6x6 wooden posts block every available turnoff except for the one close to the entrance. The only remaining parking is at the northern end of Lakeside Drive.

The entry road winds its way through tall trees that throw shade on both the road and the rocky stream to the north. Lake Roland feeds a constant flow of water into the stream to keep it 20 to 30 feet wide. At normal flows, the stream is shallow, requiring anglers to search a bit for the best trout holding locations behind rocks, in deep channels or in the scattered pools. Dense vegetation packs both banks, so plan on wading. Interestingly enough, just upstream from the junction of Jones Falls with Lake Roland, the water is cold enough to support a reproducing population of trout. To fish there, park at the Falls Road turnout and walk east to intersect the stream. Fish downstream to remain in the park.

Off entry road

Off entry road

Little Falls

Approximate Boundary: 39.626623,-76.634425 to 39.671058,-76.691245 (6.7 miles)
DNR Guidance: Mainstem from Wiseburg Road upstream to Valley Mill Road.

Type: Put and Take

Directions:
From I-83, take exit 31 onto Middletown Road heading east. To go to the first two access points, turn right on MD 45/York Road followed by a left on Wiseburg Road. Wiseburg intersects with Greystone. To go to the middle access points, turn left on MD 45. Turn left on Old York road to intersect Frederick Road on the right or Hillcrest, heading to Dairy Road, on the left. The northern access points are closest to exit 33, but MD 45 continues to be the major road connecting all of them. From MD 45, turn left on Stablers Church Road and make a left on Walker Road. From Walker Road, driving west, turn right onto Eagle Mill or, farther west a right on Valley Mill.

Access Point:
- Wiseburg Road bridge (39.626524,-76.634462)
- Greystone Road intersection with the TCB Rail Trail (39.629978,-76.636367)
- Frederick Road bridge (39.640952,-76.659417)
- Dairy Road intersection with the TCB Trail (39.64606,-76.661767)
- Stablers Church Road bridge #1 (39.658686,-76.664209)
- Stablers Church Road bridge #2 (39.659646,-76.666267)
- Walker Road (39.658816,-76.670787)
- Eagle Mill Road bridge (39.668494,-76.678391)
- Valley Mill Road bridge (39.671149,-76.691298)

Wiseburg Road

Wiseburg Road is the downstream boundary of the stocked section. Park on the broad shoulder off Greystone Road to the right of the bridge and fish upstream. Although the banks are high, the lack of vegetation on the eastern bank and the prevalence of private property to the west make the choice easy. Although wadeable at normal water levels, there is depth to the river as it moves lazily downstream. With plenty of rocks buffered by sand, Wiseburg Road hints at the opportunity for increasing trout friendly bottom structure farther north.

Greystone Road

Greystone Road runs along the east side of the river up to the junction with the Torrey C Brown (TCB) trail where the road makes a sharp turn to the north. There is a five vehicle parking area at the base of the turn adjacent to the high ridgeline supporting the trail. The entrance to the trail is 50 feet north of the parking area. Anglers can negotiate their way to the river's edge with caution, with the best place to enter being at the parking lot. After fishing the pool underneath the bridge, move downstream and hit the deep channel leading into the bend.

Wiseburg Road Upstream   Greystone Road bridge pool

Frederick Road

The Frederick Road parking area marks the transition of the streambed from small rocks and sand to rocks and boulders. The TCB trail crosses the road between concrete barriers that block through traffic. There is parking on both sides. Although there are deep pools upstream from the crossing, the river now runs through a built-up area where anglers must be sensitive to private property. A particularly attractive spot is the pool downstream of the bridge at the junction of Frederick and Hillcrest Avenue. A level, grassy bank makes it approachable for anglers who may not be as mobile as they once were.

Dairy Road

The bridge crossing is next to a parking area for the TCB trail, perfectly suited for anglers since the trail facilitates easy movement along the river for an extended distance. If you have a bike, this is a ideal place to use it since the trail parallels the river all the way down to Wiseburg Road. Upstream, it veers away from the river downstream of Stablers Church, rejoining it at Walker Road. The stream bottom is mostly rocks and the water moves with urgency down a 20 to 30 foot wide channel. The shoreline vegetation is oppressive, but look for the beaten paths through the bushes to reach the trail. The first one is immediately north of the parking area and leads to one of the deepest pools.

Frederick Road upstream   Dairy Road downstream

Stablers Church Road

The two bridges on Stablers Church Road both provide access points, each with limited parking. At the bridge closest to the Interstate, there is room for two vehicles on the west side. At the second bridge, pull off on the shoulder. Despite having a streambed consisting mostly of sand, there are enough rocks to make it attractive. The river runs through a moderate gradient producing recurring riffles with foot deep channels and glides connecting randomly scattered larger pools. The banks average five feet high with plenty of places where anglers can safely slide down to the water. Although there are overarching trees, the cover is not complete, either above the streambed or oppressively thick on the banks. Given the need to be continually sensitive to private property and maintain good landowner relations for continued permission to fish, it's always better to stay off the bank and in the water. The second bridge, the one farthest from the Interstate, is the more attractive location. The deep channel downstream from the bridge is good all the way into the first bend. Since the water compresses as it moves through the narrow underpass on the bridge, it increases velocity and keeps the river bottom from becoming sandy until it loses velocity at the bend.

1st bridge downstream   2nd bridge downstream

Walker Road

Yet another junction with the TCB trail, this one has parking areas on either side of the bridge with the largest being to the north. Closer to the headwaters, this is the first place where the river gains appreciable volume and reaches 30 feet in width. The streambed is uniformly rocky with plenty of gradient breaks adding to the velocity of the water as it moves through the channels into the various pools. If you are an angler who likes to get away from it all, fish upstream. The TCB trail provides easy access for hiking and biking with plenty of opportunities to move from the trail to the water. Be aware of your location since the river may be up to 400 feet away from the trail.

Eagle Mill and Valley Mill

Do not bother to visit either of these. I only included them because they are within the nominal stocked extent of the river based on the DNR description. At Valley Mill, the property is clearly posted and Eagle Mill "feels" posted with its "skinny" water, approximately 10 feet wide, running adjacent to a large field.

Little Gunpowder Falls

Approximate Boundary: 39.459788,-76.38711 to 39.514619,-76.477786 (8.9 miles)
DNR Guidance: Mainstem from Jericho Road upstream to Route 165.

Type: Put and Take

Directions:
From I-95, take exit 74 onto MD 152 north towards Joppatowne. Turn north on Mountain Road. The Jerusalem Road, Belair Road, Harford Road, Pleasantville Road, and Baldwin Mill Road access points are all left turns off of MD 152. To reach Bottom Road, turn left on Harford Road, go past the Harford Road access and turn right on Fork Road. Follow Fork Road to Bottom Road and turn right onto Bottom Road.

Access Point:
- Jericho Road bridge (39.459821,-76.387468)
- Jerusalem Road Mill (39.462816,-76.390118)
- Belair Road bridge (39.474782,-76.408411)
- Harford Road bridge (39.478553,-76.420318)
- Turnouts on Guyton Road near Bottom Road (39.502822,-76.42938)
- Turnouts on Bottom Road (39.504744,-76.430727)
- Pleasantville Road bridge (39.507166,-76.459276)

Jericho Road

Jericho Road, like the other interesting places to fish the Little Gunpowder Falls, is close to the southern end of the Gunpowder Falls State Park. The bridge crossing is unique since it is one of the few covered bridges in the State. Despite its scenic value, the lack of parking eliminates this as a viable access point.

Granted, there is a small turnout south of the river on the east side of the road, but using it for requires a high clearance vehicle to bump over the starkly cut drainage ditch separating the grassy "parking" from the road (good probability for "no parking" signs in the future).

Even though the river looks idyllic upstream from the bridge, the better choice is to bounce up to Jerusalem Road and work downstream. At the covered bridge, the river is approximately 30 feet wide running over a rocky bottom between banks that are a mix of large rocks and sand. Fishing upstream from this crossing requires entering the river. There is a well defined trail from the north side of the bridge to the water.

Jerusalem Road

The intersection of the river with Jerusalem Road is a "big deal" historical site. It features the 237-year-old mill that was at the heart of a Quaker settlement and operated for over two centuries. The rambling visitor center and surrounding buildings offer up numerous educational activities to include blacksmith and carpentry demonstrations. As a result, there is a large parking area anglers can use before walking 500 feet over to the river and its extensive trail system.

The key trails are the Little Gunpowder Falls trail moving north from the road on the east bank and the Horse Trail leading south on the west bank. The river runs 20 to 30 feet wide over a bottom that is a mix of rocks cushioned by a small amount of sand. The view downstream is idyllic. Tall trees lean at impossible, precipitous angles over the center of the river, throwing ample cooling shade onto the water. The deep pool under the bridge is a must fish destination immediately after stocking for those who are unable to negotiate the trails. Even after heavy rains, the water clears up quickly and runs clean and clear.

Downstream   Upstream

Belair Road

Like its sister parking area farther south where the Belair crosses the lower Gunpowder Falls, the parking area at Belair Road is huge and well-developed. The State recognized the need to provide a safe crossing for the large numbers of people who exploit this access point onto the trail system and created an underpass adjacent to the water. The river runs close to the parking lot, but a steep bank, requiring an almost suicidal leap to reach the water's edge, protects it. Unless you are a daredevil, walk to the southern end of the parking lot and move to the river down a less precipitous slope. Alternatively, use the trail system on the north side of the river to move downstream.

To fish upstream, walk through the underpass and onto the two foot wide trail that parallels the river west. Be sure to take the right fork in the trail to stay near the river. The river has the same characteristics as Jerusalem Road with plenty of rocks, riffles, deep channels and scattered pools across its 20 to 30 foot width. A dense canopy of trees continues to offer protective shade to the water, the trout and anglers.

Harford Road

There is a large, well marked parking area on the north side of the bridge. After the great-looking water downstream, this spot is a shock to the system. While it continues to be visually attractive with tall trees providing a scenic backdrop, the bottom undergoes a metamorphosis at the bridge crossing. Instead of the ubiquitous rocks and boulders downstream, the area near the bridge is a sandy mess. I attribute this to the massive, complex logjam sitting 25 yards downstream. As the water scrambles through a convoluted set of channels to penetrate the logs, it loses velocity and drops sediment. While the gouged pools in front of the logs provide an obvious holding location for trout stocked at the bridge, the immediate area downstream runs flat and shallow across a cobble and sand bottom into a deeper area at the bend where there are additional riffles. My bet is most trout will hold near the bridge, making this another good location for anglers who cannot negotiate the uneven trail along the high north bank.

Sandpit near bridge   Farther downstream, more rocks and gravel

Guyton/Bottom Road

In addition to the two turnouts on Guyton Road, the shoulder of Bottom Road upstream of the bridge is completely accessible. It is clear that the 20 to 30 foot wide river is struggling mightily to regain the trouty character that was prominent downstream. Unfortunately, sand dominates the landscape with a "beach like" area, complete with an eroded rope swing, just south of the bridge. The most fishable section is downstream from the deep pool under the swing to the bend where there are three large boulders at a riffle. Upstream from the bridge, there are more rocks and boulders, but the river bottom remains a mix of sandy channels.

Downstream past the swing

Upstream from the beach

Pleasantville Road

There is only room for two vehicles in the turnout on the west side of the bridge. The trail to the river is on the northeast side of the bridge marked with white blazes. As with most bridge crossings, there is a deep hole underneath the bridge. Even though the river runs shallow into downstream riffles that connect sandy shorelines, one cannot discount the continued beauty of the park. The tall trees, steep hillsides and general atmosphere make this a pleasant place to wander up or downstream in search of better water.

Baldwin Mill Road

Even though the DNR guidance specifies that the upper limit of the stocked water is at Baldwin Mill Road, do not bother to drive up there. There is no parking.

Patapsco River

Avalon

Approximate Boundary: 39.221748,-76.713367 to 39.246961,-76.761095 (3.23 miles)
DNR Guidance: Mainstem from the B&O Viaduct upstream to Blodes Dam.

Type: Put and Take

Directions:
From I-95, take exit 47 for I-195E towards the BWI Airport/MD 166/Catonsville. Merge onto I-195. Take exit 3 for Washington Boulevard/US 1 toward Elkridge. Turn right on US 1 (south). Turn right onto South Street. Turn left onto River Road. From there:
- To go to the Avalon Pond access, turn right onto Gun Road. Turn left onto Glen Artney Road and follow it to the parking lot.
- To go to the River Road access, turn left onto Gun Road and right on River Road.

Access Point:
- Parking lot at Avalon Pond on Glen Artney Road (39.230541,-76.729075)
- Parking lot on River Road west of the intersection with Gun Road (39.2274,-76.725599)
- Parking lot on River Road at the dead end near Blodes Dam (39.242046,-76.751433)

Whether it is Spring or the Fall, on a sunny day the clean, clear water rolling downstream mirrors a bright sky framed with towering trees. Of the two seasons, Fall is the better option for both fishing and photography. With no evidence of civilization within eyesight of the river, you will feel as if you are in the middle of the wilderness. Enjoy it!

After paying the fee to enter the Patapsco Valley State Park, you have a decision to make based on the limited parking. It boils down to fish up or downstream? The first two access points are essentially at the same place, but on opposite sides of the river. If you prefer fishing upstream, start there. Otherwise drive all the way to the end of River Road and walk up to the Blodes Dam. Since the road runs adjacent to the river, the DNR is able to distribute fish across the entire length. Because this area receives over 5,500 trout in the typical Spring season, the fishing is usually good.

The strip immediately downstream of the dam is the most scenic and contains more of the rocky structure naturally associated with trout. In the upper reaches, the river runs 50 to 60 feet wide, gradually compressing as it moves downstream towards Gun Road. Since it is a 0.75

mile walk on an easy, open trail from the upper parking lot to the dam, working downstream from the dam back to the parking lot provides a good day of fishing. With a large pool at the base of the dam and deep water in the first 200 yards, it is a favorite spot for shoreline anglers. In the days immediately after stocking, you can count on seeing plenty of people packed into that small area. Move away from the dam and the crowds thin out, the river becomes wadeable and the fishing improves. Typically, every bend is fishable.

Blodes Dam section   Downstream of the Blodes parking

Jumping to the eastern end and looking upstream from the Avalon Pond area, you would not think it is the same river. This area is low gradient with a streambed consisting of more sand than rocks as a result of velocity lost when the terrain flattened below the narrow gap between two high ridgelines approximately a mile upstream (39.23237,-76.73916). The first deep pool is adjacent to the pond with others within an easy walk upstream. Those who do not mind hiking typically walk up the trail on the north side of the river and then cut over once they are beyond their perception of pressure. Remember, even though the road runs adjacent to the river on the south side there is no parking. Therefore, riding a bike up the trail is an easy way to move quickly to the better spots. The trail is far enough from the water to conceal the river behind the foliage, but there are plenty of fisherman's trails providing hints to the popular places.

Near Avalon parking   Near Avalon parking

The Avalon section is the 17th most heavily stocked stream in the State.

Daniels

Approximate Boundary: 39.29545,-76.778741 to 39.319641,-76.826087 (4.4 miles)
DNR Guidance: Patapsco River from Route 40 upstream to Brice Run.

Type: Two fish a day

Directions:
From I-70, take exit 87 onto MD 99/Rogers Avenue heading east at the "T" intersection. Turn left on Old Frederick Road. Options are:

- Turn left onto Daniels Road. Daniels Road is a bit confusing since it leads to an industrial area. Keep going and it will eventually go to the parking area at the Dam.
- Continue on Old Frederick Road to the river. Turn right into the parking lot near the railroad tracks or continue across the river. Old Frederick Road becomes Hollofield Road. Turn left on Dogwood Road. The small turnoff is at the intersection with Alberton Road.

Access Point:
- Daniels Dam parking lot (39.315269,-76.815602)
- Alberton Road and Dogwood Road turnoff (39.31546,-76.793308)
- Old Frederick Road turnoff by the railroad tracks (39.310114,-76.793468)

Fishing the Daniels section of the Patapsco Valley State Park is easy as a result of the 1.3 mile long improved trail that parallels the northern bank of the river. Starting in the north at the Daniels dam, it is confusing to find a spot to cross the river. Do not use the railroad bridge! The best approach is to walk east at the edge of the tracks until you find a good place to cross. You can also start at the dam and find a low-water crossing. When the water is high, the river can be 75 to 100 feet wide in the lower reaches. Even at low water, the eastern section runs wide while the western end narrows where the river twists and turns through the canyon that guides its path. This is another river where a wading staff is mandatory - not because the rocks are excessively slick, but because they are jumbled.

The first 0.75 miles downstream from the dam is the most scenic. It is here where large boulders provide landmarks and guide the river into channels and pools. While the path provides easy transit from east to west, the river bank is high and steep in places. Exercise caution as you approach the riverbed. During high water, wading is impossible and fishing is difficult as a result of the combination of high bank and overgrown shoreline.

The challenge of high banks, high water and wide river is more obvious at the eastern end near the Alberton Road access point. The asphalted trail picks up around the corner from the parking lot and runs next to the river. As you walk, eyeball the water to pick the right spot to get in. You should be able to see the tops of many large boulders strewn across the river bed. If they are covered, the water is too high to wade. As soon as rising water covers the flat area at the base of the tall banks, the oppressive shoreline vegetation joins the conspiracy to prevent you from fishing from the bank.

Dangerous wading during high water   High water prevents bank access

Although the stocked section nominally extends all the way to US 40, it is not worth fishing downstream beyond the I-70 bridge since the last logical stocking point is at the Old Frederick Road bridge crossing. An interesting tidbit for year-round anglers is that the river from I-70 downstream to MD 144 (Frederick Road) is a catch and return bass fishing area. Frankly, I've never had much luck there since the river bottom is mostly sand starting approximately 0.75 miles below the I-70 bridge.

Downstream to the I-70 bridge   Inside the bass catch and release area

The Daniels section is the 15th most heavily stocked stream in the State.

Patterson Park Pond

Approximate Boundary: 39.287151,-76.580582 to 39.288741,-76.58092 (1.6 acres)

Type: Put and Take

Directions: From I-895, take exit 11 for O'Donnell Street. Turn right onto S Highland Street. Turn left onto Eastern Avenue. Park along the side of the road.

Access Point: Roadside parking on Eastern Avenue (39.286096,-76.581807)

Patterson Park is in the heart of Baltimore's Greektown. The pond is a sideshow to the other activities in the park and may or may not be on the stocking plan. The southern end of the pond tends to become clogged with scum, floating vegetation and the normal assortment of trash from slobs who mistake the pond for a garbage can.

Elsewhere along the shoreline, dense beds of cattails, lily pads, small trees and large bushes create additional obstacles. However, there is plenty of shoreline adjacent to a paved path. The pond is a wildlife nesting area and is it illegal to remove wildlife (confused urban ducks or geese that could not find a better place to go?). All in all, the pond, when combined with the park, is a good choice for those who need to air out their kids and take a few casts.

Stansbury Park Pond

Approximate Boundary: 39.260162,-76.501195 to 39.261923,-76.499929 (9 acres)

Type: Put and Take

Directions:
From I-695, take exit 43 for MD 158/Bethlehem Boulevard. Turn left onto Bethlehem Boulevard. Turn left onto the Peninsula Expressway. Turn right onto Chesterwood Road. Turn left onto Stansbury Road. Turn right into the park at the ball field. Do not turn into the road to the east of the park entrance. Your Garmin vehicle GPS will want to take you that way.

Access Point: Parking lot on southern edge of the pond (39.259859,-76.500547)

The Stansbury Park Pond sits at the edge of a 35 acre park that was established in 1974. Adjacent to the Baltimore metropolis, it was originally a horse farm and riding academy. Unfortunately, it was sold in the 1960s to a paint company that used the site for waste disposal.

Even though the site was remediated in the late 1980s, there were lingering concerns about toxic soil. This prompted the Maryland Department of the Environment to retest in early 2008. Those tests confirmed that the level of contamination remains acceptable. However, I would not eat anything pulled from this water other than recently stocked trout.

The shoreline, congested with thick bushes and trees, limits fishing. The pond features a large fishing pier that is the primary platform most people use to attack the water. There is a walking path around the pond that provides additional access to the few other places where anglers bushwhacked paths to the water's edge. Be careful where you fish. The bay, just over the eastern berm, requires a tidal license. Anglers need a freshwater license for the pond itself.

Calvert County

Calvert Cliffs

Approximate Boundary: 38.394678,-76.434322 to 38.395435,-76.434848 (1 acre)

Type: Put and Take

Directions: From I-95/I-495, take exit 11A onto MD 4S/Pennsylvania Avenue. Pennsylvania Avenue eventually turns into Southern Maryland Boulevard and remains marked as MD 4. The name changes again when the road joins MD 2 where it becomes Solomons Island Road. Follow MD 4/MD 2 south past Port Republic and St. Leonard. Signs for the Calvert Cliffs State Park appear a few miles down the road from the Calvert Cliffs Nuclear Plant. Turn left on MD 765/H. G. Trueman Road to enter the park. Follow the road around to the right and the lake will be visible down the hill from the public restrooms.

Access Point: Parking area next to the pond (38.394964,-76.434966)

The 1,400 acre Calvert Cliffs State Park is a popular destination offering visitors a unique activity - *fossil hunting*. The park includes 13 miles of hiking trails with some leading to substantial cliffs along the mile long public bayside shoreline. There are plenty of picnic areas, nature trails and a distinctive playground built out of recycled tires that offer diversions from fishing. After a quick glance at the one acre pond, any angler will instantly appreciate the need for other activities.

The Calvert Cliffs Pond is tucked next to the trailhead that leads along Grays Creek to the bay and the tidal marshland lining the coast. During the Spring season, the DNR stocks the pond with 500 fish and all of them instantly dart to the southern side of the lake with most moving to the southeast corner where the water is deepest.

The northern pipe stem of the lake is shallow and muddy as is the western shoreline near the parking lot. An active angler will find the pond interesting to fish for, at most, an hour or so. Of course, given the proximity of the pond to the Calvert Cliffs Nuclear Power Plant, any angler who is also a fan of *The Simpsons* TV show will take great joy in looking for, or making wisecracks about, the three-eyed fish featured in the cartoon. Thankfully, there are none ... Yet!

Given the tiny expanse of fishable water, any angling visitor to this park should plan on making the two-mile hike to the shoreline and become an amateur archaeologist. The area around the cliffs is a veritable treasure trove of fossils with over 600 different species being discovered over the years. Sharks teeth, along with shells, are the most popular fossils. The State allows you to both hunt for and keep anything you find, and asks that you do not go overboard.

Hutchins Pond

Approximate Boundary: 38.702176,-76.604031 to 38.701506,-76.602657 (2.3 acres)

Type: Put and Take

Directions:
From I-95/I-495, take exit 11 onto MD 4/Pennsylvania Avenue toward Upper Marlboro. Follow MD 4 to eventually merge onto MD 260E/West Chesapeake Beach Road using the ramp to the North Beach/Recreation areas. Turn right on MD 2/Solomans Island Road. Be alert. Turn left onto the small Mt Harmony Lane in approximately 1.4 miles. Follow Mt Harmony Lane for a short distance (0.1 miles) to turn left on an unmarked road that looks like a driveway. Follow it past the homes toward a stand of trees. There is a small parking area just past a set of poles comprising a "gate" that may or may not be chained from dusk to dawn.

Access Point: Parking area next to the pond (38.702176,-76.604031)

As you enter the small parking area, tip your hat and give thanks to Harry and Grace Hutchins who donated the use of the pond to the State for fishing. In addition to the trout stocked during the season, it also is home to bass and bluegill. If you expect to find an old farm pond, your expectations will be met. It is surrounded by a manicured, gently sloping bank that makes access easy except at the extreme southern end near a stand of trees overlooking a small trickle of water bubbling into the pond.

The deep water is adjacent to the parking lot. Be alert for aggressive geese lurking nearby who do not take kindly to intruders. There are a few picnic tables spaced around the lake providing a holding position for gear, a picnic lunch or a place to take a break. However, there are no other activities to provide families additional diversions. Anyone who comes here is coming only to fish.

Carroll County

Beaver Run

Approximate Boundary: 39.490071,-76.902927 to 39.5009,-76.902798 (5,123 feet)
DNR Guidance: Upstream of Route 91.

Type: Put and Take

Directions:
East: From Baltimore, take exit 19 from I-695 onto I-795N/Northwest Expressway towards Owings Mills. I-795 eventually turns into MD 140/Westminster Road. Continue on Westminster Road to the intersection with MD 91/Gamber Road/Emory Road. Turn left onto Gamber Road followed by a right onto Hughes Road.

West: From Frederick, drive east on I-70 and take exit 80 onto MD 32N/Sykesville Road. Follow MD 32 to MD 91/Gamber Road. Turn right on MD 91. Follow MD 91 and turn left onto Hughes Road.

Although you can see Beaver Run on the left across a field, do not park on the side of the road and walk across since the field is private property. Follow Hughes Road until it crosses the creek at 39.489696,-76.902936. The first public section starts on the north side of the bridge and extends to the orange sign at 39.492146,-76.901134. The remainder of the public section is accessible from the intersection of Hughes Road with Old Kayes Mill Road at 39.495317,-76.901981.

Access Point: Turnouts on Old Kays Mill Road and Hughes Road (39.497775,-76.90175, 39.495188,-76.902029, 39.491648,-76.901476, 39.490071,-76.902927)

For the casual, put-and-take an angler, there is no more pleasant location close to Baltimore than Beaver Run. A short 20 minute drive from the I-695 Beltway puts you on the banks of a placid, smoothly running stream with a rocky bottom and clear water. There is no annoying hum of traffic, only the chirping of birds and the fresh odors associated with a rural setting. As a result of the intrusion of private property (Beaver Run Fish and Game) in the middle, Beaver Run is split into two distinct sections. The main section is fishable along Hughes Road while the northern stretch lays adjacent to Old Kayes Mill Road. The Kayes section features shoreline vegetation that could be problematic if it were not for the width of the creek. The creek runs 15 to 25 feet wide and most of the shoreline trees grow up, not over, the water. This allows for unobstructed casting.

Hughes Road parallels Beaver Run and the public section starts on the north side of the bridge. The only parking off Hughes Road is immediately north of the bridge where there is a turnoff on the right that will hold three vehicles. A quick scan of the water's surface from any point along the road reveals a disappointing fact– the creek is shallow. After fishing the bridge pool, enter the water from the low bank that is the eastern boundary of the road. Fish rapidly upstream, focusing on the few scarce and random pools. If you fish this section, taking a quick walk upstream along the creek to discover the good places to fish pays off since you will waste less time fishing spots that look good from creek level. Once done, move upstream to the intersection of Hughes Road and Old Kayes Mill Road.

Bridge pool

Upstream from the bridge

At Old Kayes Mill Road, there is plenty of parking; at least eight vehicles can squeeze into the broad shoulders that sit on either side of the bridge. The best water is accessible from the faint trail that strikes south, downstream, from the bridge while there is another more obvious trail north to the large bridge supporting the updated section of Old Kayes Mill Road.

Old Kayes Mill upstream

Old Kayes Mill downstream

Since the stocked section extends approximately 1,500 feet north of the large bridge, there is plenty of fishable water in that direction. If you prefer to attack it in the middle, there is another, but limited, access point across the street from a private driveway on Old Kayes Mill Road immediately to the east of the new bridge. Usually there is a DNR sign cautioning anglers to the respectful of private property that confirms the landowner's willingness to allow you onto their property to fish this portion of the stream. However, given the biological propensity of stocked trout to swim downstream, fish upstream with low expectations.

Farm Museum Pond

Approximate Boundary: 39.555829,-76.995065 to 39.556929,-76.996749 (5.7 acres)

Directions:
East: From Baltimore, take exit 18 from I-695 onto I-795/Northwest Expressway towards Ownings Mills. I-795 will merge into MD 140. Turn left onto MD 97/New Washington Road. Turn right onto Mary Avenue followed by a right onto North Denton Drive. Turn left onto Margaret Avenue and right to remain on Margaret Avenue when it merges into Doris Avenue. Turn left on Gist Road and follow it to the entrance to the park.

South: From I-70, take exit 68 onto MD 72N/Ridge Road. Turn right onto Kate Wagner Road followed by a left onto Gist Road. Follow Gist Road to the entrance to the park.

There is formal parking at the baseball field. The road runs along the southern boundary of the lake to end in another large parking area.

Access Point: Parking area at the baseball field (39.555812,-76.993348)

This location is the perfect place to mix education and recreation. The pond is adjacent to the Carroll County Farm Museum complex. Constructed in 1964 and modified in 1992, the Farm Museum complex provides a window into 19th-century rural life. It includes all of the typical structures one would encounter on a farm from the last century to include a farm house, barn, smokehouse and other commercial operations typical of the era. You can visit a broom shop, wagon shed, general store as well as a firehouse and a one room school. After getting a dose of history, drive next door to the Landon C Burns Park and dip a line in the water since the lake offers an idyllic setting for a family outing.

There are no obstacles to fishing this lake. It features a manicured lawn that leads to the lake's edge with scattered groves of trees at the southern end and the western corner. The lake is most approachable from the south given the sloping hill that leads to the bank in the western section or along the berm separating the lake from the museum complex to the north. The sandy bottom allows you to retrieve your lure without picking up underwater vegetation. There are picnic tables and a playground near the parking area in case young anglers need a diversion.

Morgan Run

Approximate Boundary: 39.451922,-76.955895 to 39.479112,-76.999319 (3.62 miles)
DNR Guidance: From bridge on London Bridge Road upstream to bridge on Maryland Route 97.

Directions:
Jim Bowers Road: From I-70, take exit 76 north on MD-97 towards Westminster/Olney. Turn right on E. Nicodemus Road. Follow Nicodemus and turn right on Jim Bowers Road. Follow it to the end.

Klee Mill: From I-70, take exit 76 north on MD-97 towards Westminster/Olney. Turn right on Bartholomew Road. Turn left on Klee Mill Road. Continue on Klee Mill to the stream. The formal parking area is on the left.

London Bridge: Follow the directions for Klee Mill except turn right on Cherry Tree Lane from Klee Mill Road. Follow Cherry Tree Lane and make a left turn onto London Bridge Road. Follow the road to the stream.

Note: There used to be an additional access point off Old Washington Road. However, it is outside of the current DNR boundaries of the stocked section.

Access Point:
- Jim Bowers Road: At the end of the road (39.474619,-76.983728)
- Klee Mill: Parking lot on east side of the stream (39.466529,-76.970253)
- London Bridge: Road shoulder on south side of the stream (39.451849,-76.955394)

Cradled inside the 1,400 acre Morgan Run Natural Environment Area, the special regulation section is a little over three miles long and extends from London Bridge Road north to MD 97. At the northern end, the freestone stream starts out as a narrow, shallow run cradled by high dirt banks, speckled with logjams, and is lucky to be 20 feet wide with the typical width being between 10 and 15 feet. By the time it drifts under London Bridge Road, not only does the physical structure change to large boulders framing a cobble bottom hemmed in by steep hills, but it expands 30 feet wide. Over the years, the tree canopy closed in over the stream, blocking the summer heat, to keep the water cool and the fishing hot. The DNR stocks Morgan Run heavily to augment the limited brown trout annual holdover.

London Bridge upstream   London Bridge upstream

Starting in the south at London Bridge, there is a limited amount of parking on the shoulder of the road to the south of the bridge with the faint fisherman's trail starting along the north side. This is also where the stream is deepest with chest waders required to cross the stream without restriction. Follow the dim trail as it jumps from one side to the other before it eventually fades into the underbrush. Klee Mill, in the middle, has a formal parking area with a disabled angler platform and ramp near the parking lot. There is a well defined path moving downstream from the parking area for over two miles. The small parking lot at Jim Bowers Road rests at the end of a dirt road. Follow the obvious path from the lot further south to reach the river. There is no path on the northern side, but once you wade across the stream, hop on the easy walking trail set back 25 yards from the stream. As the water warms, a popular holding area for trout is at the junction of Joe's Branch (39.473098,-76.985044) where cooling water spills into the pool adjacent to the path from Jim Bowers Road.

Jim Bowers pool   Low gradient upstream from Bowers

It is amazing how the scenery changes from south to north. In the south, the stream gains velocity as it runs through a narrow slash separating the surrounding hills. This causes the water to carve out channels and push sand downstream. The banks are forested with enough rocks to give a true "trout water" feel that continues through Klee Mill. A half mile above Klee Mill, the stream breaks out into traditional wide, flat farmland where it loses velocity and the sand returns. The banks remain heavily forested all the way up to the end of the special regulation section at MD 97.

Klee Mill downstream

Klee Mill - wide and rocky

Piney Run

Approximate Boundary: 39.366431,-76.911471 to 39.352429,-76.895549 (1.39 miles)
DNR Guidance: Mainstem downstream from Arrington Road.

Type: Put and Take

Directions:
From I-70 east of Baltimore, take exit 83 north onto Marriottsville Road. Keep right at the fork and continue on Marriottsville Road. Eventually, you will see a large parking area on the left. Continue across the Patapsco River and take the second left onto Marriottsville Road Number 2. Piney Run parallels the road. Pull off at any wide spot on the shoulder that looks good.

Access Point: Numerous along Marriottsville Road Number 2. I prefer to fish upstream from 39.36194,-76.90527.

The great thing about Piney Run is that you actually have three fishing choices and can postpone your decision on where to fish until you arrive. You can fish the long stocked stretch of Piney that parallels the oddly named Marriottsville Road Number 2 or, take a hop, skip and a jump down the road and fish up or downstream on the Patapsco from the large parking area at

the bridge. After turning left to head north on Marriottsville Road Number 2, your instant impression will be disappointment. In the initial section, the stream looks like a typical central Maryland flatland creek - sandy and shallow, about 20 feet wide. 100 yards from the junction, the terrain and the quality of the water changes dramatically.

As soon as the stream picks up a little bit of gradient as it flows through the two cuts between the high hills to the north, it takes on the appearance of a traditional trout stream – full of rocks and small plunge pools. In fact, between the start of the stocked section at Arrington Road and the junction with the Patapsco, the stream drops 60 feet. At flood levels, that quick change in gradient attracts hard-core kayakers who enjoy cheating death. The most dramatic drops and pools are within the first quarter mile downstream from Arrington Road.

Shallow sections where the stream temporarily bottoms out and gathers energy for the next downward plunge separate each set of pools. There are plenty of narrow seams, sheltered by boulders and fallen logs, to hold the stocked fish. In the springtime, the water runs with sparkling velocity and is usually clean and clear.

Piney Run Reservoir

Approximate Boundary: 39.407172,-76.990657 to 39.388136,-76.976151 (300 acres)

Type: Put and Take

Directions:
From I-70, take exit 76 for MD 97 north toward Westminster. Turn right on West Obrecht Road. Turn left on White Rock Road. Turn right on Martz Road and follow it to the end.

Access Point: Parking area near concession area (39.397623,-76.987878)

Piney Run Reservoir is a spectacular, man-made lake that is the anchor and main attraction of the surrounding 550 acre Piney Run Park. According to the experts, Piney Run is one of the best fisheries in the State with citation-size bass, perch, channel catfish and crappie. In addition, there are tiger muskies, stocked in 1996, as well as good numbers of striped bass. The fact that different organizations hold regular fishing tournaments on the lake is a tribute to its quality.

This is a lake for boaters and there are enough of them to keep the dual boat ramps at the end of Martz Road busy during the peak season (electric motors only - the concession stand rents boats). The shoreline is tight, heavily wooded and terminates on private property along the northern stretches. In late summer and fall, vegetation packs large portions of the bank, creating an obstacle limiting casting. Fishing is not permitted within the boundaries of the wildlife management area at the north end of the lake or within the Nature Center Education Cove.

Anglers who want to fish from the bank may exploit several of the hiking trails along the shoreline. Specifically, the Field Trail leads north from the boat launch to the northern boundary of the park while the Lake and Inlet trails lead south. If you take the Inlet trail, do not fish until the trail leads away from The Nature Center Cove.

The fees to use the park are substantial if you are not a resident of Carroll County. In 2011, the entry fee was $10 per vehicle for nonresidents versus five dollars for residents. It costs an additional eight dollars to launch a boat.

South Branch Patapsco River (Upper)

Approximate Boundary: 39.350272,-76.882503 to 39.362085,-76.966488 (6.19 miles)
DNR Guidance: Mainstem from West Friendship Road (Howard County side) and Main Street (Carroll County side) at Sykesville downstream to its confluence with the North Branch Patapsco River.

Type: Put and Take

Directions:
Sykesville: Head west from Ellicott City on I-70 and take exit 80 towards Sykesville on MD 32N. Turn right on River Road. The Patapsco follows River Road. Turn left on W Friendship Road to fish the short section between Sykesville road and W Friendship Road.

Freedom Park: Continue north on Sykesville Road and turn right on Raincliffe Road. Turn right into the park on Buttercup Road.

Marriottsville: From I-70, take exit 83 to drive north on Marriottsville Road. Follow it to the river.

Henryton:
- North side: Continue east on Raincliffe Road. Turn right on Slacks Road followed by a left on Arrington Road. Turn right on Henryton Road. Turn right on Henryton Center Road. Follow it to the river.
- South side: From Marriottsville Road, turn left on MD 99/Old Frederick Road. Turn right on Henryton Road and follow it to the end.

Access Point:
- W Friendship Road above Sykesville Road (39.363062,-76.968566)
- On the shoulder of River Road south of Sykesville Road with the last turnoff at the corner (39.357041,-76.958463)
- At the south end of Buttercup Road in Freedom Park (39.363025,-76.950992)
- Henryton Center Road on the north side of the river (39.351496,-76.913521)
- Henryton Road on the south side of the river (39.350764,-76.913908)
- Marriottsville Road parking lot on the south side of the river (39.351698,-76.898767)

The South Branch offers numerous access points with plenty of parking. While the river is not classic "trout water", there is enough structure distributed throughout its length to provide an interesting day of fishing. The bottom is composed of rock and gravel with a good mixture of silt and mud in places. The deep holes occur wherever the river crashes into a bend with fallen trees creating additional compelling places.

The McKeldin Area in the Patapsco Valley State Park provides the easternmost access point to the stocked section. There are numerous trails extending throughout the McKeldin Area that lead to the mainstem of the Patapsco (not stocked) to the north as well as parallel the South Branch along its southern boundary. Non-anglers can take advantage of the numerous activities offered by the park including mountain bike trails, hiking trails and an 18 hole disc golf course. In addition, there are many large and small picnic areas scattered around the park that may be reserved. To reach the stocked section of the South Branch, follow the appropriately named Rapids Trail that begins at the southern end of the park. The 0.7 mile trail leads to the only dramatic vista on the South Branch – a cascading set of rapids feeding into a deep pool. Obviously, this is a popular spot that attracts plenty of photographers, hikers and anglers.

If you do not want to pay the entry fee to the McKeldin Area Park, pull your vehicle into the broad parking area at the bridge crossing on Marriottsville Road. Pick up the trail on the north side of the bridge or just walk along the southern edge of the river and survey the scene. Most of the southern bank feels manicured with a thick carpet of tall grass under shade. Unlike on the neighboring Patuxent, anglers do not need to deal with the challenge of tangled, wader ripping thorn bushes endemic there; just watch out for the poison ivy. The best strategy is to walk as far downstream as you can tolerate, checking out the river as you go, and then fish upstream. Target the good spots noted on the walk downstream. Most of the pressure comes from the McKeldin Area on the northern bank. Fewer people attack the river from the south.

Downstream from McKeldin

View towards McKeldin

Just above the bridge crossing, there is a deep pool that gets plenty of attention immediately after stocking. In fact, the entire river upstream from the Marriottsville crossing to the railroad bridge is highly pressured, slow moving water running across the same sandy bottom with deep water at the bends. Each bend will be packed with anglers during the week after stocking with most of them, and the trout, within 100 yards of the parking lot. If you are willing to walk, take the easy, beaten trail that moves away from the railroad tracks and parallels the river. Without any undergrowth to impede progress, you can move quickly upstream away from the pressure. The most scenic spot is directly downstream from the railroad bridge. At this point, there is a sharp bend in the river full of large boulders that underpin a small cliff where the river cuts right to begin its slow crawl back towards the parking lot. The river upstream of the bridge is shallow and sandy. Just remember that any trout probably migrated from downstream, so the number will not be significant.

Railroad bridge pool

Bridge pool near parking

Switching focus to the western end of the river, the river adopts a more "trouty" character. The section downstream from Sykesville Road is full of rocks and other trout friendly structure. It is easy to wade at normal water levels - without the dramatically deep spots prevalent farther downstream. As you walk downstream from the last small, two vehicle informal parking area at the eastern end of River Road, the river quickly returns to sand and mud with random fallen logs. Since the road directly parallels the river and allows for easy access, the angling pressure is more intense than at the other access points.

Upstream from last Sykesville turnout   Sykesville area

The best strategy for fishing the South Branch is to capitalize on the fact that stocked trout migrate downstream several days after being inserted into the river. Depending on how far you are willing to walk, you may want to take a short 500 foot hike in from the Buttercup Road sports complex to reach the river and then move upstream. Otherwise, the later in the season you visit, the farther east you should start, with the McKeldin Area always being a good choice.

This is the 12th most heavily stocked stream in the State.

Taneytown Pond

Approximate Boundary: 39.654047,-77.158046 to 39.654716,-77.156416 (2 acres)

Type: Put and Take

Directions:
East: From Baltimore, follow the I-695 beltway to exit 19. At exit 19, merge onto I-795/Northwest Expressway toward Owings Mills. Continue onto MD 140 when I-795 ends. Turn right onto Divern Street followed by a right on Stumptown Road. Turn into the Roberts Mill Park.

South: From I-270, continue onto US 15N. Take exit 17 onto MD 26E/Liberty Road toward Libertytown. Turn left on MD 194N/Woodsboro Pike. Turn right on East Baltimore Street. Turn left on Divern Street. Turn right on Stumptown Road. Turn into the Roberts Mill Park.

Access Point: Parking area next to the pond (39.654047,-77.158046)

The pond is the main feature of the 19.3 acre Roberts Mill Park on the eastern edge of the small village of Taneytown. The spring-fed pond is accessible via an asphalt path that encircles its perimeter. There are plenty of benches dotting the shoreline to provide places for parents to rest while watching children fish. In addition to the lake, the park includes a fenced playground, a volleyball court, picnic pavilions, restrooms and plenty of parking. The lake is shallow at the shoreline with the minimum of underwater vegetation.

Cecil County

Big Elk Creek

Approximate Boundary: 39.657309,-75.82222 to 39.721929,-75.84209 (5.47 miles)
DNR Guidance: Mainstem from the bridge at Route 277 upstream to the Pennsylvania State Line.

Type: Put and Take

Directions:
With over five miles of water, there are multiple access points. To get to the southern boundary of public water, follow these directions.

From I-95, take exit 109 toward Elkton. Merge onto MD 279W and turn right onto Belle Hill Road. Take the jog to the left to stay on Belle Hill Road. Turn right on MD 316N/Appleton Road.

The Fair Hill State Natural Resources Management Area is a striking 5,633 acre outdoor wonderland. The fishing available in Big Elk Creek is only one of the many activities available to those who make the trip to the eastern border of Maryland to use this facility. Appleton Road runs along the eastern boundary while Gallaher Road delineates much of the western. There are three primary and one secondary road leading to the various parking areas near the creek. These are:

- Elk Mills Road
- Brewster Bridge Road
- Telegraph Road
- Jackson Hall School Road (secondary)

All these roads are turns to the west off of Appleton Road. Gallaher Road has its own parking lot at the junction of Gallaher and Big Elk Chapel Road.

There is a small day use charge collected on the honor system at the key parking lots whose locations are (extracted from DNR website; all addresses are in Elkton, MD):

- *Parking Lot #2 (793 Tawes Drive) - Located at the Covered Bridge. From the Rt. 273/Rt. 213 intersection, travel East on Rt. 273 one half mile to Entrance Road #3. Turn right and make an immediate left on Ranger Skinner Drive. Turn left on Kennel/Training Center Road. Travel one-half mile and turn right on Tawes Drive.*
- *Parking Lot #3 (2895 Appleton Road) - Also known as the North Appleton parking Lot. From the Rt. 273/Rt. 213 intersection, proceed East on Rt. 273 to the intersection with*

Appleton Road. Turn left on Appleton Road, proceeding approximately one mile to the intersection of Appleton Road and Black Bridge Road. Parking lot is located immediately on your left.

- *Parking Lot #4 (483 Gallaher Road) - Also known as the Gallaher Road parking Lot. From the Rt. 273/Rt. 213 intersection, proceed East on Rt. 273 to the intersection with Gallaher Road. Turn right on Gallaher Road and proceed to the Gallaher Road/Big Elk Chapel intersection. Parking lot is located at the intersection.*
- *Parking Lot #5 (1987 Appleton Road) - Also known as the South Appleton parking Lot. From the Rt. 273/Rt. 213 intersection, proceed East on Rt. 273 to the intersection with Appleton Road. Turn right on Appleton Road, proceeding approximately one half mile. Parking lot is located on the right side of the road.*

Parking Lot #1 is too far from the fishing to list as an access point.

The map posted at the parking lots indicates an additional place on Union Road that would provide the most rapid access to the portion of Big Elk Creek near Telegraph Road. That access point does not exist. Instead, park at the North Appleton lot and follow the path south.

There are no honor boxes to pay the fee at the other access points described, but you are still expected to have made payment someplace.

Access Points:
- West side of the bridge at Elk Mills Road (39.657433,-75.822392)
- East side of Brewster Bridge on Brewster Bridge Road (39.667694,-75.82543)
- End of Booth Road (turn north from Brewster Bridge Road) (39.669577,-75.829872)
- End of Jackson Hall School Road (39.67748,-75.82416)
- Black Bridge (39.71255,-75.83688)
- Parking Lot #2, Covered Bridge Lot (39.710029,-75.837795)
- Parking Lot #3, North Appleton Lot 39.71417,-75.82249)
- Parking Lot #4, Gallaher Road parking Lot (39.68831,-75.84155)
- Parking Lot #5, South Appleton Lot (39.68807,-75.81598)

Elk Mills Road

The management area extends north of the bridge on the west bank of the creek. The east bank is all private property. There is one small turnoff on the shoulder on the west side of the bridge, but it does not really put you outside of the traffic pattern and is not a good place to park. In fact, the only defined trail is at the east end of the bridge on private property. The creek is deep with overgrown banks on both sides. If you really want to fish, a better place to park is at the Post Office in the town to the north. Follow Elk Mills Road to the west across the bridge to the Post Office near the railroad tracks at 39.659021,-75.826535. Avoid the private property to the south of the tracks and walk east to hit the creek. Whatever you do, do not attempt to gain access to the creek by following Creek Road to the west from the school. There are plenty of aggressive "posted" signs to include what I hope is a humorous, large billboard that threatens trespassers with automatic weapons fire, a plague of venomous snakes or both.

Brewster Bridge Road/Booth Road

There are two primary access points at Brewster Bridge. The first one is on Brewster Bridge Road and is a small two car turnoff on the east side of the bridge. The trail to the creek is on the south side of the bridge. The alternative is to turn north on Booth Road and drive to the end where there is a small skateboard park constructed by local residents. The stream at the dead end is Gramies Run and it joins Big Elk Creek a short distance to the east.

This is the first location where Big Elk Creek begins to reveal its "trouty" character. The creek is approximately 30 feet wide with a boulder strewn, rocky bottom and periodic gradient breaks creating riffles and pools. Most of the access is from the west bank since the eastern bank is steep and stark with rock cliffs making foot travel impossible.

Downstream   Upstream

Jackson Hall School Road

Jackson Hall School Road is an informal access point where the road dead ends into the management area. At some point in the past, the road extended all the way across Big Elk Creek. The eroded remnants on the other side of the barrier become the trail to the creek. Frankly, there is no opportunity for the stocking truck to go beyond the barrier. Therefore, any fish encountered must migrate downstream a significant distance. The walk to the creek is easy. It's only 0.36 miles with a vertical drop of 40 feet to reach the creek at 39.67615,-75.82822. At the junction point, the creek runs three to four feet deep with shallow water upstream near a small riffle.

Black Bridge/Covered Bridge/North Appleton

The Black Bridge and Covered Bridge access points may be reached from the east via the North Appleton parking lot. From the west, use Tawes Drive. In either case, these locations are accessible using a vehicle, no hiking required. Black Bridge is a short distance upstream from the covered bridge. Upstream of Black Bridge, the 30 to 40 feet wide stream is mostly sand with a few scattered rocks downstream into the covered bridge area. However, this is a key access point for stocking, so there will always be fish in this stretch during the season. In particular, the deep area adjacent to the covered bridge is popular with anglers clogging the bank on the eastern side or leveraging the fishing platform on the west. There is a well defined trail moving downstream from the west side of the covered bridge that provides a quick path to move away from the bustling activity at the bridge.

Good path downstream to right   Downstream from the covered bridge

Gallaher Road

The Gallaher Road parking lot sits on the west side of the stream. Park in the lot at the junction the Big Elk Chapel and Gallaher. Pay the access fee and walk or ride a bike across the street to follow the well defined dirt road 4,100 feet to the water's edge. This crossing is the same place reachable from the South Appleton lot on the east side of the stream. The stream runs 40 feet wide, but has enough rocks to make it interesting.

South Appleton Lot

The South Appleton Lot is the last choice to fish Big Elk Creek. The stream is almost a mile from the lot following the well defined dirt road to the bridge. It is a shorter distance to the same place from the Gallaher lot on the other side of the management area. There is an honor payment box at this location. If you decide to use this lot, ride a bike to the stream.

Path from Gallaher Road   Path from South Appleton

Big Elk Creek is the seventh most heavily stocked stream in the State.

Howards Pond

Approximate Boundary: 39.611039,-75.817993 to 39.609981,-75.820225 (4 acres)

Type: Put and Take

Directions:
From I-95, take exit 109 for MD 279W and merge onto Elkton Road. Turn left onto Belle Hill Road. Follow it past the shopping and restaurants to turn right on Muddy Lane. Follow Muddy Lane to MD 281/Red Hill Road. Turn right and follow MD 281 to the Hatchery Park complex. The pond is on the left side of the street.

Access Point: Parking lot next to the pond (39.611039,-75.817993)

The Howards Pond Recreation Area includes the pond, also known as Cow Pond, and sits adjacent to Meadow Park East/Hatchery Park. Big Elk Creek runs along the northern boundary of both facilities. In addition to fishing along the unobstructed shoreline, there is a picnic pavilion with grills open for public use. The bank is two feet high with the bottom of the lake gradually sloping, with no apparent abrupt drop-offs, to the deeper area. During the season, the shoreline is unobstructed. In addition to trout, anglers can pursue large and smallmouth bass.

Principio Creek

Approximate Boundary: 39.615298,-76.03417 to 39.660459,-76.040586 (4.43 miles)

Type: Put and Take

Directions:
To reach the northern access point (Post Road), take exit 93 from I-95 toward MD 222/Perryville. Turn right onto MD 275N/Perrylawn Drive. Turn right onto MD 276. Turn right onto Hopewell Road. Hopewell Road veers left 1.5 miles after the turn. Continue straight onto Post Road and follow it to the creek.

To reach the southern access point (Belvedere Road), take exit 93 from I-95 toward MD 222/Perryville. Turn left onto MD 275S/Perrylawn Drive. Turn left on Heather Lane followed by another immediate left onto MD 222N/MD 824N. At the fork, stay right onto Principio Road. Turn right on Linton Run Road. Turn right onto Belvedere Road and follow it to the creek.

Access Point:
- Post Road bridge crossing (39.660273,-76.040602)
- Red Toad Road bridge crossing (39.65128,-76.038915)
- Principio Road crossing and roadside (39.649396,-76.039599 and 39.638746,-76.043523)
- Theodore Road bridge crossing (39.633959,-76.037525)
- Belvedere Road bridge crossing (39.626306,-76.040479)

As a general comment, fishing Principio is problematic as a result of private property issues. In fact, in 2005, the DNR proposed removing the creek from the stocking schedule as a result of the increasingly limited access allowed by landowners. This is sad since Principio and Big Elk Creek are the only streams stocked in Cecil County. Big Elk Creek is clearly a better destination and the small number of trout stocked in Principio confirm its secondary position. On a recent visit in 2011, I was unable to find any DNR "stocked water" signage other than at the Post Road access point. Therefore, exercise caution and obey any "posted" signs that may sprout up at the stream/road crossings providing the only access to the water. In short, it's probably not worth going here.

Post Road

In 2011, this was the only access point that still had the DNR "stocked water" signage. The stream is small enough to jump across, optimistically being four to five feet wide. Parking is limited; the turnoff will only hold two vehicles on the south side of the road. There is a fisherman's ladder spanning the fence on the other side of the street, but that section is currently outside of the stocked water limits. The stream twists and turns as it runs through a 200 foot wide wooded section that divides several fields.

Red Toad Road

There is limited parking on the side of the road and I recommend you ask the business owner at the corner for permission to both park and fish if posted signs exist and you are convinced trout may have migrated this far down. The creek continues to be small and tight as it runs around the corner to rejoin Principio Road a hundred yards to the south. At Red Toad, the shoreline vegetation is thick and overhangs the shallow creek, making casting difficult. The streambed is rocks and sand, with sand predominating farther downstream.

Post Road downstream   Red Toad Road downstream

Principio Road

After crossing Principio Road, the creek moves away from the roadway to dodge around large open fields and does not rejoin the road until shortly after the intersection of Principio with Pioneer Ridge Drive where there is a small turnoff that will hold three vehicles. There is no velocity to the stream as it winds its way through the flat, picturesque valley. Sand predominates on the streambed and there is no interesting structure other than some overhanging vegetation.

Theodore Road

The bridge volunteers a small, three-car parking area on the west with an additional slot to the east. As a result of a small drop in elevation, the stream regains its velocity and the associated rocky bottom. Shoreline vegetation is thick, but does not overhang the stream to the point of becoming a significant obstacle.

Principio Road   Theodore Road

Belvedere Road

There is no parking adjacent to the bridge crossing on Belvedere Road, but the shoulder at the intersection of Linton Run Road offers a slot or two. The stream has an idyllic, trouty look to it with good shade thrown over the rocky bottom by tall trees. The stream runs 10 to 20 feet wide and has regained depth as it scurries farther downstream. Deeper pools are visible from the road.

Rising Sun Pond

Approximate Boundary: 39.697485,-76.072207 to 39.69779,-76.071461 (1 acre)

Type: Youth, Senior or Blind

Directions:
From I-95, take exit 93 toward MD 222/Perryville. Turn right onto MD 275N/Perrylawn Drive. Turn right onto MD 276. At the traffic circle, turn right onto MD 273E/Rising Sun Road. The pond is on the left.

To avoid the toll over the Susquehanna, take US 1 east from Belair and stay on MD 273 when it splits to the west of Rising Sun. Follow MD 273 to the pond.

There is limited parking at the entrance to the pond that fits three or four vehicles.

Access Point: Parking lot next to the pond 39.697212,-76.071547

Depending on when you arrive during the Spring season, Rising Sun Pond may have a unique green/blue sheen to it. Each year, the DNR treats the pond to reduce the growth of elodea that would clog the entire pond if not controlled. The chemical used is not harmful and is biodegradable.

If you wanted, you could put a boat on this small pond as long as you do not use a gas motor. However, that is overkill given the small size and the universal accessibility provided by the manicured bank. The pond is only 11 feet deep, so the fish have nowhere to hide. In addition to trout, you can also catch large and smallmouth bass.

Charles County

Hughesville Pond

Approximate Boundary: 38.549119,-76.803275 to 38.547642,-76.803232 (0.8 acres)

Type: Put and Take

Directions
North: From I-95/I-495 take exit 7 onto MD 5/Branch Avenue towards Waldorf. Follow Branch Avenue to the outskirts of Waldorf and turn left on the Mattawoman Beantown Road (still on MD 5). Make a final left on Leonardtown Road and follow it approximately 7 miles. After passing the Hughesville Pond Recreation Area, be prepared to turn right approximately 500 feet farther east. The pond is on the right, marked by a brown sign that designates the area as the Hughesville Community Park. The turn comes up quickly, so be alert.

South: Locate the town of Hughesville on the map. Follow MD 5 north from Hughesville approximately a mile and a half. The lake is on the left. If you pass the Hughesville Pond Recreation Area, you have gone too far.

Access Point: Parking area next to the pond (38.549119,-76.803275)

If there were ever a more pathetic small pond, I have not seen it. The Hughesville Pond is 400 feet long and approximately 75 feet across at its widest point. It is not much to look at. The vista looking south from the parking lot is one of a small, almost stagnant pond lying in a large ditch between a commercial area to the east and a wooded lot to the west. The northern end abuts directly on MD 5, a major road that serenades anglers with the constant, throaty roar of truck engines. A narrow grassy belt surrounds the pond and transitions gently into the shallow shelf that protects the shore. The shoreline is usually thick with matted algae and grass, making casting a lure problematic. The best place to fish is adjacent to the road where the pond is deepest. The distant southern end, near the woods, runs up on a shallow shelf that supports a greater volume of algae than anywhere else in the lake. That is not an issue with most of the anglers who broke the code and realized that bait is the only way to yank fish out of this sad body of water.

Unlike other local parks, there are no facilities to speak of adjacent to the pond. Granted, the formal Hughesville Pond Recreation Area is 100 yards to the west, but there is nothing here other than a picnic table with a single, isolated barbecue stand along with several benches created by suspending a large, board between posts poking out of the ground. All this may sound horrible, but it is really all any angler needs given the situation. If you come here, you are not here for a pleasant experience, you come to catch a few stocked trout. On the positive side, the commercial area adjacent to the pond features an insurance broker, an OB/GYN and a church. The opportunity to fish would amplify the enjoyment of attending religious services and minimize the pain associated with visiting the other commercial operations!

Myrtle Grove Pond

Approximate Boundary:
- Main Pond: 38.565224,-77.08133 to 38.566331,-77.076952 (23 acres)
- Secondary Pond: 38.55774,-77.072103 to 38.558949,-77.073562 (10 acres)

Type: Put and Take

Directions:
North: From I-95/I-495 take exit 3 onto MD 3S toward Indianhead. Turn left on MD 225/Hawthorne Road and follow it approximately five miles to the entrance to the wildlife management area. The left turn into the WMA is well marked.

South: From La Plata, MD, go north on US 301 to make a left turn onto MD 225/Hawthorne Road. Follow MD 225 for approximately 5.5 miles to reach the turn.

Follow the hard packed dirt road for a mile to reach the lake. Do not be confused when, after traveling 0.9 miles, you drive into a building complex. Continue to follow the road through the built-up area to the lake another 0.1 mile north.

The road to the smaller pond is approximately 0.8 miles to the east of the main entrance.

Access Point:
- Main Pond: Parking area near pond (38.565224,-77.08133)
- Secondary Pond: Parking area near pond (38.55774,-77.072103)

The Myrtle Grove Wildlife Management Area is a 1,723 acre preserve in the heart of Charles County. It contains a mixture of wetlands and hardwood forests consisting of oaks, hickories, maples and numerous other tree species. In short, it is a wonderful island of wilderness, protected by the surrounding rural area, that deserves a trip. While there are plenty of other things to see and do in the WMA with its hiking trails and shooting range, anglers focus on enjoying the two ponds.

There is plenty of parking at the edge of the lake with easy access along the western shoreline via the built-up berm. Even though a gate protects the berm from vehicular travel, you are welcome to walk around the perimeter. Wandering to the east, the path leads to the marsh that marks the right-hand boundary of the lake. During the trout season, the shoreline will not be empty. On the busiest days, plenty of anglers take advantage of the 2,000 fish that the DNR inserts in the two ponds. The heaviest population of anglers speckles the western shoreline, having taken advantage of the smooth trail along the top of the berm to reach their favorite spots. Aggressive hikers can attack the lake from the eastern shoreline with the easiest access being to walk all the way around the lake on the berm instead of trying to fight through the marsh to the east.

There is no need to limit visits to the trout season since both bodies of water contain bass, pickerel, bluegills and catfish.

Wheatley Lake

Approximate Boundary: 38.486354,-76.854454 to 38.496361,-76.85545 (75 acres)

Type: Put and Take

Directions:
North: From I-95/I-495, take exit 78 to merge onto MD 5 South/Branch Avenue towards Waldorf. Stay on Branch Avenue for approximately 20 miles to eventually turn right on Olivers Shop Road. Turn left onto MD 6/Charles Street and follow it approximately one mile to the entrance to the park on the left.

South: From Charlotte Hall, follow MD 6 west to the park. MD 6 is initially called New Market Road, but eventually changes its name to Charles Street.

Access Point: Parking area near concession (38.488862,-76.856512)

Wheatley Lake (aka Gilbert Run Lake) is the centerpiece of the 180 acre Gilbert Run Park. It is an older, mature body of water constructed 40 years ago as a floodwater management impoundment. After paying the entrance fee, take the left fork in the road to drive to the children's play area (the first right) or continue around the lake to the main concession operation near the fishing piers. The well-developed concession includes pavilions, picnic tables and barbecue areas as well as two volleyball courts. Along the shoreline, there are plenty of benches that will be fully occupied by busy anglers during the trout season.

Wheatley Lake, although big to look at with its 2.5 miles of shoreline, is only deep adjacent to the dam. The northern end of the lake is shallow and full of bass-holding stumps reachable via the nature trail that runs around the entire circumference. As the summer progresses, the vegetation around the shoreline grows and eventually forces anglers into boats to pursue the indigenous bass, crappie and catfish. The solution to the shoreline dilemma is to rent one of the canoes or Jon boats from the concession stand or plop your own into the lake using the improved boat launch next to the pier. The boat rental operation begins in April (weekends) with the number of days of operation increasing to run from Wednesday through Sunday starting in mid-May. If you decide to rent a boat, the operation is open between 8 AM and 6 PM. Be off the water before dark since the gates slam shut at 8 PM.

Another diversion suitable for families with younger children is the children's playground next to the first parking lot on the right. It is robust - full of slides, swings and even a small kid size climbing wall. There is a large bridge that joins the play area to the concession area, allowing plenty of freedom of movement for those who want to fish versus those who want to play. You may access the lake outside of the "fee paying" season that extends from April through November if you are willing to walk in. Park outside and do not block any of the other facilities or the dumpsters.

Eastern Shore

Caroline County

Tuckahoe Lake and Creek

Approximate Boundary: 38.926231,-75.950464 to 38.96715,-75.943211 (4.13 mile creek, 20 acre lake)
DNR Guidance: Tuckahoe Creek and impoundments above abandoned stone railroad bridge upstream of Route 404.

Type: Put and Take

Directions:
From US 50, turn left on MD 404E/Queen Anne Highway. Turn left on MD 480E/Ridgely Road. Turn left on Eveland Road.

Access Point:
- Crouse Mill Road at the south edge of Tuckahoe lake (38.966943,-75.942324)
- South side of Crouse Mill Road near the equestrian center (38.960043,-75.946526)
- Adkins Arboretum (38.953552,-75.933436)
- Horse Shoe Road parking lot (38.944791,-75.957524)
- Park Visitor Center (38.945659,-75.936263)
- Cemetery Road north of MD 404 (38.922502,-75.943589)

Tuckahoe Creek splits the center of the 3,800 acre Tuckahoe State Park and features a well developed trail system including several miles of paths that either cross or parallel the creek. To reach the creek from the Cemetery Road parking lot, follow the Tuckahoe Valley Trail and make a left just north of the railroad tracks onto the Creek Side Cliff Trail. It will eventually lead along the creek. At the northern end of this trail, a turn to the west on Turkey Hill Trail leads to a ford across the water. The Office Spur Trail, moving west from the Park Visitor Center, leads to a bridge across the creek and intersects with Greiner's Fishing Trail wandering in from the east from its trailhead at Horse Shoe Road. The Adkins Arboretum has its own convoluted network of trails and at least one leads to the creek. There is no direct trail to the creek from the Crouse Mill Road parking lot near the equestrian center.

Assuming an interest in trout, that was a long discussion to come to the bottom line that the only worthwhile place to park is near the lake and fish downstream. There is a fishing trail on the east side of the bridge. Since the stocked trout will not move far, relatively speaking, from this primary stocking location, this is your best bet to catch them. Elsewhere in the creek, bass, perch and catfish stand ready to provide action. If you have a canoe or kayak, the spillway is the start of the 5.4 mile long Tuckahoe Creek Water Trail. It starts out shallow and narrow, but eventually opens up.

Do not forget to fish Tuckahoe Lake. It receives a portion of the stocked trout and there is easy access to most of the lake from several different boat launches. The lake is shallow with a maximum depth of seven feet near the spillway and a consistent five to six feet elsewhere. The bottom drops off quickly from the shoreline. In addition to the planted trout, the standard assortment of other fish swim in the lake including bass, bluegill, yellow perch, crappie and chain pickerel.

Wicomico County

Beaverdam Creek

Approximate Boundary: 38.35283,-75.572469 to 38.360268,-75.579379 (3,649 Feet)
DNR Guidance: In Salisbury, from Schumaker Dam downstream to the bridge crossing at Memorial Plaza Road.

Type: Put and Take

Directions:
From US 50, turn south onto Davis Street. Turn left onto Glen Avenue. Turn right onto Beaver Dam Drive. Turn left at the bridge and follow the stream east to S Park Drive. Go across the bridge and turn left to continue on S Park Drive heading southeast. All the access points are off of S Park Drive.

Access Point:
- Museum parking lot to the north of S Park Drive next to the bridge (38.359883,-75.579029)
- Parking area north of the baseball field on S Park Drive (38.358593,-75.577704)
- Side of the road onto Park Drive (38.358802,-75.575908 - if "no parking" signs have been posted, turn north and park in the lot across the street)
- Parking lot at the intersection of Beaglin Park Drive and S Schumaker Drive (38.352111,-75.572781)

The stocked area of Beaverdam Creek is only interesting during the trout season. Once the water warms up, action moves either upstream to the lake or downstream to the bank fishing available from the Canal Walk Park on West Carroll Street. The best way to fish Beaverdam Creek is to work upstream from west to east. At the eastern boundary of the zoo, there is a path (Salisbury Urban Park Greenway) that runs along the north side of the creek all the way up to Schumaker Park. It is the best way to get from place to place with easy access to the trail from the parking lot at the intersection of Beaglin Park Drive and S Schumaker Drive. The side of the road parking on Park Drive, opposite the baseball field, is a good spot to approach the middle section if you do not mind bushwhacking since the Greenway trail is on the other side.

The creek is tight and closely overgrown with thick vegetation. This makes fishing a hit or miss activity depending on where you can wedge your way between the thick bushes. The stream runs slow with thick, scummy vegetation increasingly coating the bottom as the weather and the water warms. At most points, the stream runs around 10 to 20 feet wide, spiking to 30 feet near the ball field, across a muddy bottom with variable depth following the main channel.

Worcester County

Shad Landing Pond

Approximate Boundary: 38.139561,-75.438847 to 38.139999,-75.439695 (1 acre)

Type: Put and Take

Directions:
From US 13 on the east side of Salisbury, take MD 12S/Snow Hill Road. Turn right onto US 113 Business/W Market Street. Turn right to enter the park and follow the road to the right to reach the boat launch and pond. There are no directional signs for the boat launch near the entrance.

Access Point: Parking lot to the west of the pond (38.140472,-75.439814)

Shad Landing State Park, along with its neighbors the Milburn Landing State Park and the Pocomoke River State Forest, border the convoluted, lazily flowing Pocomoke River. Shad Landing Pond is a sideshow when compared with the superior fishing available in the river. The lake is inconsequentially small with fewer than 900 fish planted in the typical Spring season, a trivial number in the grand stocking scheme of things. But, when you realize that 900 trout is a lot of fish to pack into a pond is small, your opportunity to catch something skyrockets.

If you have a canoe, kayak or a "real boat," you would not pay the pond a second thought as you plop your craft into the water in your eagerness to attack the vibrant population of largemouth bass hunkered in the still and quiet backwaters. Since the cool months of the Spring and the Fall are the best times to pursue Pocomoke bass, it is not surprising that the pond may be a second choice during the trout season. Wait for a falling tide and paddle 500 feet north from the boat launch to enter the Pocomoke River complex. When fishing the river, focus on the weed edges. During high water conditions, throw to the inside edge, otherwise outside. Fish downstream towards Dividing Creek (38.08931,-75.540841 - east of Pocomoke City) since that is the best part of the river near the pond. Note that fishing in the Pocomoke River requires a tidal license while the pond demands a freshwater permit.

The pond features the standard easy accessibility that anglers expect in Maryland. The bank is gentle and rolls easily down to the shoreline where the bottom drops off quickly to an uncertain depth. There are three small fishing piers that enable disabled anglers and children to fish without the need to dodge the small amount of vegetation that grows along the bank. Clusters of large trees break up the monotony created by the wide, sandy path encircling the pond. After the season warms up, grass grows with abandon to the edge of the mowed section.

Shad Landing Pond

Ramp complex leading to the river

Frederick County

Big Hunting Creek

Approximate Boundary:
- Lower section below the lake: 39.620169,-77.429852 to 39.632234,-77.453896 (2.47 miles)
- Upper section above the lake: 39.628821,-77.461962 to 39.636431,-77.483188 (1.41 miles)

DNR Guidance: All waters of Big Hunting Creek and its tributaries within Cunningham Falls State Park and Catoctin Mountain Park except Owens Creek, Little Hunting Creek, Cunningham Falls Lake and Frank Bentz Pond.

Type: Fly Fishing Only

Directions:
From Frederick, head north on US 15. Exit onto MD 77W and follow it into the park. MD 77 parallels Big Hunting Creek. To fish below the falls in the upper section, turn left onto Catoctin Hollow Road. Follow Catoctin Hollow to the right-hand turn for the park. There are parking lots adjacent to the trail system.

Access Point:
- Above the lake
  - Parking lot on MD 77 (39.632167,-77.46828)
  - Small turnout on north side of MD 77 where the creek crosses the road (39.632969,-77.47514)
  - Cunningham Falls trailhead in the State Park (39.627683,-77.463948)
- Below the lake
  - Turnout on south side of MD 77 across from Park Central Road (39.633376,-77.449754)
  - Parking lot on Park Central Road (39.633787,-77.449725)
  - Parking lot on MD 77 (39.632438,-77.447171)
  - Various turnouts (39.630376,-77.44385, 39.629407,-77.443994, 39.627112,-77.444778, 39.621023,-77.434739)
  - Parking lots on both sides of the bridge (39.62593,-77.440982)

One of the few tailwater fisheries, Big Hunting Creek is a premier catch and return fishing location that also holds the distinction of being one of the first streams stocked in Maryland. The section above the lake remains the solitary domain of wild trout since all stocking is done on the lower river to complement the wild browns in the tailwater. Even though the name includes the word "big," it is a small stream. In the lower section, it runs 15 to 20 feet wide and shrinks to nothing at the headwaters high in the Catoctin Mountains. The stream bottom is perfect trout habitat consisting of rocks and clean gravel. The banks are low and usually easy to traverse. Anglers can fish the stream from rocks that jut out into the streambed, but most wade.

For the mile immediately below the dam, the creek runs down a gentle grade, dropping about 90 feet, creating a meandering flow with most of the pools at the bends. Once past the Camp Peniel bridge, the creek descends over 208 feet in the next 0.75 mile. The steep section features an amazing complex of narrow runs and plunge pools protected by an abrupt bank supporting the road that makes entry and exit moderately challenging. Across its entire length, the stream flows through thick forest that spreads protective shade to keep the water, fish and anglers cool.

Upper section is shallower...   but there are still plenty of pools

Brunswick Pond

Approximate Boundary: 39.334656,-77.612852 to 39.334033,-77.612235 (1 acre)

Type: Two fish per day

Directions:
East: From Frederick, take US 15/US 340 west towards Brunswick. Exit onto MD 180 south towards Petersville. Turn left onto MD 79W/Petersville Road.

South: From Leesburg, VA take US 15N to Point of Rocks. At the traffic circle, take the third exit onto MD 464/Point of Rocks Road. Stay on MD 464 and make a right turn when the name of the street changes to Souder Road. Turn right on Petersville Road.

The Brunswick Pond is located in the Lions Park.

Access Point: Parking area near the pond (39.334245,-77.613152)

Brunswick Pond is located just north of the town of Brunswick and provides a limited option for fishing that is clearly targeted at the local population. In addition to trout, the small pond supports bass and catfish. It is a few steps from the parking area, features a manicured, 100% accessible bank with a shaded children's playground perched in the southeast corner. As a result of the small size, it is not a destination for more than an hour or two of fishing, mostly lounging in a chair on the bank. The northern section of the lake becomes overgrown with subsurface vegetation, making it more suitable for bait fishermen. The eastern and western banks pitch a little bit more sharply down and that additional depth keeps the bank clear during the early part of the year. In short, a good place to bring a kid to catch a trout, but not worth the gas as a long-distance destination.

Carroll Creek

Approximate Boundary: 39.429536,-77.436236 to 9.416176,-77.423512 (1.2 Miles)
DNR Guidance: From a red post located 300 yards upstream of Baughmans Lane, downstream to the dam at College Avenue.

Type: Youth and Blind

Directions:
East: From I-70, merge onto I-270N. Take exit 14 for Rosemont Avenue. Keep left at the fork and follow the signs for Frederick/Hood College/Historic District/Visitor Center. Park anywhere along the road.

South: From Leesburg, take US 15N all the way to Frederick and merge onto I-270N. Take exit 14 for Rosemont Avenue. Keep left at the fork and follow the signs for Frederick/Hood College/Historic District/Visitor Center. Park anywhere along the road using the red covered bridge as the landmark designating the center of the stream.

Access Point:
- Shookstown Road (39.425873,-77.432211)
- Baughmans Lane (39.428058,-77.432684)
- Anywhere along W 2nd Street or from the Frederick High School on the south side of the stream

Carroll Creek is a narrow, shallow stream, running over a rocky bottom, with limited accessibility in the northern reaches. The best place to approach the water is in Baker Park upstream from W College Terrace near Culler Lake. North of US 15 in the 18 acre Waterford/Rock Creek Park, the creek runs through dense thickets whose overhanging vegetation makes casting problematic. Above Shookstown Road, the terrain opens up with restored accessibility. Rather than try and beat the bush, take your children to the groomed 44 acres in Baker Park below US 15.

With broad visibility as result of the open field, it is easy to keep an eye on the action as your children fish. Move from spot to spot using the asphalted trail that parallels the creek. In the park, the banks are low and easy to negotiate. There are plenty of other recreational activities including baseball fields and playgrounds to round out a good family outing.

Catoctin Creek

Approximate Boundary: 39.506148,-77.562858 to 39.508632,-77.557644 (1,850 Feet)
DNR Guidance: Catoctin Creek extends from US 40 downstream 0.35 miles to a red post at the downstream boundary of the park.

Type: Delayed Harvest

Directions:
From I-70, take exit 42 north towards Myersville on MD 17/Main Street. Turn right on Ellerton Road to stay on MD 17. Turn into the parking lot at Doubs Meadow Park and walk east to intersect the creek.

Access Point: Parking lot at Doubs Meadow Park 39.508613,-77.561129

The 31 acre Doubs Meadow Park sits in the eastern corner of Myersville and was assembled by combinations of gifts and outright annexation between 1996 and 2006. The park is jammed into the small corner formed by the intersection of MD 17 and US 40 that includes a wetland along with a playground, basketball court, soccer and baseball field as well as trails and a gazebo. Despite those distractions, Catoctin Creek is the draw for anglers. It is a wide freestone stream bordering the western edge of the park protected by delayed harvest regulations. The creek is approximately 30 feet wide with a boulder strewn bottom supporting enough flow to push out sand. In short, it's perfect trout water. During the season when the creek is running full, the volume and velocity create obvious pools and pockets between the large boulders that are liberally sprinkled throughout the length of the stream. One caution is that, at normal levels, the creek is not deep, causing the fish to be wary. Anglers who move carefully and quietly will do just fine. The best tactic is to walk to the southern end of the park, find the red post and fish upstream to the US 40 bridge.

Only the west bank of the stream is open for angler travel since the east bank sits on private property. That is no big deal since the topography of the private land is mostly steep and unfriendly, protected by a layer of thick brush and trees. Be sure and fish the area just downstream of the junction of Catoctin Creek with Little Catoctin Creek. The next fishable landmark moving upstream is a large rock cliff face that creates a sharp eastern edge to the creek. In the northern reaches, as one wades closer to the bridge, the vegetation thins out and wading and walking becomes easier.

Cunningham Falls Lake

Approximate Boundary: 39.62809,-77.456256 to 39.622868,-77.464303 (43 acres)

Type: Put and Take

Directions:
From Frederick, MD head north on US 15. Exit onto MD 77W and follow it into the park. Turn left onto Catoctin Hollow Road. Follow Catoctin Hollow to the right-hand turn for the boat launch and, farther down, the park itself.

Access Point:
- Boat launch on Catoctin Hollow Road (39.624405,-77.461427),
- Parking lot in the State Park (39.626372,-77.462264)

Cunningham Falls Lake (also known as Hunting Creek Lake) is the major feature of Cunningham Falls State Park. The man-made lake catches the water from the scenic Cunningham Falls that can be viewed at the end of a half mile hike. At 78 feet, Cunningham Falls is the largest cascading waterfall in the State. In addition to stocked trout, the lake includes a good population of bass, crappie and catfish. While there are places to fish from the shoreline, this is primarily a boating lake, electric motors only. The boat launch is well-maintained and offers quick access to the lake for a small service fee. A concession rents boats during the busy summer season.

The park has plenty of picnic areas surrounding two white sand beaches. The beaches are a major attraction and cause the park to reach capacity early in the day on summer weekends and holidays. In addition to being prohibited in the beach area, fishing is also prohibited from the junction of MD 77 and Catoctin Hollow Road to the output of the dam. Fishing is permitted above the lake downstream of the falls.

Fishing Creek

Approximate Boundary: 39.52803,-77.467275 to 39.550601,-77.481523 (1.68 miles)
DNR Description: Left fork (also known as Steep Creek) above the confluence with Little Fishing Creek upstream of Fishing Creek Reservoir.

Type: Put and Take

Directions:
From I-270, merge onto US 15N in Frederick and continue towards Thurmont. Turn left onto Stull Road after passing Utica Park on the right. Follow Stull Road to its dead end on Mountaindale Road. Turn right and follow Mountaindale past the Fishing Creek Reservoir. The stocked section begins at the confluence of Little Fishing Creek with Fishing Creek.

Access Point: Numerous turnouts along Mountaindale and Fishing Creek Roads (39.527831,-77.467189)

Tucked into the Frederick Municipal Forest, the 15 foot wide Fishing Creek offers spectacular "trout water" scenery and is a popular place for fly, spin and bait anglers during the season. In addition to stocked trout, the upper reaches hold brookies in the scattered tributaries that feed a push of cool water into the larger creek. In the Spring, the creek runs swift and strong down a freestone course that includes a calm, flat section in the north with a quick transition into a dramatic canyon just south of the intersection of Fishing Creek Road and Mountaindale Road. The stream exits the canyon near 39.52943,-77.47226 for its final run to the junction with Little Fishing Creek and Fishing Creek Reservoir.

The terrain surrounding the creek is extremely rocky and broken with thick brush protecting the stream from anglers as well as the heat of the sun. Unfortunately, by late summer, the creek runs low and slow, limiting trout survival more so than the summer heat. For those who would rather not walk a great distance to reach the water, this is the ideal stream. The road parallels the creek throughout its entire course, with the maximum distance from the road to water being approximately 30 yards except in the canyon section. The steep hillside that juts starkly upward from the western edge of the creek limits movement to the eastern bank. In most areas, the creek is easily approachable since the water level is just below the height of the eastern bank.

Above the intersection with Delauter Road, the creek runs flat through a narrow, level valley. It is shallow, and offers pools wherever there is a slight drop in elevation. There are plenty of fallen trees to provide additional holding structure.

Upper end at high Spring water   Delauter Road at high water

For the more adventurous, the canyon section supplies a mountain trout setting with dramatic plunge pools sheltered by severe, steep cliffs on either side. The best place to enter the canyon is at the turn near 39.53549,-77.47339 where there is room for a couple of vehicles to pull off on the side of the road. Look for and follow the small, dry streambed from its intersection with the road to the canyon. What awaits at the end of this short hike are spectacular small waterfalls, plunge pools and clusters of logs. Another option is to drive farther south to start fishing into the canyon at 39.53410,-77.47433 where the road enters a left-hand turn.

At entry to canyon   High gradient through the canyon

The lower section is unremarkable, but pretty. The creek lies adjacent to the road with plenty of turnoffs as it runs towards the junction of Little Friends Creek. The creek narrows to become 10 to 15 feet wide, running shallow near the confluence. Anglers must walk to discover the dispersed pools. Unlike farther upstream, anglers can walk on either bank.

Frank Bentz Pond

Approximate Boundary: 39.621554,-77.425279 to 39.62131,-77.424142 (2 acres)

Type: Put and Take

Directions:
From Frederick, MD head north on US 15. Exit onto MD 77W and follow it to the Pond.

Access Point: Parking off of MD 77 (39.620895,-77.424469)

This small pond was created in 1908 when Big Hunting Creek was dammed to power electric generators for Thurmont. In 1955, it was dedicated to Frank Bentz Sr., the public relations director for the Game and Inland Fish Commission, who was a key figure in the original restoration of the pond. Sadly, the pond is slowly filling up with silt and eventually will become unfishable without dredging. In 2011, Thurmont approved a plan to conduct a second restoration that will stabilize the pond for least another 50 years.

Given the pond's small size and location in a residential community bordering a well-established, large trailer park, this pond sees more than its fair share of pressure. As a result of the siltation, the pond is shallow with the deepest area near the water outtake at the southeast corner of the lake. The bank is reachable where it borders the parking area on the south and from a short patch of grass adjacent to the trailer park on the north. The remainder of the shoreline is packed with dense brush.

View from main road   Looking upstream

Friends Creek

Approximate Boundary: 39.711786,-77.427657 to 39.715605,-77.398775 (2.12 miles)

Type: Put and Take

Directions:
From Frederick, drive north on US 15. Take the exit onto MD 550 and turn left onto Sabillasville Road. Follow this road for approximately 6 miles and turn right on Harbaugh Valley Road. Turn right on Sunshine Trail. After a quarter mile driving south, Sunshine Trail forks with Friends Creek Road on the left and Eylers Valley Road on the right. Friends Creek Road continues east, paralleling the creek.

Access Point: Turnouts along Sunshine Trail and Friends Creek roads (39.70964,-77.424476, 39.706289,-77.418939, 39.708632,-77.411294, 39.715396,-77.402067)

Located in the distant northern backwoods of Maryland only a few feet from the Pennsylvania border, Friends Creek is one of the most heavily stocked streams in Frederick County. The stream runs through private property and there are numerous Maryland DNR signs cautioning anglers to the respectful to ensure continued public access to the creek.

At its western end, there is a small amount of parking, adequate for four or five vehicles, next to the bridge that is approximately 300 feet north of the triple intersection of Sunshine Trail, Friends Creek Road and Eylers Valley Road. Access to the stream is via the fisherman's trail that starts at the southern end of the bridge. To walk along the creek is to fall in love with it. In general, the topography of the stream is consistently rocky, matching the stereotype of good trout water. It winds its way through a level valley that has just enough change in gradient to create dramatically different structure moving from west to east. At the western end, the stream runs fairly flat through forested farmland and transitions to a more mountain-like appearance a mile to the east. It follows the typical run, riffle, pool pattern that makes fishing a joy.

Driving east along Friends Creek Road, the road veers away from the creek with a 100-200 foot forested buffer separating the water from the road. The road eventually leads to the next access at the intersection of Friends Creek Road and what appears to be a private driveway extending across an open field to a small bridge. This spot is easy to find since it is the first left driving east from the western bridge (39.706289,-77.418939). Parking is limited at this spot, so exercise care and find a safe place to pull completely off the road.

Middle access upstream

Middle access downstream

In the middle, the most popular section of the entire stream starts were Friends Creek Road rejoins the creek at 39.708632,-77.411294, just west of a large house whose owner thoughtfully speckled the landscape with plenty of "no parking" signs on either side of the road. This is the section of the creek that is most mountain-like. Here, the creek tumbles down a gentle drop that features the small plunge pools, large boulders and tight runs characteristic of an ideal mountain setting. The best fishing is to the west, upstream, since it moves away from the road and the easy access it provides. However, you must wait a week or two for the trout inserted upstream to migrate into this area.

Near "no parking" area

Near "no parking" area

Continuing east, the road crosses a bridge near the Friends Creek Church of God. The creek is only fishable for a thousand feet to the east of the bridge as a result of private property restrictions. Instead of rocks, sand and small gravel form the streambed for a brief period with the creek resuming its rocky character once it charges around the bend near a cliff to rejoin the road and reach the end of the public section.

Hamburg Pond

Approximate Boundary: 39.515432,-77.488478 to 39.51453,-77.488596 (0.9 acre)

Type: Put and Take

Directions:
Head north on I-270 towards Frederick, merging onto US 15 to take exit 13B onto US 40W/Baltimore National Pike. After driving through a built-up area that features several stoplights, US 40 eventually turns into a decent high-speed road. Follow it for approximately 8 miles to turn right on Harmony Road. Turn right on Coxey Brown Road and follow it until it dead ends on Gambrill Park Road. Turn left. Be alert for the right-hand turn onto Hamburg Road. The pond is on the right approximately 0.6 miles from the turn onto Hamburg.

Access Point: Parking north of the pond on the "service road" (39.515432,-77.488478)

After the turn, be alert since the entrance to the pond is unmarked. The only indicator is a 25 yard stretch of side road and the glimmer of water through the underbrush. If you do not have a high clearance vehicle, take care as you cut right onto the "service road." There is plenty of room for parking here – both on the service road or on the main dirt road.

The first thing to notice is the excessive amount of trash piled up at the northern edge of the lake adjacent to the parking area. Please do not add to the mess when you visit. Other than that, the pond sits in an attractive location surrounded by dense forest. There is an easy access berm that leads around the eastern edge of the pond extending all the way to the southern tip.

The adventurous can continue beyond the trail, into the woods, to reach the southwest corner of the pond. During periods of high water, a wide puddle forms on the berm within 20 yards of the parking area blocking access to those who do not wear waterproof boots and care about getting their feet wet.

In addition to walking on the berm, there is a faint trail leading directly west to disappear into the thick brush after approximately 15 yards of travel. It is problematic to fish from the western bank as a result of the densely packed vegetation that limits access to the water. In fact, fly rodders will have a tough time fishing anywhere on the pond since the trees are close to the shoreline. The best gear to use is a spin rod.

Little Catoctin Creek

Approximate Boundary: 39.508811,-77.562041 to 39.506858,-77.561751 (746 Feet)
DNR Guidance: Little Catoctin Creek extends from MD 17 downstream to the junction with Catoctin Creek.

Type: Delayed Harvest

Directions:
From I-70, take exit 42 north towards Myersville on MD 17/Main Street. Turn right on Ellerton Road to stay on MD 17. Turn into the parking lot at Doubs Meadow Park and walk west to intersect the creek.

Access Point: Parking lot in Doubs Meadow Park (39.508613,-77.561129)

The Little Catoctin Creek shares Doubs Meadow Park with its larger sibling, Catoctin Creek, that forms the southeastern boundary of the park. The excitement you may have had associated with locating two streams under delayed harvest regulations that are also easily accessible will quickly evaporate when you see the small, dribbling stream that is Little Catoctin Creek. There is no way that any fish inserted into this water could survive to the end of the delayed harvest season on May 31. Although the stream is 10 to 15 feet wide and runs over a rocky bottom, it is shallow throughout most of its length. There are three small pools that might hold fish before poachers or wildlife pluck them out, but nothing else of interest.

One positive aspect is that the banks are not clogged with vegetation. Granted, they are not mowed and manicured like the banks of many of the fishing ponds in the State, but the tall weeds present no obstacle to movement. As a result, this could be a good place to take a beginning fly fisher to practice on-stream skills without the challenge of densely overhanging, fly catching vegetation. Therefore, if you fish here, pay attention to the stocking schedule and visit this small water within a week or two of the date when fish are planted. You must be alert for the announcement since both creeks are usually only stocked with a small number of fish.

Little Fishing Creek

Approximate Boundary: 39.52803,-77.467103 to 39.555952,-77.462418 (2.02 miles)

Type: Two fish per day

Directions:
From I-270, merge onto US 15N in Frederick and continue towards Thurmont. Turn left onto Stull Road after passing Utica Park on the right. Follow Stull Road to its dead end on Mountaindale Road. Turn right and follow Mountaindale past the Fishing Creek Reservoir. Turn onto Gambrill Park Road immediately after passing the reservoir and before crossing the bridge.

Access Point: Along Gambrill Park Road - numerous across entire length of the stream

Little Fishing Creek is a native trout stream that wanders for over two miles through the heart of the City of Frederick Municipal Forest. The topography of the stream makes fishing it an interesting experience. At the southern end, the creek runs through a tight, narrow canyon whose aperture gradually opens into a moderate width valley. While not as well known as the adjacent Fishing Creek, Little Fishing Creek offers a true wilderness fishing experience within an easy walk from the road. This small freestone stream ranges from five to fifteen feet in width with the narrowest portion being just upstream of the junction with Fishing Creek. The dense forest throws plenty of shade in the summer to keep the stream cool and protect the native trout population. The stream bottom ranges from moderate sized boulders and rocks near the junction to a sand and cobble mix at the northern extremity.

Fishing the stream is simple; pick a challenge or have an easy day. For a challenge, fish upstream into the canyon from the junction with Fishing Creek where there is a broad turnout near the bridge. The creek features a stair step of small plunge pools that continue upstream to approximately 39.52955,-77.46664 where the road heaves back into view. From that point up to 39.55514,-77.46209, the road follows the stream and offers plenty of parking close to the water. The banks do not present a challenge to enter or exit the stream. Typically, they are only a foot or two above the level of the water.

In the northern section, where the valley flattens out, the creek runs wide with broad, one to two foot deep glides leading to the gradient breaks. Each gradient break is worth checking out since the disruption in the flow creates a fishable pocket of water. As the road climbs away from the creek to the right, the distance from road to water increases and the pressure drops a proportional amount. Water levels decrease substantially as the season transitions from Spring into Summer. For the best experience, visit early in the year.

Little Hunting Creek

Approximate Boundary: 39.581006,-77.432374 to 39.586331,-77.436858 (2,254 feet)
DNR Guidance: Mainstem from a red post located approximately 0.25 mile downstream of MD 806, upstream approximately one mile to the upper boundary of Cunningham Falls State Park Manor Area.

Type: Catch and Return/Artificial Lures

Directions:
From US 15, turn east onto Catoctin Furnace Road. Follow the road south to the main access points. Turn west to enter the Manor Area Park to use the parking area at the south end of the park.

Access Point:
- Bridge crossing over the creek on Catoctin Furnace Road (39.582847,-77.433959)
- At the Catoctin Furnace (39.581478,-77.433685)
- Parking area at south end of Cunningham Falls State Park (39.587263,-77.435966)

The Manor Area, that includes Little Hunting Creek, is best known for its proximity to the 200-year-old Catoctin Iron Furnace. In fact, the parking lot near the furnace provides access to the creek from the west. Since the fishing is not extensive on Little Hunting Creek, you may also be interested in taking advantage of the visitor center, aviary, picnic area and playground.

Little Hunting Creek is managed as a wild trout stream. It has not been stocked since 1994 and offers anglers the opportunity to catch small brown trout and brookies. Even though the only publicly fishable section is less than a half mile, fish exist on five miles of the creek. Sadly, the upstream fishing in the public area ends quickly as the creek leaves the park and enters the 450 acre Trout Run private section that was a favorite of President Eisenhower. Given that the fish are wild, it is important to abide by the catch and return ethic to maintain the population.

Below the bridge

Above the bridge

The creek is 20 feet wide, scenic and runs over a rocky bottom that is devoid of sand. There is a trail adjacent to the creek that offers easy access. Tall trees grow to the water's edge and the low hanging vegetation is not oppressive, allowing anglers to move either in the creek or on the bank. The creek is shallow with fish available in the deeper pools. Those same pools are popular with hikers who want to flop into the creek and cool off during the warmer months.

Middle Creek

Approximate Boundary: 39.571104,-77.532542 to 39.517559,-77.548034 (4.73 miles)
DNR Guidance: From the MD 17 bridge near the junction of Bittle Road upstream to the confluence of Spruce Run.

Type: Put and Take

Directions: From I-70, take exit 42 north onto MD 17/Myersville Road. Stay on MD 17 when it jogs right onto Ellerton Road in the town of Myersville. The stocked section begins at the bridge crossing approximately 1.3 miles after turning onto Ellerton Road.

Access Points: MD 17 parallels the creek for most of its length with numerous turnoffs. The best spots include:
- Spruce Run Road (39.569391,-77.532375)
- Highland School Road (39.546124,-77.526147)
- Several turnouts along the highway south of Highland School Road
- Small four vehicle turnout adjacent to the bridge at Bittle Road (39.517595,-77.547534)

Middle Creek is a wonderful 30 foot wide body of water, routinely stocked with over 5,000 trout, that stretches a lazy five miles through the narrow valley framed by the Catoctin Mountains on the east and the South Mountain National Environmental Area to the west. The creek runs clear over a uniformly rocky, boulder strewn bottom. Depending on the wind, the sweet odor of fresh cow manure provides both an aromatic caress as well as a reminder that you are in the heart of a rural area.

MD 17 hugs the bank tightly for most of its length, allowing frequent access to the stream. As a result, this is a popular destination and experiences heavy pressure during the height of the season. Even if you wait a week, there are usually still decent numbers of stocked trout remaining to provide an enjoyable experience. The best, most productive stretch lies in the middle section between the junction of Harp Hill Road (39.526991,-77.543077) and Highland Hill Road (39.546169,-77.5258). There are plenty of spots to pull off and safely access the stream, just be cautious of private property. In general, this creek is at its best when the Catoctin Creek Middletown gage (downstream of the stocked area) is running near 115 cfs.

Middle Creek is the 19th most heavily stocked stream in the State.

Middletown Community Pond

Approximate Boundary: 39.444542,-77.529767 to 39.446154,-77.528888 (6.5 acres)

Type: Put and Take

Directions:
North: From I-70, take exit 42 and merge onto MD 17S/Myersville Road. Turn left on E Green Street. Turn left onto Schoolhouse Drive and follow it to the park.

South: From I-70, take exit 49 onto US 40 Alt W. Turn right on Coblentz Road. Make a left turn into the park.

Access Point: Parking lot to the east of the lake (39.44576,-77.52829)

The pond is the centerpiece of Middletown Park. The park offers a broad set of amenities to include fields and courts of all types, a disc golf course, picnic shelters, grills and everything else one would expect in a well run and maintained community park. The lake sits at the southern end of the property and is bordered on the right by soccer fields and the disc golf course. The left side contains all the picnic areas and ball fields. The bank is forested on the west, open on the east with unrestricted access to the entire perimeter. The deep section of the pond is near the dam at the south. The lake is muddy at the upper end where a small stream feeds the lake.

Owens Creek

Approximate Boundary:
- **Section 1:** 39.643976,-77.413452 to 39.642732,-77.406925 (4,368 feet)
- **Section 2:** 39.643976,-77.413452 to 39.651212,-77.435853 (1.62 miles)
- **Section 3:** 39.65826,-77.445302 to 39.663206,-77.449758 (2,395 feet)
- **Section 4:** 39.667368,-77.452977 to 39.675428,-77.458169 (3,983 feet)
- **Catoctin Mountain National Park:** 39.66887,-77.47806 to 39.653691,-77.488167 (1.48 miles)

DNR Guidance: Mainstem from Raven Rock Road downstream to Roddy Road.

Type: Sections one through four are Reverse Delayed Harvest with two fish per day in the Catoctin Mountain National Park

Directions:
Head north from Frederick MD on US 15. Once past Thurmont, turn right onto Roddy Creek Road. Follow it to the covered bridge that marks the southernmost public section of Owens Creek.

All of the other sections are west of US 15. Instead of turning right on Roddy Creek Road, turn left onto N Franklinville Road, followed by another left onto Franklinville Road. Follow it to the "T" intersection on Kelbaugh Road. Turn left followed by a right on Sabillasville Road/N Church Street.

Stay on Sabillasville Road until it reaches a fork at the railroad tracks with Foxville Deerfield Road. Follow Foxville Deerfield road to the bridge crossing that is the publicly accessible upper end of the stocked section.

To reach the Catoctin Mountain National Park portion of Owens Creek, continue to drive west. A sign announces entry into the park and the transition to public property.

Access Point:
Section 1:
- Below the intersection of Albert Staub and Roddy Creek Roads (39.639687,-77.398851)
- Covered Bridge at Roddy Creek and Roddy Road (39.641026,-77.393812)
- At least four different turnoffs along Franklinville Road north of US 15

Section 2:
- Just east of the railroad overpass on Sabillasville Road (39.649078,-77.426287)
- Just east of the first residential property on the right (39.651414,-77.435801)

Section 3:
- Turnoffs on the west side of the road at 39.66111,-77.44745 and 39.66270,-77.44839

Section 4:
- At the bridge on Foxville Deerfield Road (39.675239,-77.457903)

Catoctin Mountain National Park
- There are at least eight turnoffs adjacent to the creek. The first one is immediately south of the sign announcing entry to the park (39.66887,-77.47806) with the last one being at 39.653058,-77.488056.

Owens Creek, a mere valley away from Big Hunting Creek, is managed under remarkably different regulations. The creek downstream from the church next to the bridge on Foxville Deerfield Road is managed as reverse delayed harvest. Elsewhere in the State, May 31 marks the end of the delayed harvest restriction and the start of the opportunity to keep fish. The reverse is true on Owens Creek. In this stream, the Spring season is "put and take" while the remainder of the year is artificial lures, catch and return. This allows for some of the trout to hold over if the water does not become excessively warm in the hot Maryland summer and provides an extended opportunity for trout fishing when other anglers are in hot pursuit of bass.

The lower section is fragmented into four fishable areas because some landowners do not authorize angler access (their right, but sad nevertheless). This places an additional obligation on each angler to be alert for private property and to respect property rights. Besides, the DNR will not stock on private property unless the landowner offers access, so there will not be significant numbers of trout given the holdover rate outside of the public areas anyway.

The section in the Catoctin Mountain National Park is managed under traditional two fish a day regulations and is not stocked to encourage the reproduction of wild fish. Therefore, I strongly encourage anglers to ignore the two fish a day permission and practice a strong catch and release ethic.

Reverse Delayed Harvest Section

Except where it runs through the level valley just downstream of the Foxville Deerfield Road bridge, Owens Creek is a high gradient channel stuffed into a narrow bed speckled with boulders and cobble.

Section 1

Make a right turn from US 15 to drive all the way to the covered bridge and throw an eyeball on the small stream to the right of the road. It all looks good. The water dribbles downstream across a solid rocky bottom with plenty of shade thrown by tall trees lining both sides of the bank. Below US 15, there are at least four different turnoffs with the largest one being at the covered bridge. Although the stream runs through the Roddy Road Park, the bank at the northern edge of the park is steep and inaccessible. Ignore that side and stick with the turnoffs on Roddy Creek Road.

With all of the private property issues encountered farther upstream, it is reassuring to see the numerous DNR "stocked water" signs confirming both public use and the promise of stocked trout. In addition to fishing at the covered bridge, the other good location is at the deep pool on the other side of the metal barrier east of the intersection of Roddy Creek Road and Albert Staub Road. Park at the turnoff located at 39.639687,-77.398851 and walk upstream to fish. Except for those two spots, anglers must walk the stream to find the pools.

Above US 15, after dodging around a small shopping complex, the creek parallels Franklinville Road. The public section continues to be well marked even though it is set back farther from the road. Dense forest protects the creek as it flows across the same rocky bottom seen farther downstream. The transition back from public use to private property is clearly marked by the presence of houses at the northern end.

Near the bridge

Deep spot near Albert Staub Road

Section 2

Although the stream was trout friendly in the first section, the best part of Owens Creek is the stretch below Eylers Valley Flint Road. Not surprisingly, this section sees the most pressure. The stream runs away from the distractions of private property through a steep, forested valley framed by railroad tracks. The stream cuts deep pools and good runs as it winds its way down a high gradient parallel to the road. The only good place to park is just east of the railroad overpass. This also happens to be adjacent to the best pool. While there are other places to fish for those who are willing to walk and look for holes, this particular spot experiences the heaviest pressure. There is another narrow, deep slot a short distance upstream underneath the railroad bridge.

The other primary access point is at the extreme northern boundary (39.651414,-77.435801). If you park there, fish downstream since upstream is posted. It is productive given the fractured nature of the creek. As it runs down the hill, boulders create numerous holding positions – both stocked and wild. Look for the bends where the downstream rush of water carves out deep cuts.

Under the railroad bridge   Downstream into the corner

Section 3

The next section north of Eylers Valley Flint Road is hardly worth fishing as a result of the obstacle presented by the dim trail running down the steep hill to eventually join the stream. The DNR used to stock the creek from the railroad, but I do not know if that practice continues. The one time I fished it, I only caught fallfish. While a scenic view of a small creek shaded by a full canopy of dense trees greets you as you break out of the brush onto the water, that water is mostly a stagnant mess. This section is in a gentle, level stretch between the surrounding steep mountains causing the water to slow as it spreads out with a few random deep spots hiding near rocks or the bends. There are only two access points, both on the west side of the road.

Section 4

In this, the last section of lower Owens Creek, the stream winds lazily through open fields. It is remarkably slim, being only 10 to 15 feet wide as the stream crosses the upper boundary of the stocked section at the bridge on Foxville Deerfield Road. On the north side of the bridge, there is a deep pool that is 15 to 20 feet wide fed by cool water from the thickly shaded area immediately upstream. While there are two turnoffs south of Lantz, the major access point is at the bridge. The rocky bottom becomes mixed with more sand as the velocity slows in the flat valley.

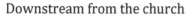

Downstream from the church   Upper stream runs through this field

The mainstem of Owens Creek is the 14th most heavily stocked stream in the State.

Catoctin Mountain National Park

If it were not for the prevalence of Maryland license plates, you could imagine that you were in the Shenandoah National Park in Virginia. The rocky bottom, narrow cuts, moderate sized boulders and a steep cliff pushing traffic to one bank, all are common sights in the Blue Ridge Mountains. There is a decent volume of water running through the cut that frames the creek as it charges into the valley. The dark forest throws cool shade and retains humidity. In addition to looking like a Blue Ridge stream, Owens Creek has the same failing – it's a long walk between pools. Given the high gradient, the majority of the stream runs shallow across slick rocks. Anglers can find deep areas at the bends or below the infrequent dramatic drops in elevation. Where the stream broadens in the rare flat section, it shallows and sand becomes pervasive. As expected, there is less water upstream than down. Be sure and tone down expectations and prepare for a significant amount of exercise as you move into the higher elevations.

Rainbow lake

Approximate Boundary: 39.695454,-77.388407 to 39.694397,-77.392098 (8 acres)

Type: Put and Take

Directions:
From Frederick MD, drive north on US 15. Once past Thurmont, turn left onto North Franklinville Road followed by a right onto Orchard Road. Continue onto Kelbaugh Road and make a slight left onto Black Road. Take the right fork from Black Road onto Three Springs Road. The road undergoes a name change to Eylers Valley Road shortly after the fork. Eventually, Eylers Valley Road will make a 90° turn to the left at a "T" intersection. Do not turn. Continue straight ahead on Hampton Valley Road. The lake is on the left about 1.2 miles from this intersection.

Parking is available on the southern side of the lake along Hampton Valley Road. You will have to dodge pricker bushes if you park in a turnoff that does not have a beaten trail leading to the lake.

Access Point: Several turnoffs on Hampton Valley Road (39.695454,-77.388407)

Rainbow Lake is also known as the Emmitsburg Reservoir. The most important thing you need to know before fishing is that the town requires anglers to have a special permit in addition to a State fishing license. To obtain the free permit, go to the town office with your fishing license. The reason is that Rainbow Lake is a conservation area and provides water to the surrounding community. There is no boating, swimming or camping allowed in the vicinity of the lake.

Once you deal with the hurdles of being legal, you will be pleased to discover that Rainbow Lake is a large and vibrant fishery. Happily, the shoreline is not clogged with underwater vegetation. Instead, it features clear water and a sand/gravel shelf that drops quickly into the deep water. The western end of the lake is shallow while the east holds the deep water. At the eastern end, the lake butts up to the high dam whose manicured summit provides a direct path and easy access to the far shore. Once off the spillway on the northern shore, follow the narrow, well beaten fisherman's trail that leads part of the way around the perimeter of the lake. The shoreline is forested, but not enough to restrict access to the water. Instead, the pricker bushes comprise the greatest challenge. Be prepared to contort your way through them if you do not want to use the established access points. The most frustrating thing is knowing that the biggest fish are probably smart enough to remain outside of casting range.

Urbana Lake

Approximate Boundary: 39.300553,-77.340707 to 39.297896,-77.340835 (2.8 acres)

Type: Put and Take

Directions:
North: From I-270, take exit 26 onto MD 80 toward Urbana. Stay on MD 80W at the traffic circle (Fingerboard Road). Turn left onto Thurston Road. Turn left onto Dixon Road. Look for the dirt road where Dixon Road joins a golf course to the east. You should be able to see the wooden sign announcing the lake. If you continue on Dixon Road, it will dead end on Dr. Perry Road. If

this occurs, make a U-turn and drive carefully along the golf course to discover the dirt road. Once on the dirt road, follow it to the end.

South: From I-270, take exit 22/MD 109S/Old Hundred Road. Turn right on Slate Quarry Road. Turn right on Thurston Road. Turn right onto Dr. Perry Road. Turn left onto Dixon Road. 0.5 miles after turning left on Dixon Road, take the slight right onto a dirt road with the golf course on your right. You will not see the sign for the lake since it is facing away from your direction of travel. Follow the dirt road to the end.

After parking, follow the shaded trail to the lake from the northeast corner of the lot.

Access Point: Parking lot at the end of the road (39.298262,-77.343003)

In 2004, Urbana Lake (also known as Chevy Chase Lake) was declared to be a potential excess property the State could sell. It's now 2011 and the property remains under DNR control. Therefore, I do not think this interesting fishing lake will be abandoned anytime soon. The lake sits at the southeast edge of the 60 acre Urbana Lake Fish Management Area. The entire area has a remote feel even though it is within 500 feet of the buzzing traffic on I-270.

After bouncing over the scattered pine straw on the dirt road to end at the parking area at the edge of the dense forest surrounding the lake, walk north from the parking area onto the flat trail leading down a slight grade to the lake. It is a short walk (0.2 miles) with a total drop in elevation of 59 feet. The forest is thick in all directions and throws plenty of cooling, protective shade to minimize sweating even on the hottest summer day.

Once on the shoreline, there is an option to follow a small trail around the lake, but fishing from the shore can be problematic given the dense forest that crowds to the water's edge. There is a substantial mat of underwater vegetation blocking the shoreline on both the eastern corner near the dam as well as at the southern tip. At the northern end, the water is slightly deeper along the dam line. However, casting will be obstructed by a congested mess of cattails at the edge of the dam.

Whiskey Springs Pond

Approximate Boundary: 39.566646,-77.495044 to 39.565645,-77.496057 (1 acre)

Type: Put and Take

Directions:
North: From I-70, take exit 32A onto US 40E (or just take US 40E from Hagerstown). Turn left onto MD 17N/Wolfsville Road. At the intersection of Wolfsville Road with Harmony Road/Middle Creek, bear left and take an immediate right to stay on MD 17/Wolfsville Road. Turn right onto Middlepoint Road. Turn right onto Tower Road when Middlepoint ends. Make a sharp left onto Gambrill Park Road. The pond is approximately 500 feet from the turn on the right.

South: From I-270, take Exit 32 onto US 15N/US 40W. Merge onto US 40W by taking exit 13B. Turn right on Harmony Road. Turn right onto Wistman Lane. It eventually turns into Crow Rock Road. Turn left onto Highland School Road. Turn right onto Rum Springs Road and then left onto Gambrill Park Road. Follow Gambrill Park for approximately 1.3 miles to reach the pond.

Access Point: Small turnoff adjacent to Gambrill Park Road (39.566646,-77.495044)

The Civilian Conservation Corps excavated Whiskey Springs during the Depression to provide a source of water to combat forest fires. The pond experienced a brief moment of fame in 2003 when the FBI drained it in search of some of the components used to make the anthrax found in letters mailed following the attack on September 11, 2001 to political leaders and media outlets. All that is history now and the lake sits quietly in a level valley where the 26 mile long Catoctin Trail provides a highway for hikers and bikers near the pond.

Since the pond is small, it may or may not be stocked depending on the amount of rainfall. Therefore, pay attention to the posted stocking schedule to ensure that it gets a dose of fish before making the effort to drive here. The turnoff to the pond is unmarked except by the intersection of the gravel road that joins Gambrill Park from the south. There are only a few parking spaces. Follow the remnants of the dirt road over the rough berm to cross the small spillway to stand on the southern bank of the pond. Most anglers fish from the south side, along the berm, since the northern bank is packed with trees and dense bushes that leave few openings.

The pond remains reasonably clear of lure clogging vegetation during the season. From the southern bank, the depth drops off quickly to become approximately five feet deep within ten feet of the shoreline. The western end of the lake is shallow and, as the season progresses, becomes scum-clogged sooner than the rest of the pond.

Woodsboro Community Pond

Approximate Boundary: 39.532335,-77.306774 to 39.533684,-77.307176 (1.6 acres)

Type: Put and Take

Directions:
From I-270N, merge onto US 15N, exit 13B. Continue on US 15 and take exit 17 to merge onto MD 26/E Liberty Road toward Walkerville. Make a left onto MD 194/Woodsboro Pike. Turn right on MD 550/Woodsboro Road. Cross over Israel Creek and look for the entrance to the park on the left.

Access Point: Parking lot near pond (39.531272,-77.306007)

The Woodsboro Community Pond sits in the middle of the Woodsboro Park. The town did a great job using State grant money to improve the entire facility. While most parks have ball fields and playgrounds, Woodsboro is one of the few places that features a well developed disc golf course. Think Frisbee, but improved and customized to incorporate the organization and rules of golf.

The pond receives a robust stocking of fish with normal post-insertion pressure being exacerbated by superior angler access via the asphalt path that runs around the entire perimeter of the lake. The northern part of the pond is shallow and becomes clogged with underwater vegetation as soon as the water begins to warm. In addition to trout, the pond contains bass and bluegill, so fishing extends well into the summer and fall. After a heavy rain, a second, smaller pond will appear at the southern edge of the main pond. No matter how attractive it looks, do not bother to fish it since it is just a big puddle that will dry up as soon as the sun comes out.

Garrett County

Accident Pond

Approximate Boundary: 39.629872,-79.316255 to 39.630143,-79.316928 (1 acre)

Type: Put and Take

Directions:
North: From I-68, take exit 14 onto US 219S toward Oakland. Turn left on Cemetery Road followed by a right onto South Street. The parking lot is on the left.

South: From Oakland, drive north on US 219. Turn right on Cemetery Road followed by a right onto South Street. The parking lot is on the left.

Access Point: Parking lot to the west of the pond (39.6306,-79.317411)

Accident Pond is a typical small-town pond that sits in the middle of an open field. The entire perimeter of the lake is accessible. Some underwater vegetation grows in the northern corners, but other than that, casting is unobstructed since the bottom drops off quickly from the shoreline and the depth controls the growth. A cluster of trees to the east offers a scrap of shade with scattered benches providing welcome seating for those who would rather not stand or sit on the ground.

Bear Creek

Approximate Boundary: 39.654408,-79.330069 to 39.660718,-79.396361 (4.45 miles)

Type: Put and Take

Directions:
East: From I-68, take exit 14A to merge onto US 219S. Turn right on Bear Creek Road. The stocked section starts approximately 1.6 miles from the junction of Bear Creek Road and US 219.

West: From I-68, take exit 4 to merge onto Friendsville Road. Turn left onto 1st Avenue. Turn right on Maple Street. Maple turns into Bear Creek Road. The stocked section begins on the east side of I-68 where the road crosses the creek.

Access Point: Various turnoffs on Bear Creek Road to include: 39.6554,-79.30426 39.66028,-79.3163, 39.65695,-79.35625, 39.65767,-79.3586, 39.65835,-79.36073, 39.65653,-79.36457, 39.65859,-79.36878, 39.65585,-79.38821, 39.65377,-79.38399, 39.65308,-79.38511, 39.65396,-79.38659, 39.65542,-79.3885, 39.65593,-79.39149, 39.66095,-79.39686

At the time of publication, there is a disconnect between the published boundary of the stocked section and the reality on the ground. I extracted the boundary GPS coordinates from what was published by the DNR on the Internet. However, on the ground, the first DNR signage actually occurs a little over a quarter mile west of US 219, not 1.6 miles from the landmark as quoted above. Therefore, the fishable stretch of Bear Creek extends beyond 4.45 miles - all scenic, all good. Do not bother to fish east of US 219, it is all posted. At the narrow headwaters near the first turnoff, there is room for two cars to park. It runs 25 feet wide over a bottom composed of small rocks with a minimum of sand. Gradient breaks occur at regular intervals, producing deep spots below the riffles as the creek drops almost 800 feet between US 219 and the I-68 bridge. After that first opportunity to fish, the road moves away from the creek, gaining altitude and limiting admittance. To fish the western stretch, anglers must walk from the small turnoff with no easy path along the creek. The next access point is east of the junction of Harmons Road (39.66028,-79.3163) and features another two car turnout. It is set back from the river with a well defined path to the creek. The amount of flow increases as a result of the contributions of two small streams feeding in from the north. Bear Creek now runs 30 feet wide with a increasing number of rocks and boulders strewn across the streambed. Shoreline vegetation lightens, making movement along the northern bank much easier – especially 20 yards back from the creek where the forest thins out. The southern bank runs along the precipitous mountainside that leads up to Hickory Ridge and Wagner Hill.

The road resumes its upward climb and the creek is not approachable until the road drops around the corner near a sparsely populated residential section in the vicinity of Everly Road. Given the obvious issues with private property, continue to follow the road until it enters the narrow gap between Winding Ridge and Oak Hill. For the next mile, there are scattered, small turnoffs with the largest one able to accommodate six vehicles. It is immediately prior to the sharp left where the protruding ridgeline pokes to the south off Winding Ridge.

There is plenty of good fishing in this stretch with one spot being the deep pool next to a supersized boulder close to the large parking area. A small ATV trail runs next to the river for a short distance and connects anglers to good holes in both directions. The southern bank remains relatively inaccessible as it continues to be braced by the mountainside. Movement is easy through the flat forest along the northern shore.

Once "civilization" returns, parking opportunities disappear until the road takes a sharp turn to the right near Friendsville with the junction of Bear Creek Road and Accident Friendsville Road being a significant landmark. The creek flows deep and wide with plenty of room for vehicles in well spaced turnoffs along both roads (Accident Friendsville Road is on the south side of the creek). In fact, one of the most popular places to fish is immediately downstream of the junction where there is a series of stairstep pools that extend west approximately 100 yards. Immediately after stocking, this is where you will see plenty of anglers.

Bridge at Friendsville-Addison Road   Below the bridge

As the creek moves through another drop in elevation, it tightens again, offering deep water with rhododendrons packing both sides. The next parking is at the bridge crossing over Bear Creek where there is room for two cars to pull off on the side of the road. Upstream, the river runs down a drop in elevation to create an additional staircase of pocket water marked by medium-size boulders. Downstream, the number of pools increases as the stream moves underneath the I-68 bridge (a few parking spots) and begins to parallel Walnut Street. At that point, there is urban roadside parking next to a gentle, grassy slope.

Bear Creek is the third most heavily stocked stream in the State.

Big Run

Approximate Boundary: 39.543268,-79.138516 to 39.603043,-79.167831 (5.11 miles)

Type: Zero Creel

Directions: From Westernport, take MD 135 west towards Bloomington. Turn right onto Savage River Road. Turn left on Big Run Road.

Access Point: Various turnoffs and campsites adjacent to Big Run Road

Big Run drops 1,162 feet as it wanders 5.1 miles from its source on the south side of Meadow Mountain through the gap between Middle and Peapatch Ridges. Given that huge drop, Big Run meets all expectations for a high gradient stream and pairs up with its major tributary, Monroe Run, to be the key water feature inside Big Run State Park. The DNR stocked almost 17,000 brook trout in the 40 years between 1948 and 1988 to reestablish their presence. Like the rest of the Savage Reservoir watershed, it is protected by a Zero Creel fishing regulation. The name "Big Run" is an appellation that recognizes the width of the stream rather than the depth. In most places, the shallow stream runs 15 to 20 feet wide across a rocky bed. Given the sharp drop in elevation, anglers must hike to find pools deep enough to hold fish. Most of the park facilities are located at the junction of Big Run Road and Savage River Road and include improved campsites, restrooms and a potable water source.

Near the Savage Reservoir   Farther upstream

Broadford Lake

Approximate Boundary: 39.407484,-79.372408 to 39.423332,-79.359491 (140 acres)

Type: Put and Take

Directions:
From US 219 in Oakland, turn east on Memorial Drive and follow it to Broadford Road. At the intersection of Memorial and Broadford, turn left to go to the Memorial Drive access point or right for the public access and boat launch on Recreation Lane.

Access Point:
- Intersection of Memorial Drive and Broadford Road (39.420244,-79.371319)
- Parking lots adjacent to Recreation Lane (39.41637,-79.374135, 39.412805,-79.373529, 39.411168,-79.37436, 39.407799,-79.374425)
- Boat launch on Recreation Lane (39.410776,-79.374382)

Broadford Lake offers easy access to the shoreline from Recreation Lane with the best fishing opportunity going to anglers with boats (electric motors only) that allow them to cover the entire body of water. No boat? The park is happy to rent one to you. For those willing to walk along the shoreline, the entire perimeter of the lake is accessible with how far to go limited only by the energy you want to invest. In general, the northern end is shallow and contains the preponderance of bass holding structure – stumps, lily pads and other aquatic vegetation. The proper habitat for smallmouth bass is adjacent to the dam in the south, and you never know where you may pick up a tiger musky. Caution! The DNR introduced 2,000 striped bass fingerlings in 2008, so get ready to pour water on your smokin' drag when one of those bad boys grows up and rips into your lure!

The lake receives a decent dose of trout during the season, but in a lake this large, you will probably catch something else before you find a trout. For the family oriented, the park has the normal collection of facilities including picnic areas, swimming and biking.

Casselman River

Approximate Boundary: 39.694782,-79.139265 to 39.722427,-79.111716 (4.1 miles)
DNR Guidance: From a red post located on the south side of the I-68 eastbound bridge downstream to the Pennsylvania State Line.

Type: Delayed Harvest

Directions:
From I-68, take exit 19 onto MD 495N/Bittinger Road towards Grantsville. Turn right on US 40 Alt E/Main Street. Turn left into the Casselman Bridge State Park parking area prior to crossing the river or proceed across the river and turn right into the parking adjacent to I-68. To fish downstream, continue east on Main Street and turn left on River Road. River Road parallels the river.

Access Point:
- Casselman Bridge State Park parking (39.696274,-79.144777)
- I-68 lot parking (39.695299,-79.140611)
- River Road bridge parking (39.702179,-79.136712)
- Various turnoffs along River Road (last one at 39.716144,-79.120648)

Fishing on the Casselman River was destroyed in the 1800s by acid runoff from mining. The DNR corrected this through aggressive management and reclamation efforts and, by 1989, the river had become a "go to" trout fishing destination. The great joy of the Casselman as opposed to its siblings farther to the west, the North Branch of the Potomac and the Savage River, is that wading is much easier. The "rock snot" that forms a treacherous coating over every rock in the other two rivers is not as prevalent on the Casselman. The smaller rocks and cobble that form the streambed are a refreshing change from the larger boulders on the other rivers that were designed by the devil to twist ankles and pitch anglers head first into icy water. While the Casselman has plenty of large rocks, they serve the positive purpose of creating holding areas for fish rather than obstacles for anglers. Although the river is narrow as it winds its way underneath the I-68 bridge, it quickly grows from 20 to over 80 feet as it enters the flat farmland upstream of the Pennsylvania State line. Sadly, the river warms to the point of trout mortality in the summer, so reserve time on your cold weather calendar to fish when the DNR stocks the river with large numbers of brown and rainbow trout, including many of trophy size. As the weather and the water warms up, the trout migrate to the cool water trickling into the river from a few random springs. If you can find those, you can find late-season fish. The local Trout Unlimited chapter is active in supporting the DNR by float stocking the river. Therefore, it pays to walk away from the road. Start your day in the four acre Casselman River Bridge State Park. The manicured grounds make fishing easy. Once south of the US 40 bridge, the bank becomes a steep, jumbled cluster of large rocks making it tough to negotiate unless you wade. To fish that side, start from the I-68 parking lot.

I-68 bridge downstream

Upstream from park towards US 40

Moving north from the River Road bridge, the steep hills to the west push the shaded road close to the river. The protective band of vegetation is not thick, with minimal bush and vine undergrowth making it easy to approach the river. The eastern bank borders open fields and the rural noises of farming and cattle mixes with the nose-nipping aroma of manure to complete the picture. Once on the river, do not be fooled by the shallow appearance. The water is crystal clear and runs deeper than it looks. The secret to success on the Casselman is to find the deep cuts and protected structure. Do not ignore the banks, since the big fish huddle near cover, causing experts to advise anglers not enter the river at all since the fish tend spook on the sound of gentle splashing. There are no rushing rapids to conceal your approach since the gradient is flat and gentle.

At 39.70776,-79.12589, the road briefly touches the river and is the last place to walk to the shore until the road winds its way through a farm and returns to the river at 39.71469,-79.12332. Start fishing at any of the obvious parking areas with the last one being adjacent to a path at 39.716144,-79.120648 where the road veers left and a large field becomes an insurmountable protective cushion of private property. The river deepens at this location and it may be problematic to wade depending on the water levels. According to the DNR, flows lower than 150 CFS on the Casselman River gage at Grantsville are optimum for fishing.

The Casselman River is the body of water that receives more trout than any other in the entire State. It is number one in terms of stocking with over 9,100 fish inserted in the Spring.

Crabtree Creek

Approximate Boundary: 39.503974,-79.155296 to 39.457684,-79.226967 (4.85 miles)

Type: Zero Creel

Directions
From Westernport, take MD 135 west towards Bloomington. Turn right onto Savage River Road. At the first hard, hairpin turn at the west end of the reservoir, take a right onto Spring Lick Road. Crabtree Creek runs on the south side of the road.

Access Point: Various turnouts along Spring Lick Road to include 39.49994,-79.16156, 39.49924,-79.16175, 39.49439,-79.16781, 39.49187,-79.17212

Crabtree Creek rivals Middle Fork as a top brook trout fishing destination. It runs wide and clear across a rocky bottom that provides ideal habitat for brook trout. In fact, this is one of the streams identified in the Maryland DNR Brook Trout Management Plan as having a robust, self sustaining brook trout population. Please obey the Zero Creel limit admonishments that the DNR posts at all of the turnouts! As you drive up Spring Lick Road, the creek scratches its course through dramatic scenery that includes deep runs and plunge pools. Avoid fishing near any of the residential areas even if they are not specifically posted.

Near reservoir   Plenty of good pools

The Potomac State Forest lies to the south of the creek and includes the land between the mountain and the road for the first 1,400 feet of the stream. At approximately 39.501011,-79.159781, the creek flows through private property with angler access permitted at landowner discretion. As of early 2011, there are no "posted" signs adjacent to the DNR turnoffs identified above. In addition, DNR signage is at each location, confirming access, *for now*. I urgently request anglers to be gentle with this stream, leave no trace, pick up any garbage you see and do everything you can to protect it.

Risky road leading to stream   Next to road

The Potomac State Forest northern boundary runs along the old rail bed that rides a precarious ridgeline on the northern side of Backbone Mountain. There is a gap in public ownership starting at 39.480759,-79.185426 extending to 39.468402,-79.201047. However, according to American Whitewater, aggressive kayakers plop their boats into the creek at the bridge using the railroad right-of-way at the town of Swanton. In the past, they reported friction with one of the landowners in that area.

Exercise caution on how you enter the water since the Potomac State Forest property does not begin until 39.457071,-79.221261, approximately 0.3 miles east from the bridge. Any creek that gets kayakers excited based on the number of ledges and drops is usually a good indicator of promising water for hiking anglers once the level drops enough to make the stream uninteresting to kayak borne adrenaline junkies.

For those who enter the creek from the Savage River Reservoir side, the best turnoff is 1,000 feet prior to Spring Lick Road taking an abrupt bend to the north. Do not be tempted to follow the old road adjacent to the bend that hangs off the ledge leading to the creek. It is narrow, severely eroded and while you might be able to drive to edge of the creek, chances are you may find yourself upside down instead of right side up when the fragile roadbed collapses under the weight of your vehicle. At this spot, Spring Lick Run slams into Crabtree Creek and creates a set of good pools that will, appropriately, lure you farther west into the deep gorge between the surrounding mountains.

In the gorge

Robust flow, high gradient

Deep Creek Lake

Approximate Boundary: 39.451385,-79.307613 to 39.556286,-79.356365 (3,900 acres)

Type: Put and Take

Directions:
North: From I-68, take exit 4 onto MD 42/Friendsville. Turn left onto Maple Street and follow it to the start of MD 42S. Merge onto US 219 and continue south to the lake.

South: From Oakland, MD head north on US 219 to the lake.

Access Point: Too numerous to document. However, the easiest, most obvious place is the shoreline of Deep Creek Lake State Park (39.516401,-79.310224). It includes one mile of shoreline with easy access for fishing.

Initially constructed in the 1920s to run a hydroelectric plant, the lake is now the top vacation destination in western Maryland. According to the DNR, the lake is 13 miles long with over 69 miles of shoreline. It reaches a maximum depth of 75 feet and averages 25 feet. In addition to the trout that hold over from year-to-year in the cold water, it also supports a vibrant fishery consisting of large and smallmouth bass, walleye, yellow perch and some northern pike. *Most* of the shoreline (the buffer strip) is owned by Maryland although anglers must avoid boat docks and the area near the lake outlet. State ownership of the buffer strip is emphasized via the requirement that property owners adjoining it must obtain an annual permit. Therefore, the vast majority of the shoreline is open for fishing.

Dry Run

Approximate Boundary: 39.523078,-79.144485 to 39.537278,-79.158347 (1.76 miles)

Type: Zero Creel

Directions: From Westernport, take MD 135 west towards Bloomington. Turn right onto Savage River Road. Turn left onto Dry Run Road.

Access Point: Single turnoff on Dry Run Road (39.52355,-79.14719)

Dry Run drops 670 feet into the gash between Solomon Ridge and Mount Nebo. The stark terrain creates an abrupt canyon that squeezes the creek and the road beside it into a tight, thin line with limited parking. Other than at the confluence with the Savage River Reservoir, the only convenient turnoff is at 39.52355,-79.14719, merely 500 feet from the intersection with Savage River Road. In fact, once past 39.52488,-79.15022, the road rises sharply to claw its way along the southern hillside, moving far away from the valley floor and the trickling creek below. While the creek remains fishable upstream from that point, it is up to you to decide how much sweat to invest to find the widely distributed pools. In the lower reaches, the creek ranges up to ten feet wide, compressing to a small dribble no more than two feet across in the higher elevations. The water runs across a freestone bottom flecked with large rocks surrounded by cobble.

Elk Lick

Approximate Boundary: 39.60175,-79.08742 to 39.620202,-79.113114 (2.41 miles)

Type: Zero Creel

Directions: From Westernport, take MD 135 west towards Bloomington. Turn right onto Savage River Road.

Access Point: Elk Lick Campsite (39.60175,-79.08742)

Tumbling 556 feet across its 2.4 mile course inside the Savage River State Forest, the creek does not pause to create many fishable pools. Look for the start of the State property on Elk Lick Road and pull off at the campsite located just northwest of the park border. From there, walk over to the stream and slide down the ten foot tall bank to reach the water's edge. It is not wide and the terrain only allocates five to ten feet to hold the streambed. The hillside is steep; prepare to sweat to find a fishable pool.

Glades Park Pond

Approximate Boundary: 39.415151,-79.415737 to 39.416444,-79.415898 (1 acre)

Type: Youth and Blind

Directions:
From US 219 in Oakland, turn left on E Center Street and follow it across its intersection with N Bradley Lane (road changes name to Bradley Lane as it turns to the south). Turn right on Liberty Street. Turn right on Spruce Lane to enter the park.

Access Point: Parking lot off of Spruce Lane (39.415632,-79.415265)

This small pond is across the street from the Oakland water treatment facility. It is L-shaped with easily accessible banks. A fence protects most of its perimeter with the entrance on the east side. The town's running/walking path snakes along the southern bank, but a fence separates it from the pond. There are a few places where large trees restrict fishing along the shoreline.

The bottom of the pond transitions quickly from the shoreline into deep water with the shallow shelf extending no more than five to ten feet from the bank. Thankfully, during the season, there is a minimal amount of vegetation to obstruct casting. For safety, there are strategically placed life preservers around the perimeter of the pond. The small park includes basketball courts and a large pavilion in addition to the running trail.

Herrington Creek

Approximate Boundary: 39.460517,-79.447271 to 39.461031,-79.423302 (1.73 miles)

Type: Put and Take

Directions:
North: From I-68, take exit 4 onto MD 42. Follow MD 42W to the intersection with Blooming Rose Road and turn left to go back underneath the Interstate. Turn left on White Rock Road. Turn right onto Cranesville Road. Cranesville Road becomes Herrington Manor Road. Park either at the dam inside the State Park or go past the entrance to the State Park to the large parking area on the north side of the creek.

South: From Oakland, turn west on E Center Street. Follow it through the intersection with N Bradley Lane onto Bradley Lane to turn right on Liberty Street. Head west on Liberty Street across the river and into the park. The name of the road changes to Herrington Manor Road. The large parking area is on the north side of the creek prior to reaching the entrance to the State Park. Another option is to park near the dam in the State Park.

Access Point:
- Parking lot on the east side of Herrington Manor Road adjacent to the creek (39.464106,-79.443864)
- Herrington Manor Lake Road near the north end of Herrington Lake (39.459146,-79.449607)

Herrington Creek is lightly stocked for its length, only receiving 480 fish in the Spring season, but all those fish are inserted in a very small area. A DNR kiosk marks the large turnout on the north side of the creek. There are no trails paralleling the stream downstream other than the faint fisherman's trail that leads directly from the parking area to the water. At the turnout, the creek is approximately 15 feet wide and thoroughly overgrown with dense vegetation. The stream bottom is a mix of sand, rocks and small boulders.

The upstream side is tied into the formal trail network of the Herrington Manor State Park and offers easier access where the trail parallels the creek. Between the dam on Herrington Lake and the turnout, the stream is low gradient, flowing through an open valley. After crossing the road, the elevation drops approximately 40 feet in the 1.4 mile stretch to the junction of the Youghiogheny River. Unlike the upstream section, downstream runs through a deep valley with no exit point other than the original turnout. The most dramatic section begins 0.8 miles from the road.

According to the Eastern Brook Trout Venture, Herrington Creek has good enough water quality, equivalent to the Savage Reservoir watershed, to support natural reproduction of trout. However, the DNR 2005 Brook Trout Management Plan did not identify this creek as having a self-sustaining population. Maybe that will change in the future, but it means that if you hike a significant distance from the road, you may not encounter any fish.

Herrington Lake

Approximate Boundary: 39.453575,-79.461862 to 39.457982,-79.452914 (53 acres)

Type: Put and Take

Directions:
North: From I-68, take exit 4 onto MD 42. Follow MD 42W to the intersection with Blooming Rose Road and turn left to go back underneath the Interstate. Turn left on White Rock Road. Turn right onto Cranesville Road. Cranesville Road becomes Herrington Manor Road. Turn right at the entrance to the State Park. Stay to the right to get to the boat launch and the area near the dam.

South: From Oakland, turn west on E Center Street. Follow it through the intersection with N Bradley Lane onto Bradley Lane to turn right on Liberty Street. Head west on Liberty Street across the river and into the park. The name of the road changes to Herrington Manor Road. Turn left to enter the park on Herrington Manor Lake Road. Stay to the right to get to the boat launch and the area near the dam.

Access Point:
- North end of the lake near the dam (39.457568,-79.451872)
- Parking area adjacent to the boat launch (39.454971,-79.453657)

The lake is another project we can thank the Civilian Conservation Corps for creating in the 1930s when they threw a dam across Herrington Creek to create the impoundment.

It sits inside the 365 acre Herrington Manor State Park and fishing is only one of the many activities available. There is a beach for swimming, picnic areas, hiking trails as well as tennis, volleyball and furnished log cabins the State rents out to visitors who prefer a roof thicker than nylon.

The best way to fish this lake is from a boat. In season, the concession stand rents canoes and kayaks during daylight hours between 10 AM and 5 PM – electric motors only. The deepest part of the lake is between the boat launch and the dam. At its southern extremity, the channel of Herrington Creek cuts its way across the muddy bottom. The channel is skewed to the north side of the lake and not fishable from the shore.

Jennings Randolph Lake

Approximate Boundary: 39.406356,-79.164062 to 39.43321,-79.122519 (952 acres)

Type: Put and Take

Directions:
Maryland Side
- North: From Westernport, take MD 135 west towards Luke and follow it across the Savage River in Bloomington. Continue on MD 135 for a little over 8 miles and then turn left onto Mt. Zion Road. It dead-ends at the launch.
- South: From Oakland, follow MD 135 east for a little over 12 miles and turn right on Mt. Zion Road. It dead-ends at the launch.
- Maryland Overlook 1: Turn east onto Walnut Bottom Road from MD 135. Walnut Bottom joins Chestnut Grove Road as it turns to the south. Follow the road another 1,000 feet to the overlook.

West Virginia Side
- North: From Westernport, take MD 135 west towards Luke. On the other side of Luke, turn left (south) on WV 46. Turn right at the sign for the Howell Boat Launch.
- South: From Elk Garden, WV, turn north on WV 46. Turn left at the sign for the Howell Boat Launch.

Access Point:
- Maryland boat launch (39.419685,-79.12993)
- West Virginia Howell Run boat launch (39.409556,-79.12008)
- Maryland Overlook 1 at the end of Chestnut Grove Road (39.440626,-79.121638)
- Eastern shoreline near the dam using the Paul Sarbanes Trail (39.444081,-79.119201)

Authorized in 1962, the Army Corps of Engineers completed construction of this massive facility in 1981. The lake is big with a depth exceeding 270 feet in places, a characteristic that allows it to produce hulking fish. Four Maryland State records trace back to the lake - a 14 lb 4 oz walleye, a 13 lb 7.5 oz brown trout, 7 lb 4 oz cutthroat trout and 6 lb 2 oz brookie. A key factor contributing to the spectacular results was the release of over 2.5 million walleye fry by the WV Fisheries that was matched by an additional stocking of thousands of trout fry from the Maryland DNR.

The first challenge is to determine how to move from point to point. From talking to other fishermen, the best spot for smallmouth is up at the mouth where the North Branch flows into the lake from Kitzmiller. Running five or six miles up the lake is not a big deal in a high powered bass boat that can go fast enough to make your cheeks flap, but it is a heck of a challenge in a canoe pushed by paddles or, at best, a trolling motor churning hard to reach three mph. If all you have is a canoe, you could spend an hour or more just getting across this huge body of water. Therefore, without power, stick to the shoreline close to the two launches.

Sadly, bank fishing is a nonstarter since it is impossible to fish the lake from the shoreline in the upper section simply because there is no shoreline to walk on. The lake is in a deep, steep valley. The closeness of the contour lines on the map provides a dramatic indication of how abruptly the mountains drop to the water. The only good shoreline access I am aware of is near the dam, reachable by following the road down from Maryland Overlook 1 to transition to the Paul Sarbanes trail. Go through the gate and take the left fork to intersect the fishing access trail near the dam.

If you are on foot and in search of trout, a better choice is to head up or downstream to fish the North Branch of the Potomac. The ultimate, detailed reference is my book, *Trout and Smallmouth Fishing on the North Branch of the Potomac* that provides step-by-step, detailed coverage from Westernport, MD to Wilson, WV (traditional print available from the normal online booksellers, eBook from www.CatchGuide.com).

Little Youghiogheny River

Approximate Boundary: 39.394949,-79.398433 to 39.420953,-79.424331 (2.91 miles)
DNR Guidance: Mainstem from Route 219 downstream to the Youghiogheny River.

Directions:
In Oakland, turn south from US 219 on South 3rd Street and follow it to the river.

Access Point:
- South 3rd Street bridge (39.405803,-79.408389)
- Town Park on South 2nd Street (39.40852,-79.409384)
- Oakland Rosedale Road bridge (39.412391,-79.416353)

Starting from the south, even though the stocked section begins downstream of US 219, the river is not publicly approachable. There is no parking since the road runs over a high bridge with industrial areas to the east and private property to the west. The first opportunity to fish the 20 to 30 foot wide river is near the 3rd Street bridge. There are a small number of parking areas adjacent to the bridge that will hold three or four vehicles. Upstream of the bridge, the river runs deep through a tight section that features a high northern bank clogged with vegetation. Downstream, the river flows over a rocky bottom through a small gradient break into a larger pool with high, relatively clear banks farther downstream.

The Town Park provides the best access point. In addition to fishing, feel free to participate in the farmers market that usually runs Wednesdays through Saturdays from 10 AM until 2 PM. Obviously, being there during that window of time allows you to experience the greatest congestion and competition for parking. The park is on the east bank of the river and overlooks a deep section. Despite being at the edge of town, it presents a scenic picture since the river drifts underneath two bridges surrounded by bright green vegetation.

For anglers who are not mobile, there is a fishing pier at the northwest corner of the park directly adjacent to the parking lot. The deep channel pushes against the west bank. Immediately north of the Town Park sits the small Rotary Park. It provides additional shoreline access to the river near a spot where the river shallows out below the set of riffles that is the watery dividing line between the two facilities.

3rd Street bridge   Town Park

The final access point is near the bridge supporting the Oakland Rosedale Road and is connected to the Town Park by an improved running trail that offers easy walking to the east where the path hugs closely to the river for a thousand feet prior to moving away towards MD 39. At most, two vehicles can park in a small turnout adjacent to the bridge. The banks are high, the river runs slow and heavy vegetation makes fishing a challenge. To fish downstream, use the northern bank on the property associated with the Oakland water treatment facility.

Path that leads to the Oakland-Rosedale
Road bridge

Oakland-Rosedale bridge downstream

Middle Fork

Approximate Boundary: 39.512683,-79.154227 to 39.51447,-79.216068 (5.32 miles)

Type: Zero Creel

Directions: From Westernport, take MD 135 west towards Bloomington. Turn right onto Savage River Road. Middle Fork crosses Savage River Road north of the junction of Spring Lick Road.

Access Point:
- Small roadside turnout at the Middle Fork bridge (39.512683,-79.154227)
- Dry Run Road (not personally confirmed - 39.54982,-79.17637)

Dropping 871 feet, Middle Fork starts in the Middle Fork Wildland and ends at the Savage River Reservoir. The stream is famous enough to be written up in Ann McIntosh's book, *Mid-Atlantic Budget Angler*. According to her, there are 2,400 trout per mile, making this top producing water. A key reason for that vibrant population may be the long hike to reach the best water cradled in the deep valley of the Middle Fork Wildland. There is no easy choice since you must choose between a grueling 45 minute hike from the top via a gate on the south side of Dry Run Road near 39.54982,-79.17637 (not personally confirmed) or a two-mile walk from the parking area near the reservoir.

Lower section   Below the road intersection

As with all of the Zero Creel water feeding the reservoir, Middle Fork runs through a tight cut between two large mountains - Mount Nebo to the north and Chestnut Knob to the south. It is a mountain freestone stream that varies in width depending whether you are near the headwaters or at the junction with the reservoir. At its confluence with the Savage River Reservoir, the creek can run 30 feet across during periods of high water. At the end of a dry summer, the flow reduces to a mere trickle or even disappears, with trout desperately trying to survive, huddled in widely spaced community pools. Other than the large rocks and steep cliffs that demand careful movement, the creek side vegetation is not oppressive and will not be a major obstacle to a stealthy approach or an accurate cast. The initial path from the Savage River access point is wide for the first half mile before it degenerates into a typical hiking trail. This is remote country. Be prepared for anything as you move farther and farther away from the road.

Above the road intersection   Same location as the cover picture in a dry year

Mill Run

Approximate Boundary: 39.714516,-79.384561 to 39.715209,-79.346055 (2.38 miles)
DNR Guidance: Mainstem downstream of Frazee Road.

Type: Put and Take

Directions:
From I-68, take exit 4 toward MD 42/Friendsville. Turn right onto Maple Street. Turn left onto 2nd Avenue. 2nd Avenue turns into Friendsville-Addison Road. Follow it to the stream and turn either left or right on Mill Run Road to fish the stream.

Access Point: All access if off of Mill Run Road
- Access points to the east on Friendsville Addison road include: 39.71517,-79.34505, 39.71369,-79.34641, 39.71035,-79.3481, 39.70937,-79.36351
- Access points to the west, towards the lake, include: 39.70978,-79.36851, 39.71052,-79.37001, 39.71391,-79.37791, 39.71446,-79.38044

The stocked section of Mill Run starts within a few feet of the Pennsylvania border. Unlike many of the streams in the state, the 2.38 miles quoted by the DNR is an honest number. Very little of the stream is posted and most of the access points are well marked with DNR signage offering reassuring confirmation of permission to fish.

At the upper end, the stream is small and languid, wandering lazily down a freestone course through a narrow valley. Unlike some of the other streams in Garrett County, this one is not as clogged on the banks with dense rhododendron foliage or other impenetrable vegetation. Instead, it is passably open with the intermittent rhododendron bushes only being a minor obstacle. Instead of vegetation, the topography of the valley presents a greater challenge with steep hillsides leaping up from the edge of the stream.

Moving downstream from the border, the creek winds its way through a sparsely populated rural area. The few homes should still trigger awareness of private property and remind you to make an effort not to walk into somebody's backyard. The next good spot downstream is adjacent to a bend in the road near a concrete embankment (39.71517,-79.34505) where the river picks up velocity as it pitches down a drop in elevation to level out briefly in an open valley.

Continue to the next bridge crossing at 39.71369,-79.34641. The stream is 15 to 20 feet wide, running shallow across the rocky streambed. Walk in either direction, up or downstream, to locate the deep pools and channels carved out during high water. At the bridge crossing, the stream tightens up and narrows, showing more overhanging vegetation. As a result of the narrow valley with the steep eastern mountainside, the only access to the river is from the road to the west. Below 39.71035,-79.3481, all the way to the intersection with road, the stream tapers, becomes rockier and requires more walking to find the fishable spots. Exercise care not to exit from the stream to walk back to the road across private property. This may require you to remain in the water longer than you like.

Friendsville–Addison Road

West of Friendsville-Addison Road

Below the intersection, the creek begins to adopt the look and feel of a Blue Ridge mountain stream. The velocity abates, producing more level sections with pools. One of the best ones is at the intersection of Mill Run and Chet Kelly Road (39.71052,-79.37001). Fish the deep pool underneath the bridge as well as the downstream deep section.

At 39.71391,-79.37791, there is a sign marking the start of the Mill Run fish habitat improvement project. The Corps of Engineers created several dams and water flow deflectors to improve fish habitat. Do not get too excited since the construction was not extensive and there are only a few dams between the sign and the campground on the lake. Each features a deep pool on the downstream side. The stream is more accessible than it was at the headwaters as a result of the greater dispersion of vegetation in the flat valley. The banks are low, presenting no obstacle to entering or exiting from the stream. The road runs all the way to the Youghiogheny River Lake. There is a developed campground with picnic tables and fire rings at the end of the road.

East of improvement project   Waterflow deflectors and dams

Muddy Creek

Approximate Boundary: 39.500878,-79.416329 to 39.519801,-79.477934 (5.13 miles)

Type: Put and Take

Directions:
North: From Deep Creek Lake, head southwest on US 219S/Garrett Highway. Turn right onto Mayhew Inn Road. Turn left onto Oakland Sang Run Road. Turn right onto Swallow Falls Road. After crossing the bridge over the river, turn right onto Maple Glade Road.

South: From Oakland, take MD 39W. Turn right onto Oakland Rosedale Road. Follow it through several turns. Turn left onto Liberty Street. The name of the street changes to Herrington Manor Road. Turn right onto Swallow Falls Road. Turn left to enter the park on Maple Glade road.

Access Point: Swallow Falls State Park (39.499206,-79.419057)

The Maryland DNR teamed up with the Youghiogheny Trout Unlimited Chapter and Garrett College to dump limestone into the stream to mitigate acid deposition to support a year-round fishery. Begun in 1999, the recovery program continues with tons of limestone placed in the stream over the years. The successful program allows the DNR to stock "put and grow" brown trout fingerlings. Therefore, in addition to the stocked fish that may have drawn you to this spot in the first place, you may end up tangling with cranky wild browns.

Others have noted, and I will add my voice to theirs, that Muddy Creek must have been named by an angler intent on protecting spectacular fishing water by giving it the most boring name imaginable. After all, it conjures up visions of a slow-moving, silt filled backwater that would be the last place in the world to fish for trout. Perhaps the name was assigned by an early settler gazing at the languid drip of the stream running across a muddy bottom as it exited the Pine Swamp complex on the West Virginia border. From there, the creek runs through a wide valley hemmed in by Snaggy Mountain to the south and Lewis Knob to the north. While this stretch is theoretically within the extent of the stocked section, there is no place to turn off the road and no DNR signage indicating that it is stocked water.

Unless you want to see the muddy trickle at the top end, do not bother to drive farther north than the Swallow Falls State Park since all the roads that could lead over to the creek are gated or posted. Considering this, you are bound to wonder about how the DNR stocks the creek given the distance from traditional stocking points at bridge crossings. According to the Park Ranger I discussed this with, they use ATVs and manpower to spread the fish.

The creek undergoes a dramatic transformation from muddy top to rocky bottom as it plunges over 200 feet in elevation from Cranesville Road to the Muddy Creek Falls. After paying the fee to enter the park, pull into the lot and walk through the arch at the northeast corner to transition onto the well-developed, easy walking trail system that not only leads to the upper and lower Swallow Falls on the Youghiogheny River, but also to the Muddy Creek Falls and the great fishing upstream.

Within a few steps of leaving the parking lot, the roar of multiple waterfalls assaults your ears. Since the Muddy Creek Falls is the highest freefalling waterfall in the State, it is well worth the 10 minute diversion to throw a glance and take a picture. Continue down the wooded path to the observation platform overlooking the falls for the best view. Once you make your mother proud by completing that obligatory cultural diversion, follow the rough, three foot wide path to the next bridge upstream.

Your casting arm will begin to twitch as your eyes touch the 30 to 40 foot wide free-flowing stream roiling crystal-clear over a rocky bottom. Spectacular water! Cross the bridge and use the rough fisherman's trail along the west bank.

Unfortunately, the trail is only good to move from point to point since dense vegetation lines both banks, forcing you onto the narrow, rock lined shoreline or into the creek itself to actually fish. Exercise considerable caution when the creek is running high since American Whitewater advertises that Muddy Creek can offer a class V whitewater experience in the lower reaches.

Mudlick Run

Approximate Boundary: 39.642694,-79.021443 to 39.66455,-79.028546 (1.71 miles)

Type: Zero Creel

Directions: From I-68, take exit 29 for MD 546 south toward Finzel. Turn right on Old Frostburg Road and make a left onto Frostburg Road at the fork. Turn right on Mt Aetna Road and drive through the gate. Follow the road across the headwaters of the Savage River to the parking lot immediately north of the bridge.

Access Point: Parking lot near the Savage River (39.643631,-79.020045)

Go through the gated entrance; it should be open during the day. Do not drive any farther than the parking lot unless you want to go to the Savage River Lodge. There are no other turnoffs or parking areas along the road. The Savage River Lodge sits at the summit of Mount Aetna and is one of the area's premier recreational destinations with comfortable accommodations, plenty of year-round activities, gourmet food and wine.

Mudlick Run is a small trout stream that winds its way through a series of beaver ponds (39.648372,-79.028988 and 39.643635,-79.023109) to eventually contribute its flow to the headwaters of the Savage River. From the parking lot, follow the Mount Aetna loop trail (red trail) to the left. It parallels Mudlick Run until it turns to the right near 39.656229,-79.028929 to circle around the top of the mountain to return to the parking lot. The trail provides an easy way to make big moves from place to place. However, once you begin fishing, it is easier to leave the stream and wander through the prolific explosion of tall grass near the water to jump to another spot.

The stream is scenic with tall trees framing uncongested banks to provide a relaxing mountain fishing experience. The deep sections are usually where the stream bends its way through a curve or enters a small gradient break to dump into a larger downstream pool. There are additional deep spots where the water gouged its way around rocks or fallen trees. The bottom is a mix of mud, sand and rocks. As with any mountain venue, there are places where the fishing becomes technical with overreaching branches and bushes providing protective cover for the skittish trout.

The Savage River Lodge website is www.savageriverlodge.com

New Germany Lake

Approximate Boundary: 39.632862,-79.122316 to 39.637075,-79.119698 (13 acres)

Type: Put and Take

Directions:
North: From I-68, take exit 24 onto Avilton Lonaconing Road. Turn right onto Lower New Germany Road heading south. Turn left onto Twin Churches Road. It becomes Westernport Road. Turn right onto McAndrews Hill Road and follow it to the lake. Parking is on the left.

South: From Westernport, drive north on MD 36/Victory Post Road. It becomes New Georges Creek Road SW. Turn right on Middle Street. Turn left on Sugar Maple Road SW. Turn left onto Moores Run Road. Turn right onto Legislative Road SW. At the "T" intersection, turn right to stay on Legislative Road SW (MD 939). Turn left on Bartlett Street (name changes to Bartlett Run Road SW followed by Russell Road). Turn right onto Westernport Road. Turn left onto McAndrews Hill Road and follow it to the lake. Parking is on the left.

Access Point: Parking lot at the south end of the lake (39.632862,-79.122316)

According to the DNR, this park is a "best-kept secret." Built by the Civilian Conservation Corps in the 1930s, it sits between the Big Savage and Meadow Mountains and definitely has a high elevation feel as a result of the crystal clear water mirroring the tall pine trees surrounding the lake. The park has ten miles of trails, but none encircle the lake. The best access is from the eastern side adjacent to the camping areas. The water is deepest at the southern end since it transitions into a muddy marshland to the north. Wild trout enthusiasts may want to follow the Green Trail that runs 1.6 miles along the headwaters of Poplar Lick, a brook trout stream.

For those who would rather float, there is a boat launch (electric motors only – 39.634169,-79.121245). The lake also has a vibrant population of bass, bluegill and catfish. Key facilities include a beach, boat rental and nature center. Visitors can rent cabins or stay at the primitive campsites (central bathhouse with restrooms and showers available).

North Branch of the Potomac

Approximate Boundary: 39.479351,-79.043008 to 39.253624,-79.39863 (33.5 miles)

The North Branch of the Potomac is one of the most significant trout rivers in Maryland. As such, there is far more to say about this water than can be covered in this high-level book. For those anglers who want to know everything there is to know about fishing the North Branch, I recommend my other book, *Trout and Smallmouth Fishing on the North Branch of the Potomac*. It is available from the normal online booksellers, with an eBook version available from www.CatchGuide.com.

The fishable part of the North Branch spans approximately 34 miles of which 13 is controlled by special regulations that include both delayed harvest and catch and return sections. Of that total, 23.8 miles are above the Jennings-Randolph dam and 9.7 are below.

The stocked section of the North Branch begins at the eastern end of the town of Westernport where the river borders 1st Street and ends miles south (upstream) at the bridge in the small town of Wilson. While the content and character of the river changes - moving from narrow to wide, fast to slow, deep to shallow - the one thing that is consistent is that it runs most of its course in a breathtaking, narrow valley full of trees that hang precariously off steep mountains. Backbone Mountain tops out at 3,220 feet, the highest point in a Maryland State Forest, and keeps a distant watch over the roiling river while the surrounding hills create an exciting, exceptionally beautiful setting for a great day of fishing. In a general sense, if you were to fly at low level from Westernport to Wilson, you would see the river change from being broad and slow in the northern reaches to tight and fast once into the delayed harvest area in the Potomac State Forest above Kitzmiller. The highlight of your day might just be sitting on a flat rock in the middle of the stream sucking down a hot cup of coffee from a thermos while you let the sun warm your face and enjoy the spectacular view.

In the Barnum section south of Westernport, the river is a cold water, year-round trout fishery supporting an active population of cutthroats, browns and stocked rainbows. It ends at the base of the Jennings-Randolph Dam where the disposition of both the river and fishing change dramatically. The lake formed by the dam supports trout, bass and walleye, cradling them in the unusually deep sections formed by the surrounding steep hills.

Above the dam, the river loses the cold tailwater advantage provided by the dam, reverting to natural temperature and flow characteristics that align the pursuit of trout to the stocking programs of Maryland and West Virginia. Your only hope for cool water in the summer rests with the pools created by feeder streams where they join the North Branch. Each of these becomes a potential target since they attract trout as the water warms. The Stony River pushes into the North Branch from the south in the Wallman section and is the reason for the significant difference in water volume measured at the Steyer and Kitzmiller gages. The amount of water diminishes farther upstream, becoming a trickle at Wilson. By August in dry, hot years, the trout are either caught or dead as a result of water temperatures that can spike up to 80°. However, the smallmouth bass shrug off the heat better than their finny cousins and cruise the deep, cooler pools, lonely and rejected when the trout hunters leave.

You do not need a four-wheel drive vehicle to poke your rod into the vast majority of the North Branch. Where I recommend a high clearance vehicle, I note it below. In addition, there are plenty of areas where you do not need to break brush, shoot an azimuth, or take exceptional measures to find good water. In fact, in the "Put and Take" section below Barnum, the river runs next the old mining road for several miles, making it an ideal stretch for those who may not be as young and robust as we all wish we still were. Farther north, below the Blue Hole, where the river transitions back to catch and release, you may want to use a bicycle to push into the remote sections. If you do that, fill your tires with "green slime" to protect against punctures since the road bed is littered with sharp objects.

The remoteness of the North Branch might make you leap to the conclusion that it is not fully supported by an active, aggressive stocking program. Thankfully, both Maryland and West Virginia stock this water, so it sees more than its fair share in a given year. Maryland stocks the remote areas from a tank truck outfitted to ride the rails via a cooperative agreement with the CSX Company. In the spring of 2011, Maryland deposited 20,425 trout into the North Branch with West Virginia adding thousands more to the mix. In some years, one or the other State will stock large brood trout as late as August to add to/extend the excitement.

Anglers who spend time on the North Branch will all agree that the rocks are shaped with carefully engineered dimensions designed to cause you to twist your ankle as you totter upstream trying to balance on their snot-slick surfaces. The North Branch has its own brand of sadistic slime that coats everything as a result of the addition of lime to offset the impact of the acid water from old, environmentally unconscious mining operations. There is no sure footing anywhere on the river. *If you fish without using a wading staff, you are a fool who will not be long for this world*.

The DNR has done a good job of carving the river into different regulatory areas. There is something for everybody whether you are a catch and return purist or need to take a few fish home for dinner. The "Put and Take" sections alternate with the special regulation areas, allowing anglers to experience the full variety of scenic settings regardless of the fishing method they choose. Depending on where you fish, you can use bait. There are restrictions on keeping fish based on the calendar date in some sections.

Finally, be aware of the river conditions. The quality of the fishing depends on the amount and temperature of the water. Fortunately, the US Geological Survey sponsors a diverse set of gages on the North Branch that provide real-time statistics on what is happening. Never, ever take the long drive to the North Branch without checking the gages! The gage readings offered below represent the extreme upper end for wading - be very careful, In accordance with disclaimer in the front of this book, *you must take full and complete responsibility for your own safety and not step into the river if it is running faster than you can handle*. Also, a single gage reading does not provide absolute certainty of safety since conditions depend on where you enter the river. Narrow sections compress the volume and make it dangerous even at a level that would be safe elsewhere.

Finally, even if you only have a Maryland license, feel free to fish from the West Virginia side since there is a reciprocal agreement covering the North Branch.

Wilson to Steyer

Approximate Boundary: 39.302657,-79.290054 to 39.253674,-79.39856 (9.1 miles)
DNR Guidance: From the uppermost boundary of Potomac State Forest at Wallman upstream approximately 8.5 miles to the bridge at Old Wilson Road.

Type: Put and Take

Directions:
Eastern: From Gormania WV, head north on MD 560. Take an immediate right onto Steyer-Gorman Road after crossing the bridge. Drive east until the road cuts north where it joins White Church Steyer Road.

Western: From Gormania, stay on US 50W and go up the hill. At the bend in the hill, turn left onto Althouse Hill Road and follow it into the valley. Althouse Hill Road parallels the river up to the inoperable bridge at Bayard. To fish the final western leg beyond Bayard, take WV 90 west from Gormania. It passes the Bayard bridge and leads to Wilson.

Access Point:
- Railroad tracks near White Church Steyer Road (39.304683,-79.311912)
- Numerous turnouts along Steyer-Gorman Road
- Turnout on Althouse Road (39.285326,-79.351494, 39.278139,-79.356417)
- Bridge at Bayard (39.273727,-79.369676)
- Bridge at Wilson 39.253624,-79.398601

If you intend to wade, do not make the trip if the river is running over 200 cfs at the Steyer gage.

On most maps, Gormania is called "Gormania", but you may also see this small town referred to as "Gorman". The difference? Gormania is on the West Virginia side of the bridge and Gorman is on the Maryland side. The entire length is theoretically fishable except for one small section of private property between Gormania and Steyer on the Maryland side. The driveway that leads to the private property looks like a turnoff to the river. Be alert for the "posted" and "private drive" signs in the vicinity of 39.302229,-79.325092.

Eastern Side

After parking at the east end of the Steyer-Gorman Road, either walk downstream towards the Potomac State Forest and the delayed harvest area or upstream towards Gormania. Downstream, there is a faint fisherman's trail next to the river, but it will eventually disappear and you have to either wade in the river or bushwhack through some high brush.

The river is broad and deep when the flow is up. In the Spring, in the midst of the normal season, expect to have plenty of water with the typical depth being two to three feet. As the water levels abate with the summer heat, the going gets easier. Given the width of the river, there are no significant landmarks to help locate any particular spot. Instead, feel your way downstream and identify hotspots based on what the current flow conditions are doing to create the instantaneous character of the river.

Instead of wading in the river all the way up to Gormania, move from turnout to turnout since the best places will change depending on the amount of water. Upstream beyond Steyer, the river remains wide with a rocky bottom. The deep channels are randomly distributed and their location is dependent on the water volume. Look for the dark green color indicating deeper water. The bends in the river are obvious deep spots and you should fish them. The first good upstream bend is at 39.30216,-79.31956.

The river maintains this look until it reaches 39.30099,-79.32723 where the bottom structure moves from rock to sand. The sand stretch is a dead zone for smallies and marginal for the stocked trout. Skip it and rejoin the river where the bottom transitions back to rock at 39.30030,-79.33181. Fish the bend and upstream until the sand reappears at 39.29771.-79.33722. The bottom remains sandy until reaching the outskirts of Gormania.

Western Side

Frankly, it is not worth fishing upstream from Gormania to Wilson. Yes, the river is stocked from the Wilson Bridge down to Gormania. In fact, the section is stocked at the Wilson Bridge, Bayard and two additional places between Bayard and Gormania. The only dependable access to the river is from the Maryland side. The West Virginia bank is protected by innumerable "posted" signs.

When approaching the river near Bayard, the first thing that jumps out is the striking red color of the river bottom resulting from years of mining operations leaching acid into the river. The acid is under control thanks to the limestone doser near Wilson that constantly adds buffering chemicals to keep the pH in a range that maintains fish survival. Upstream of Gormania, the banks are low. **However, the rocky river bottom will continue to make wading an exercise in caution – stay alert!**

Bayard bridge

Wilson bridge

Potomac State Forest

Approximate Boundary: 39.364829,-79.228964 to 39.302657,-79.290054 (7.38 miles)
DNR Guidance: That portion of the North Branch Potomac River from the lowermost boundary of the Potomac State Forest near Lostland Run to the uppermost boundary of the Potomac State Forest at Wallman.

Type: Delayed Harvest

Directions:
There are three primary access points to the river inside the Potomac State Forest - Lostland Run, Laurel Run and Wallman Road. The "roads" leading to the Laurel Run and Wallman access points are officially designated as off road vehicle trails. Unless the DNR graded the dirt tracks,

they will be rutted and rough, slick when wet. Use them with a low clearance vehicle at your own risk. All three of the roads are hard to find, hence the additional detail in the directions below.

Lostland Run:

East: From Kitzmiller heading west from West Virginia on MD 42, turn left onto West Main Street after crossing the bridge. West Main eventually becomes Shalimar Road. Follow it past the school and be alert for the fork in the road onto North Hill Road. Turn right onto North Hill Road and follow it until it dead-ends. At the stop sign, turn left onto Potomac Camp Road. After approximately 1.7 miles, be alert for a small bridge. Turn left on the dirt road immediately after the bridge (39.381814,-79.277773).

West: Heading southeast out of Oakland on MD 135, turn right onto MD 560. Follow it and turn left on Bethlehem Road. Bethlehem leads to a "Y" intersection. Stay on Bethlehem Road by taking the right branch of the "Y". Turn left onto Combination Road and then another left on Potomac Camp Road. After a mile, immediately prior to going over a small bridge, turn right on the dirt road that leads to Lostland Run (39.381814,-79.277773). Start looking for the turn after passing the headquarters building for the Potomac State Forest.

Laurel Run/Wallman

North: Head south on MD 560 from Oakland. Do not turn at the sign for Potomac State Forest; continue south.

South: Head north from Gormania on MD 560.

Regardless of the direction on MD 560, turn east onto White Church Road. Once on White Church, be alert for the place where the road takes a hard right at an acute bend. There is a small, almost invisible brown sign for the State Forest at the bend. Instead of charging around to the right, slow down and go straight (39.337617,-79.309831). This puts you onto a small road (Audley Riley Road) that turns to gravel. Follow it until you see a large brown forest service sign, "State Forest Camping". It has directional arrows pointing to Wallman on the right and Laurel Run on the left. This is also where you can self-register for one of the camping spots.

If going to Laurel Run, take the left fork and follow the road to the dead end in a small parking area separated from the Laurel Run stream by a rock wall. To reach the river, walk across Laurel Run onto the grassy trail that would have been the logical continuation of the road if the rock wall was not present. You can see the trail/road on the other side of the stream from the parking lot. The river is about 600 feet from the parking area.

If going to Wallman, drive up the hill on the road to the right of the sign. At the next "Y" intersection (marked by a sign that says "State Forest Parking"), veer right and continue to follow the gravel road. It takes you down the side of the mountain, and, as of 2009, the road was well maintained. You did not need a high clearance vehicle in 2009, but the conditions may have changed since then.

Ignore the small dirt road on the left at the base of the hill leading to a closed yellow gate. Continue on the main dirt road and be alert for a small turnout to the left. It is the parking area I call "Wallman North". It holds four trucks and overlooks the railroad tracks. Park there, gear up and walk down the small trail to the tracks that are only 20 yards away. At this point, you can see the river.

To get to "Wallman Middle", continue past the first parking area for a little over 0.5 miles to a small dirt road to the left that pitches down a steep grade (39.31453,-79.28459). Do not take the turn unless you have a 4x4 vehicle. There is no alternate parking location at this point for a normal flatland car – if you have a flatlander, proceed to Wallman South.

0.5 miles farther south, the DNR maintains the formal, large "Wallman South" parking lot. It is marked by a DNR kiosk posted with the regulations and other information. At the southern tip of the lot, there is a rough, deeply pitted road that continues south over the hill. I have not driven up it since it looks exceedingly nasty and there may not be any turnouts that would allow reversing direction easily. I do not recommend continuing unless you are good at backing up; it is just as easy to hike along the river to move farther south.

Access Point:
- Lostland Run parking lot (39.363445,-79.233128)
- Laurel Run parking lot (39.342008,-79.260124)
- Wallman north parking lot (39.32230,-79.28346)
- Wallman middle parking lot (39.31453,-79.28459)
- Wallman south parking lot (39.30861,-79.28636)

If you intend to wade at Lostland or Laurel Run, do not make the trip if the river is running over 400 cfs at the Kitzmiller gage. If wading at Wallman (upstream of Stony River), look for a flow less than 200 cfs measured at the Steyer gage.

The North Branch at Lostland Run has the appearance of a tight western mountain stream, looking and smelling like the McCloud River in California. As such, it presents a stark contrast to the river in Kitzmiller or downstream in Barnum. This is the remotest section of the North Branch and the DNR stocks it via a cooperative agreement with the railroad. No matter which access point you choose, the river is scenic and beautiful with classic looking trout water. It moves fast around boulders with the high flows carving seductive channels. If you like fishing alone and are willing to walk as little as 100 yards over difficult terrain, this is the best place in Maryland for that experience.

Adjacent to the scenic dirt roads leading to the Lostland and Laurel Run endpoints, there are small streams on the right. Those streams contain brookies as well as swimming holes. On

Lostland Run, there are two well known pools on the stream. The first is known as the "cascades" (39.36559 -79.24501) with the second being near a foot bridge (39.36140 -79.23375) close to the final left turn that leads to the parking lot. Like Lostland Run, Laurel Run also has two well known spots. The first is near campsite #29 (39.34462 -79.26657) with the other being upstream of the parking lot at the end of the road. But, the prime attraction of the delayed harvest section is the North Branch itself.

Lostland Run

At Lostland Run, the river drops down a gradient of over 100 feet from Laurel Run. This creates widely distributed deep pools with most of the river consisting of large boulders that create cuts and runs with whitewater predominating during periods of higher flow. The entire river is fishable, with the best spots being the head and tail of the large pools. Moving upstream, there are plenty of those spots to hold your attention. Most anglers find a place to cross the river and move upstream on the West Virginia side to obtain the best angles to attack the holes. If you decide to move downstream, be aware that the next major pool is at the bend north of the parking lot where the river takes a sharp cut to the east. This is a popular swimming hole (39.365061,-79.230879), so fish it early in the day before the bathers arrive.

Short distance upstream for access   Approximately 0.75 miles upstream

Laurel Run

At Laurel Run, the pattern set at Lostland Run continues. In fact, there is even a Laurel Run version of the Lostland Run swimming hole. In this case, it is immediately upstream of the entry point. Movement on the Maryland side is challenging, barely facilitated by a faint fisherman's trail that winds its way through tight trees perfectly pitched to topple you over the steep bank and forcing you to "Tarzan" your way through, clinging to each tree to keep your balance. The trail eventually disappears into the thick woods. Again, most anglers cross the river and use the West Virginia side to move up or downstream.

Wallman

A little farther upstream at the three Wallman access points, the river undergoes a minor metamorphosis. While it maintains the pattern of gradient breaks and associated pools, the high bank supporting the railroad pushes the river into a narrower channel. As such, it runs deep and fast. At times, it is a challenge to find a place to wade across the river and fishing is from the bank or protruding rock ledges. At Wallman North, the best approach is to walk beyond the railroad bridge and start fishing in the deep pools 100 yards farther north. Since the river begins its downward pitch north of Steyer, the farther south you move, the gentler the flow becomes. Between Steyer and the southern Wallman access point, the river only drops 70 feet. If you enjoy wild, crashing trout water with challenging pools and deep cuts that careen around massive boulders, the Wallman section is the first place in on the North Branch you should visit.

Kitzmiller

Approximate Boundary: 39.406887,-79.165621 to 39.364829,-79.228964 (7.29 miles)
DNR Guidance: From Jennings Randolph Lake upstream approximately 6 miles to the lower boundary of the Potomac State Forest.

Type: Put and Take

Directions:
Locate East Main Street (39.392494,-79.180398) in Kitzmiller, MD. East Main Street is the first right north of the river and runs next to west bank with reassuring "Stocked Water" signs posted to the trees. Go to the dead end at the north end of East Main and park in a small pull-off on the right (39.392494,-79.180398). Do not park on the yard of the house on the other side of the street.

While East Main leads to the parking area that is the jump off into the eastern portion of the Kitzmiller "Put and Take" area, follow West Main to move farther upstream and access the river from Shalimar Road. Be sure to turn to the left at the "Y" intersection where Shalimar joins North Hill Road. The good section of the upstream "Put and Take" section begins at the "Y" (39.389161,-79.194324).

Access Point:
- North end of East Main Street (39.392494,-79.180398)
- Park on the east side of the railroad tracks in West Virginia (39.386474,-79.180462)
- Park on the Maryland side of the bridge in Kitzmiller (39.387436,-79.181492)
- Park at the school at the end of West Main Street (39.387353,-79.189003)
- Intersection of Shalimar and North Hill Road (39.38934,-79.194626)
- Various other turnouts along Shalimar - the last one is at the confluence of Abram Creek (39.379682,-79.202455)

If you intend to wade, do not make the trip if the river is running over 400 cfs at Kitzmiller.

Eastern Side

Kitzmiller is the first place on the North Branch above Westernport providing anglers an opportunity to fish for both smallmouth bass and trout. In itself, that presents a significant dilemma. Depending on how far you want to walk, you will move from one species to the next.

The lake formed by Jennings-Randolph Dam is approximately 4.5 miles downstream from the end of East Main Street. It supports a vibrant population of smallmouth bass trout were first stocked in the mid-90s. The closer you get to the lake, the farther you move from the stocked trout clustered closer to the city where the DNR stocks them. While the DNR map depicts the stocked area in the vicinity of Kitzmiller as extending downstream all the way to the railroad bridge, the Maryland Western Region fisheries office confirmed that the DNR only stocks off the road – not from the railbed as they do in the delayed harvest area. Therefore, the likelihood of encountering trout farther than a half mile downstream from Kitzmiller is low.

As you transition upstream from the wide inlet formed by the Jennings-Randolph Lake, the river quickly tightens up as it begins to run through a deep canyon extending most of the way back to Kitzmiller. From the bridge upstream, the river is typically 50 to 60 feet across with plenty of rocks and fallen tree structure to absorb your attention and shelter fish. The river maintains that perspective until it rounds the major bend looping south towards Elk Garden. Near 39.38926,-79.16843, there is a small valley that allows the river to spread out and create a shallow (one to two feet) section dominated by flat water with numerous rocks nudging above the surface. A short distance upstream is a moderate gradient break where the river charges around the sharp bend just downstream of the town. The bend features a good deep section that is perfect trout water.

Western Side

To fish upstream, park near the bridge to gain access to the broad, shallow section bordering Kitzmiller. There is an asphalt sidewalk that parallels the river - no need to stumble across rocks while you look for the right hole. Near the town, you can fish the deep water on the West Virginia bank from the Maryland side. At the intersection of North Hill Road and Shalimar there are a series of dramatic pools that extend around the bend. To fish this stretch, park at the school at the end of W Main Street and walk west. There are some small turnouts just beyond the intersection that can hold one or two trucks. Once around the bend heading south on Shalimar Road, the river returns to being broad and flat. The next 0.75 miles contain plenty of large rocks and boulders with interesting channels.

The final landmark is the confluence of Abram Creek with the North Branch where there is a deep pool on the north side of the railroad track. Abram is listed as troubled water as a result of high concentrations of metals and acid left over from mining activity. In 2008, West Virginia began a reclamation project to remediate the creek using lime sand and dosers. Given the success of this technology throughout West Virginia, you should expect to see the return of brook trout to Abram Creek. BUT, Abram Creek is in West Virginia, so do not fish it if you only have a Maryland license since the reciprocal agreement only applies to the North Branch.

Upper Catch and Return

Approximate Boundary: 39.439242,-79.11659 to 39.431718,-79.111354 (3,423 feet)
DNR Guidance: From the mouth of unnamed tributary at Bench Mark 1218 on the Westernport U.S.G.S. Quadrangle downstream approximately 0.75 mile to a red post, located approximately 100 yards above the upstream concrete abutments at Barnum, WV.

Type: Catch and Release

Directions:
South: At Elk Garden WV, turn north on WV 46. That road runs past the lake, the dam and eventually intersects with Barnum Road. Turn left on Barnum Road (Co Hwy 46/2). Follow it to the parking lot near the river.

North: Follow MD 135 west out of Westernport towards Luke. On the other side of Luke, turn left (south) on WV 46. WV 46 will eventually intersect with Barnum Road (Co Hwy 46/2). Turn right on Barnum Road. Follow it to the parking lot near the river.

Access Point:
- Parking lot near the river (39.442503,-79.114427)
- Maryland Overlook 1 at the end of Chestnut Grove Road (39.440553,-79.121768)

If you plan to wade, do not make the trip if the river is running over 550 cfs at Barnum.

The southern catch and release area is the most popular section of the North Branch for fly fishing. Its proximity to the "off limits" stretch of the river just downstream of the old trout breeding pens increases the attraction as a result of the legendary large brown trout that cruise those waters. Every fall, the density of fishermen on this stretch increases dramatically as the browns migrate.

Most people fish upstream from the main parking area. The trail leading south from the parking lot eventually disappears into the brush. When that happens, bushwhack east to pick up an old road that continues upstream. As with any fishing spot, most of the pressure is within the immediate vicinity of the parking lot. You will be well served in putting some distance between yourself and your vehicle.

Note the cable the DNR stretched across the river just south of the parking area. It marks the start of the catch and release section. Upstream, around the bend, the river straightens into a dense mix of channels and ledges. Once the streamside trail disappears, and you transition to the old road, the bank is steep, requiring care to scramble down the loose rock slope to the shoreline. Hard-core anglers walk all the way up to the upper boundary of the catch and release area, marked by another cable, and fish for the big brown trout sulking in the pools closer to the dam. Unlike the delayed harvest area, the easiest movement is on the Maryland shore. Throughout this entire section, wading is tricky as a result of the randomly distributed deep cuts. Move carefully and you can spend the entire day fishing a 100 yard stretch.

In late 2010, the DNR established another access point to the river when the Paul Sarbanes trail opened. The trail is 1.7 miles from Maryland Overlook 1 to the edge of the river. The DNR permits bikers to use the trail and that may be the easiest way to reach the river quickly. The trail drops over 500 feet to the river's edge, so be prepared for a pretty tough day of physical activity.

Barnum

Approximate Boundary: 39.457336,-79.108522 to 39.439242,-79.11659 (1.91 miles)
DNR Guidance: From a red post located approximately 100 yards above the upstream concrete abutments at Barnum, West Virginia downstream to a red post located below a pool known as Blue Hole, approximately 1/3 mile upstream of Bench Mark 1110 on the Westernport U.S.G.S. Quadrangle.

Type: Put and Take

Directions:
South: At Elk Garden WV, turn north on WV 46. That road runs past the lake, the dam and eventually intersects with Barnum Road. Turn left on Barnum Road (Co Hwy 46/2). Follow it to the parking lot near the river.

North: Follow MD 135 west out of Westernport towards Luke. On the other side of Luke, turn left (south) on WV 46. WV 46 will eventually intersect with Barnum Road (Co Hwy 46/2). Turn right on Barnum Road. Follow it to the parking lot near the river.

Access Point:
- Parking lot near the river (39.442503,-79.114427)
- Various narrow turnouts along the road
- Parking lot at the Blue Hole (39.455182,-79.101866)

If you plan to wade, do not make the trip if the river is running over 550 cfs at Barnum.

The "Put and Take" area is perfect for those who can only walk short distances since the road parallels the river as it sweeps north to the Blue Hole. However, the eastern bank supporting the road is precipitous in places, requiring anglers to be cautiously nimble when shinnying down to the water's edge. After leaving the catch and release area, the river narrows where the high mountain on the east bank creates a constricted passage - compressing the flow, raising the depth and increasing velocity. If you're looking for a gentler experience, drive to the southern area near the Blue Hole where the gradient is moderate and the river spreads.

Starting from the main Barnum parking lot, access the river via the broad shelf on the eastern bank that incorporates a number of campsites. Once beyond them, the road carves a path 15 to 20 feet above the water from the perpendicular hillside, limiting access to anglers whose genetic heritage can be linked backwards in time to mesozoic mountain goats. To fish here, you must be feel comfortable balancing on the thin edge of river rock that constitutes the shoreline. The river eventually takes an expansive sweep to the east with an extended rough section of scattered boulders and fast current to widen into a broad lake with the deep channel on the east (road) side immediately upstream from the famous Blue Hole.

The Blue Hole is the legendary formation that marks the end of the "Put and Take" section. Its deep water glows with a unique blue tinge reflecting a large cliff on the western shore. This spot is well over 100 feet wide with no access from the Maryland side. As a result, anglers line the West Virginia bank and throw as far into the deep water as they can. There is a concrete ramp running along the southern tip of the hole to facilitate disabled access.

The Blue Hole

Looking north from the road

The put and take section is the 11th most heavily stocked stream in the State.

Lower Catch and Return

Approximate Boundary: 39.471649,-79.082644 to 39.457336,-79.108522 (3.23 miles)
DNR Guidance: From a red post located below a pool known as Blue Hole, approximately 1/3 mile upstream of Bench Mark 1110 on the Westernport U.S.G.S. Quadrangle, downstream approximately four miles to the confluence of Piney Swamp Run.

Type: Catch and Return

Directions:
South: At Elk Garden WV, turn north on WV 46. That road runs past the lake, the dam and eventually intersects with Barnum Road. Turn left on Barnum Road (Co Hwy 46/2). Follow it to the parking lot near the river and continue north to the dead end.

North: Follow MD 135 west out of Westernport towards Luke. On the other side of Luke, turn left (south) on WV 46. WV 46 will eventually intersect with Barnum Road (Co Hwy 46/2). Turn right on Barnum Road. Follow it to the parking lot near the river and continue north to the dead end.

The trail to the catch and release area is at the northern end of the parking lot. It is a wide path that used to be the railroad into the mining town of Warnock.

Access Point:
- Parking lot at the Blue Hole (39.455182,-79.101866)
- Small lot on Seldom Seen Road off MD 135 (39.474415,-79.076694)

If you intend to wade, do not make the trip if the river is running over 550 cfs at Barnum.

Before walking over to the Barnum Rail Trail, go to the west end of the parking lot where there is a gap in the trees and look downstream. This is the famous "Blue Hole"- a spot that gets hammered by folks who sometimes stand shoulder to shoulder - all fishing intently hard. There is a red post and a cable across the river downstream to mark the start of the special regulation area.

This section of the North Branch offers a scenery "trifecta." It's wide, deep and tight, sometimes all of the above at the same time. There are plenty of runs and pools that are too deep to wade, forcing movement to the side of the river. Pick crossings carefully as a result of the strong surge of water and scarcity of shallow areas during times of normal flow with the danger amplified by the thick coating of slippery slime on the rocky bottom. The trail parallels the southern bank from the Blue Hole almost all the way to Bloomington and makes this a good place to use a bike (fill your tires with "green slime" to protect from punctures).

The river widens downstream of the Blue Hole where there is a deep cut on the eastern bank near a large concrete wall followed by a quick transition around the corner into a narrow stretch. Adjacent to the old cemetery tucked in the bend, there is a cliff face with a deep pool spinning downstream into a fast, wide area where the water races two to three feet deep terminating in a boulder field. After undergoing a moderate gradient change that adds velocity to the water, it slows up briefly, entering a wider spot in the vicinity of 39.46325,-79.10443.

From there into Bloomington, the river remains narrow (40 - 50 feet wide) until it extends as it rolls around the bend upstream of the town. At the bend, high ridgelines cradle the northern end where the river surges to 80-100 feet across and shallows with deep channels on the southern bank once the river straightens for the last pitch into town. Walking into this section from the east near Bloomington requires a moderately stressful hike down the steep northern hillside from the small lot behind the apartment building on Seldom Seen Road.

Westernport/Piedmont

Approximate Boundary: 39.479434,-79.043248 to 39.471649,-79.082644 (3.58 miles)
DNR Guidance: From Piney Swamp Run downstream to the upper Potomac River Commission Wastewater Treatment Plant discharge in Westernport.

Type: Put and Take

Directions: Drive to Westernport, MD. See guidance below for each access point.

Access Point:
- Westernport:
  - Parking lot near the ball field on 1st Street (39.481135,-79.04396)
  - Dirt parking lot behind the sign for the Westernport Railroad Park on Front Street (39.48364,-79.04602)
- Piedmont: Parking lot on River Lane (39.483268,-79.048761)
- Luke: Side of the road on MD 135 (39.474921,-79.061316, 39.480065,-79.065549)
- Parking lot near WV 46 and the railroad tracks (39.478705,-79.067542)
- Bloomington: Kayak takeout at the end of Owens Avenue (39.476311,-79.06942)

Fair warning, anglers fishing here get to "enjoy" the sights and smell associated with the Westvaco Paper Plant in Luke. Piedmont offers true urban fishing where you can park, fish, move your car, go to McDonald's, fish, and move again. With dense white smoke belching out of the paper plant, you always have a landmark to use as reference.

Starting at the water treatment plant at the east end of Westernport, the river drops down a gradient break with plenty of medium size boulders with a few deep cuts on either side of the island that splits the river. Moving upstream to the area between Piedmont and Westernport, the river shallows with the bottom consisting of small rocks and cobble. There is no access to the river from the Maryland side until west of the power plant in Luke.

Between Luke and the confluence with the Savage River, the deep water hides large boulders with fishing limited to the banks in the area immediately upstream of the plant. Above the confluence, the river's depth moderates with the next deep and popular spot being underneath the railroad bridge near the kayak takeout.

Zero Creel

Approximate Boundary: 39.478871,-79.042225 to 39.562328,-78.847983 (18 miles)
DNR Guidance: From the Upper Potomac River Commission Wastewater Treatment Plant at Westernport downstream to the MD 956 bridge at Pinto.

Type: Zero Creel

Directions:
McCoole: Drive west from Keyser, WV or east from Westernport on MD 135 to the McCoole boat launch. There is an easily overlooked small sign on the south side of the highway, opposite a commercial building that had a "U-Haul" sign in 2011, marking the entrance.

Black Oak: From Keyser, follow US 220 north. Turn right on Black Oak Road, cross the railroad tracks and turn right to follow the small road to the takeout at the base of the bridge.

Access Point:
- Parking lot near the ball field on 1st Street in Westernport (39.481135,-79.04396)
- McCoole boat launch (39.45341,-78.98862)
- Black Oak boat launch (39.478067,-78.942606)

For those who like to fish on their feet, the Zero Creel area will be a disappointment. This is the domain of the float trip - partly because of the depth of the river, but mostly as a result of no walk-in access. You may be tempted to pull off on the south side of MD 135 into any of the wide turnoffs that dot the landscape. However, the CSX rail line parallels the river from Keyser all the way to Westernport. Even though the distance from the side of the road to the river is minimal, the railroad is private property with no coordinated DNR access (such as the road across the tracks at the McCoole boat launch).

To reach the Black Oak launch, make the turn to the east and bounce across the railroad tracks. Immediately turn right to roll down the short hill towards the gate. Turn left to follow the fence line to the boat launch. This is a superb facility with concrete blocks paving the way to the water. Although the river is deep, there are portions that are wadeable.

Unlike Black Oak, the McCool launch is primitive by comparison. The dirt entry road stretches 0.2 miles along a ridgeline from the railroad tracks to the turnaround. The launch point is separated from the main flow by a peninsula that creates a slack backwater for unhurried launching as well as a platform to fish the riffles on the other side. Be prepared to manhandle your boat since there is no sloped surface leading to the water. Instead, it is an abrupt drop from the top of the bank.

Modern Black Oak launch   Primitive McCool launch

As of 2011, there is no public takeout at the lower end of the Zero Creel section at the MD 956 bridge in Pinto.

Parkview Pond

Approximate Boundary: 39.700117,-79.156694 to 39.699857,-79.154757 (1.5 acres)

Type: Youth and Blind

Directions:
From I-68, take exit 19 onto MD 495N/Yoder Street. Turn left on Ravine Street. Turn right on Hershberger Lane and follow it to the library.

Access Point: Library parking lot off of Hershberger Lane (39.700375,-79.156677)

The pond is a narrow, elongated body of water that is well protected by dense cattails along the bank. Even though cattails proliferate, there are plenty of opportunities to stand adjacent to the water. A manicured trail runs around the perimeter of the pond with several benches providing strategically located places for adults to supervise the activity. The banks drop-off steeply with a minimum of underwater vegetation on the other side of the cattail beds. The pond appears to be mostly shallow and can be muddy after a rain. As with most small ponds located in parks, there are plenty of other kid friendly activities in the surrounding area.

Piney Reservoir

Approximate Boundary: 39.703576,-79.010521 to 39.712028,-78.999513 (120 acres)

Type: Put and Take

Directions:
East: From I-68, take exit 20 onto MD 546 toward Finzel. At the top of the exit ramp, continue across Beall School Road. Follow the side road to turn right onto Piney Run Road at the junction with US 40. Turn left onto Grantsville Road when Piney Run Road crosses the lake.

West: From I-68, take exit 24. At the top of the ramp, turn left onto Avilton Lonaconing Road. Turn right onto US 40. Follow it for over five miles and turn left onto Piney Run Road. Turn left onto Grantsville Road when Piney Run Road crosses the lake.

Access Point:
- Several turnouts along Grantsville Road (39.706008,-79.003845, 39.707757,-79.002418, 39.710494,-78.998931)
- At the dam at the southern end of the lake (39.701783,-79.009155)

Owned by the City of Frostburg, the 35 foot deep Piney Reservoir is also known as Frostburg Reservoir. The DNR reconstructed the lake in 1990 and it is primarily a destination for bass, perch or tiger muskies. The DNR stocks trout to provide additional variety. There is no doubt that this is a scenic setting. The northern perimeter backs up onto manicured farm fields and the entire western side of the lake hugs a thickly forested ridge.

From a fishing perspective, the fact that boats are not permitted limits fishing to the shoreline and that becomes a huge negative on a lake this large. The only opportunity to fish away from the shore comes in the winter when the ice is thick enough for ice fishing (be very careful). Thankfully, Grantsville Road runs down the entire eastern boundary and provides universal access to the tight, extended shoreline. Unlike some of the other lakes in the State, there is no well-defined path along the bank until you reach the southern end of the reservoir. In all other areas, the bank is forested with faint fisherman's trails weaving between the trees. Depending on where you stand, the bank may or may not drop off sharply.

The upper end is shallow with the section adjacent to Piney Run Road becoming unfishable as a result of the heavy growth of aquatic vegetation. Marshland also predominates east of

Grantsville Road as well as at the southern tip of the main lake. The water is deeper at the western end of the dam and, according to the DNR, walleye have been caught along that shoreline.

Poplar Lick Run

Approximate Boundary: 39.58434,-79.09181 to 39.631903,-79.12277 (6.4 miles)

Type: Zero Creel

Directions: From Westernport, take MD 135 west towards Bloomington. Turn right onto Savage River Road. Look for the kiosk that marks the trailhead approximately five miles north of Big Run Road.

Access Point:
- Marked trailhead on Savage River Road (39.58434,-79.09181)
- Parking lot at the south end of the lake in New Germany State Park (39.632862,-79.122316)

Poplar Lick is best known for the off-road vehicle trail that parallels its path. The ORV trail is permanently closed and, to the delight of trout hikers, the only way to fish this long stream is to hike or bike in. Since the trail is actually the remnants of an old Civilian Conservation Corps roadway built during the depression in 1934, walking is easy along the hard-packed surface. The trail winds its way back and forth across the stream 13 times with only five bridges, allowing you to go as far upstream as you care to, adding distance between where you stand and your personal perception of where the fishing pressure begins. There are numerous primitive campsites adjacent to the trail, just be sure to self register before you begin your trek.

Although Point Ridge looms dramatically above the streambed with the contour lines on the topographic map being close enough to make you cross eyed, Poplar Lick only drops 800 feet from its start at the base of New Germany Lake. This makes for easy hiking and biking. Like its brook trout friendly neighbors to the south, Poplar Lick is a mountain freestone stream with a good surge of water allowing it to expand to 30 feet wide at the base. There are a passel of pools that hold trout. In addition to brook trout, there are stocked trout, browns and rainbows, that run up from the Savage River in search of cool water.

Sand Run

Approximate Boundary: 39.25512,-79.400389 to 39.25924,-79.411161 (3,822 feet)

Type: Put and Take

Directions: From Gorman, MD (aka Gormania, WV) take WV 90 south. Turn right on Wilson Road.

Access Point:
- Turnout on Wilson Road north of the bridge across Sand Run (39.253787,-79.401607)
- Service road next to Wilson Road from 39.255074,-79.40468 to 39.258178,-79.408838

Sand Run is not currently stocked. Back when this creek was stocked, it routinely received around 1,000 fish. The stream is about 20 feet wide and runs over a bottom that is a mix of rocks and sand. The banks are open and unobstructed with easy access from the service road that parallels most of the eastern bank of the creek. The larger pools are in the lower section near several gradient breaks.

Savage River

Approximate Boundary: 39.481189,-79.067967 to 39.584491,-79.091957 (9.77 miles)

Type: Varies

Directions:
North: From I-68, take exit 24 onto Avilton Lonaconing Road. Turn right onto Lower New Germany Road heading south. Turn left onto Twin Churches Road. It becomes Westernport Road. Turn right onto Savage River Road and follow it to the junction with Poplar Lick. This is the northern boundary of the stocked section.

South: From Westernport, drive west on MD 135/Pratt Street. Turn right on Savage River Road. Follow it approximately 0.3 miles to the first turnout on the right that provides access to the Trophy Area.

The Savage River is the centerpiece of the 54,000 acre Savage River State Forest with the Potomac State Forest providing an additional buffer of public land at the lower boundary near the reservoir. Beyond the great fishing on the Savage River, nearly every tributary feeding into the Savage River Reservoir supports wild brook trout. I discuss the ones that are well-known elsewhere in the book. However, if you are resourceful and have access to a topographic map, you can venture off to discover your own wild brook trout wonderland by following almost any "blue line". If you intend to spend the night, be sure to obtain a backpack camping permit after self registering at one of the six sites scattered throughout the property.

The Savage River Reservoir provides a geographically massive, recognizable breakpoint between the special regulation areas below the dam and the general fishing available on the mainstem of the river. There are three distinct fishing sections. Above the dam, the mainstem of the river from Poplar Lick down to the lake operates under normal "put and take" regulations and the DNR stocks it heavily during the season. It ranks number four in overall numbers of fish. Below the dam, the first mile is fly fishing only followed by trophy trout water (artificial lures and flies only) extending to the town of Bloomington. If you fish with spin gear, do not encroach upon the fly fishing section since you will surely be reported by another angler.

The common environmental theme below the dam is "snot slick" rocks. If you do not use a wading staff, you will surely die if you try and fish without that advantage. The boulders were tailor-made to snap ankles and trip anglers who, to the sadistic enjoyment of their fishing buddies, will flail desperately in four dimensions, rod flying, only to splat unceremoniously upon the rocks. Exercise extreme caution and be sure of your footing to remain safe. As you can imagine, those same boulders channel the fast-moving water into an infinite number of deep cuts, creating plunge pools to shelter crafty, lurking monster browns and a smaller number of nimble brookies. The banks are not friendly and restrict movement.

Throughout its entire length, the Savage River runs clear and clean over a trout compatible rocky bottom with a typical width of 30 to 50 feet. Where the gradient picks up below the dam, the habitat becomes even better. During the period when the Savage River Reservoir was undergoing repairs, anglers across the State were concerned that the two foot deep blanket of silt dumped downstream from the reservoir would destroy this pristine fishery. Thankfully, torrential rainfall filled the reservoir and allowed the management to celebrate completion with an aggressive, violent 4,500 cfs flush. According to the DNR, it cleared out almost all of the sediment with the positive effect of adding clean spawning gravel from the bottom of the reservoir. Granted, the trout population suffered a 19% reduction, but there are still over 800 trout per mile and, hopefully, the density will bounce back to the near record level of 1,716 trout per mile measured in 2008 (FFO section). The vibrant insect life that spurs trout health and growth continued uninterrupted during the repair.

Trophy Area

Approximate Boundary: 39.481255,-79.068017 to 39.501027,-79.114514 (3.71 miles)
DNR Guidance: Mainstem from its mouth upstream for a distance of approximately 2.7 miles to the lower suspension bridge.

Type: Artificial Lures Only

Access Point: Various turnouts along Savage River Road to include: 39.50155,-79.10718 (lower suspension bridge), 39.49573,-79.10236, 39.49642,-79.09863, 39.49283,-79.09818 (fish upstream only), 39.49057,-79.09553 (may be posted soon), 39.49118,-79.09156 (fish downstream only), 39.48804,-79.08677 (200 feet from river), 39.48729,-79.08578 (150 feet from river), 39.48659,-79.08464 (west of first bridge), 39.48625,-79.08248 (at first bridge), 39.48308,-79.07369 (first turnout near Bloomington)

The easiest wading in the trophy area is near Bloomington. Moving upstream from the town, the first two turnouts provide the best access with the one at the bridge being preferred. The first turnout north from Bloomington sits on a high ridge approximately 50 feet above the streambed. The pitch is acute down the steep hill, so devise an exit strategy before entering the river. Access at the bridge is as easy as the first spot is hard. The best approach to fishing downstream is to enter along the southern bank and stay between the large ridge that parallels the river and the water's edge. It is fully overgrown with vegetation, so walk as far downstream as you can using the narrow gap between the rhododendrons and the rock ridge and then fish up to the bridge while remaining in the river. Fair warning. Aaron Run joins the Savage River near the bridge and is subject to acid drainage from old mines farther up the mountainside. Depending on the effectiveness of the acid mine drainage mitigation efforts that include the installation of lime dozers similar to those on the North Branch of the Potomac, there may be fewer trout downstream than upstream from this point.

At first access point below the bridge   Upstream from first access point

Above the bridge, while there are numerous turnouts, you may encounter "posted" water. Be consciously aware of private property as you fish from those locations. Between the lower suspension bridge that marks the upstream boundary of the trophy area and the transition into the fly fishing only section, the river drops almost 300 feet as it plunges towards that first turnout above Bloomington. This creates fast water, deeply cut channels and challenging pools as the river surges to reach a width of over 50 feet. Anglers can spend the entire day working a 50 yard stretch if they cover all of the water.

The water is deceptive and what appears to be shallow may actually be a deep channel. The clarity causes everything to appear unproductively shallow but, in reality, there is no dirt or muck floating in the crystal-clear water to provide an indication of depth. Each boulder shelters holding positions. This is the zone for highly technical fishing that gives the advantage to a fly angler since a spinner takes a certain amount of distance to activate once the retrieve starts.

Anglers can get a bird's eye view of the good spots from the road. On a weekend, grab the first place you see since the exceptional fishing attracts an early crowd. Those who drive the complete distance up to the dam to check out the entire river may not be able to find a parking spot on the way back down.

Fly Fishing Only Area

Approximate Boundary: 39.506491,-79.132683 to 39.501027,-79.114514 (1.18 miles)
DNR Guidance: Savage River mainstem from the Savage River Reservoir Dam downstream to the lower suspension bridge (Allegany Bridge).

Type: Fly Fishing Only

Access Point:
- Lower suspension bridge (39.50155,-79.10718)
- Upper suspension bridge (39.50117,-79.11443)
- Second bridge (39.50268,-79.12426)

Beyond the restriction on the type of tackle, the key difference between the fly fishing only section and the trophy area is the higher gradient as the river drops 157 feet in this short distance. The gradient increases the crush of the water as it charges downstream desperately looking for the first place to level out and lose energy. Large boulders speckle the landscape, all densely populated with flyrodders in search of the massive fish that call this part of the river home. In fact, it is worth taking up fly fishing just to fish here! Narrower than downstream, but with more deep channels and even deeper pools, the indigenous fish are highly educated since most fly anglers are catch and releasers.

While many believe that the best fly to use is a nymph, the big fish look for a more substantial meal and that gives the edge to streamers. However, given the rocky bottom and the robust hatches, dry fly fishing can be fantastic at the right time. Since the fish are wary, old-timers caution that 7X tippet is required to achieve the appropriately deceptive drag free drift. Others claim that you can be successful using 6X for dries and nymphs and even 5X for streamers. Who knows? Use what works. One final challenge is the thick accumulation of algae on every rock. If fishing with nymphs, they will come up covered in slime on every cast unless you tune either the indicator or the split shot to keep the nymph floating freely over the bottom. This is one of the reasons why many prefer dancing dry flies delicately across the surface.

Fly fishing only on a misty morning

Upstream from bridge

Mainstem

Approximate Boundary: 39.539131,-79.13764 to 39.586376,-79.09215 (4.88 miles)
DNR Guidance: Mainstem from Savage Reservoir upstream to Poplar Lick.

Type: Put and Take

Access Point: There are 17 different turnouts along Savage River Road between the upper end of the reservoir and the confluence of Poplar Lick.

As a general statement, turn out and park near the confluence of any tributary stream to find the largest pools and the best fishing. The mainstem of the Savage is the fourth most heavily stocked river in Maryland and received 8,185 fish in the spring of 2011. The almost five miles of fishable length above the reservoir argues for the continued insertion of large numbers of fish. In fact, it is a shame that the DNR can't move all the trout they stock in Deep Creek Lake where they instantly disappear into the depths of that massive body of water to the Savage where we have a better shot at catching them.

The river easily supports trout with a rocky bottom and widths that can be up to 60 feet. It is deeper on the mainstem than downstream, but not deep enough to keep the average sized angler from wading at normal water levels. The river runs through a fairly level valley, losing only a little over 200 feet between the start of the stocked section and the reservoir. Although the water moves quickly, it is not oppressively fast. In addition, the cold water algae that grows with abandon below the reservoir is not a problem here. Every bend in the river hides a deep pool and the best producing locations are close to the road where the stock truck has easy access to insert fish. Even then, the river runs deep enough that the fish distribute themselves pretty well across the length within 10 days of the stocking. As I discussed in the fish behavior chapter, most stocked fish move downstream and that should inform your fishing strategy. Start at the lower end and work upstream.

While the trophy sections downstream of the reservoir demanded highly technical, almost expert level skills, the mainstem is ideal for the novice angler while still being scenic enough to bring joy to the heart of anyone who values catching fish in an idyllic setting. With the exception of the few residential areas scattered along the river, there is minimal evidence of humans to reinforce a remote feel. Thankfully, people routinely pick up their trash and keep the Savage looking good.

Weekend campers find plenty of options adjacent to the river with a large camping area in Big Run State Park at the northern end of the reservoir. For those who prefer camping in a more natural mountain setting, take advantage of any of the campsites along Westernport Road (Elk Lick - 6 sites) or Big Run Road (21 sites). Although the maps show campsites along the Poplar Lick off-road vehicle (ORV) trail, the DNR permanently closed that trail to vehicles – hikers are still welcome.

The mainstem of the Savage is the third most heavily stocked stream in the state.

Savage River Reservoir

Approximate Boundary: 39.508345,-79.133849 to 39.52523,-79.138741 (350 acres)

Type: Put and Take

Directions:
North: From I-68, take exit 24 onto Avilton Lonaconing Road. Turn right onto Lower New Germany Road heading south. Turn left onto Twin Churches Road. Twin Churches becomes Westernport Road. Turn right onto Savage River Road and follow it along the shoreline.

South: From Westernport, head west on MD 135. Turn right onto Savage River Road after crossing the river. Follow it past the dam to the various access points.

Access Point:
- Small turnouts along Savage River Road to include 39.53675,-79.13944, 39.53675,-79.13944, 39.53009,-79.13739, 39.52418,-79.14149, 39.52296,-79.14379, 39.51229,-79.15431, 39.50575,-79.15341
- Dry Run boat launch off Savage River Road (39.523012,-79.143932)

For a lake this large, access is extremely restricted. Savage River Road runs along a ridgeline on the west side of the lake. Unfortunately, the ridgeline is high above the water and those who park at the numerous small turnouts, face the supreme challenge of climbing down to the water's edge while powering through thick brush and dodging steep cliffs.

The best way to fish the lake is on a boat with an electric motor. Even then, the reservoir is located in a sharp, narrow cut that looks as if somebody used an ax to chop a gash in the countryside. As a result of the narrowness and the length of the canyon created, anglers may experience high winds. The DNR cautions that those conditions make paddling difficult and dangerous.

The most significant event in recent history to impact fishing was that one of the gates in the dam needed to be replaced. Rather than draining the lake each time a single gate needed to be fixed, the management decided to not only fix the damaged gate but maintain the others as well. When all was said and done, all four of the gates and their valves were replaced. To accomplish this feat of engineering, most of the Savage River Reservoir was drained during the repairs with the gates being back in full operation in 2010.

While this could have destroyed the fishery for years, the DNR took aggressive action to restock the lake with fish lost during the low water period, inserting 12,000 bass and 18,000 black crappie fingerlings in mid-2010. Earlier, the DNR had already stocked 825,000 walleye of various sizes, 25,000 bluegills, and 9,000 sunfish along with the normal spring season stocking of 3,850 adult rainbow trout. Obviously, it will take years for the warm water species to grow to catchable size with DNR predicting the first good year being 2015. Therefore, the reservoir is only a destination for trout anglers and even they may be frustrated given the small numbers of fish in such a large body of water. A better choice is to pursue the native fish in the surrounding watershed or take advantage of the trophy trout opportunities below the dam.

Snowy Creek

Approximate Boundary: 39.387337,-79.463823 to 39.391201,-79.467632 (1.1 miles)

Type: Put and Take

Directions:
From Oakland, follow US 219 into town. Do not turn north onto 3rd Street. Instead, continue onto E Oak Street and MD 39W. MD 39 becomes Hutton Road. After crossing the Youghiogheny River, turn left on Otterbein Street and continue south on Kendall Drive. Turn left on Crellin Street and follow it to Snowy Creek. There is additional access off Crellin Mine Road.

Access Point:
- Single vehicle turnout on the west side of the Crellin Street bridge (39.389308,-79.468846)
- Various turnouts along Crellin Mine Road (39.386621,-79.470602 to 39.389018,-79.468272)

In early 2011, the DNR asserted that Snowy Creek was 2.3 miles of fishable water. I questioned that since my research revealed there is no public access outside of the short stretch along Crellin Mine Road. There was no trail or road that would allow the insertion of fish upstream from the Crellin Street bridge. In late 2011, the DNR adjusted the boundary to show the reality on the ground - 1.1 fishable miles. Despite its pristine name, this is miserable looking water with assorted trash, to include vehicle parts, strewn along the eastern bank as it runs through a bare-bones looking neighborhood.

That said, the first access point is at the bridge at the southern end of Crellin Mine Road where there is a small turnout adjacent to the creek. Moving upstream, there are numerous turnouts along the road where you can pick your spot to pull off and fish. The creek has the standard western Maryland rocky bottom and is easily wadeable after the Spring flooding. Dense vegetation overgrows the banks, making fishing from the shoreline impossible. The parking is limited at the bridge on Crellin Street with the better choice being to park on the adjacent Crellin Mine Street Road.

Lower Crellin Mine Road   Upper Crellin Mine Road

Youghiogheny River

Oakland

Approximate Boundary: 39.387188,-79.461551 to 39.500332,-79.415889 (12.63 miles)
DNR Guidance: Mainstem upstream of the junction of Muddy Creek.

Type: Put and Take

Directions:
To go to the south end, follow MD 39 west from Oakland. Turn left onto Ottobein Street. Ottobein becomes Kendall Drive. Turn right on Crellin Underwood Road.

To go to the north end, turn west onto S Center Street from US 219 in the center of Oakland. Continue onto N Bradley Lane. Turn right on Liberty Street. Liberty becomes Herrington Manor Road. Turn right onto Swallow Falls Road. Park on the east side of the bridge over the river.

Access Point:
- Parking area on the east side of Crellin Underwood Road north of the junction of Snowy Creek with the river (39.38778,-79.463742)
- Parking lot of the baseball field just south of Snowy Creek (39.38606,-79.462529)
- Junction of MD 39 and Ottobein Street (39.391039,-79.463801)
- Bridge crossing on Liberty Street (39.424158,-79.421808)
- Bridge crossing at Swallow Falls Road (39.494247,-79.416273)

Unless you fish from a canoe or kayak with a greater interest in paddling than fishing, do not become elated at the prospect of over 12 miles of stocked water. There are only a few accessible points for kayakers, the stock truck or wading anglers. Moving west, away from Oakland, the worse it becomes. At the start of the stocked section in the tiny village of Crellin, the river is a muddy, silty mess with little to recommend it. The river is wide and shallow consisting of high banks with scattered trees throwing some shade over the water. Since the river runs through town, a mix of residential and industrial buildings peppers the banks conspiring to create an unfriendly, unattractive vista. In short, not a compelling or pleasant fishing location.

Thankfully, by the time the river reaches the Liberty Street bridge crossing miles downstream, it is dramatically different. The bottom is now uniformly coated with a layer of rock with large boulders providing random points of interest, creating pools and holding locations. Access the river via the fisherman's trail on the west side of the bridge. Rocks and boulders line the banks and hold back the vegetation. There are still plenty of trees to provide interesting scenery as well as a little bit of shade.

Liberty Street bridge upstream   Liberty Street bridge downstream

The next access point is at the Swallow Falls State Park. There is a small turnout, outside of the park (no fee), on the east side of the bridge. Only a fool would wade in the river downstream since Swallow Falls is only a short distance away. There is a trail leading from the parking lot to the north side of the bridge providing access to the upstream river. However, unless you are willing to walk over a mile, be prepared for a total waste of time. Upstream of the bridge, the river bottom consists primarily of a slick, flat rock shelf that holds no structure and prevents the creation of pools or the generation of forage to attract fish. In the far distance, you can see some large boulders poking up out of the streambed and those mark the first place where the fishing becomes acceptable. The flat shelf continues upstream until 39.486957,-79.408566 where rocks and pools take control.

Swallow Falls upstream

Swallow Falls downstream

If you walk across the street from the parking lot, follow the trail down the east side of the river to get a bird's eye view of Swallow Falls and fish the downstream river outside of the danger zone. Exercise extreme caution if you choose this option and wear a PFD.

The Oakland section is the 25th most heavily stocked stream in the State.

Hoyes Run - Sang Run

Approximate Boundary: 39.565967,-79.429372 to 39.52427,-79.414551 (3.71 miles)
DNR Guidance: Mainstem beginning at a red post approximately 100 yards upstream of the Deep Creek Lake tailrace and extending downstream four miles to the Sang Run Bridge.

Type: Catch and Return - Artificial Lures

Directions:
- Hoyes Run: From I-68 take Exit 14 for MD 219 South. Turn right on Sang Run Road. Turn left on Hoyes Run Road. Turn right on Oakland-Sang Run Road. The parking area is across the bridge.
- Sang Run: From I-68, take exit 4 for MD 42S near Friendsville. Turn right on Bischoff Road followed by another right on Sang Run Road about two miles later. Follow Sang Run Road to the parking area a couple hundred yards up from the bridge.

Access Point:
- Sang Run parking lot off of Sang Run Road near the bridge (39.565574,-79.426642)
- Hoyes Run kiosk parking lot 200 feet west of the intersection of Hoyes Run Road and Oakland Sang Run Road (39.529344,-79.41025)

This section of the Youghiogheny River is popular with anglers as a result of the catch and return regulations that contribute to trout densities of over 1,000 trout per mile near Hoyes Run with the lower Sang Run area holding 500 trout per mile. A good number of these brown and rainbow trout measure over 20 inches long. In addition, the recurring rush of water from the Deep Creek power plant, to include special summer releases to maintain the cold water habitat, provides a continual churn and refresh of the food that makes it an attractive place for trout.

Hoyes Run

Hoyes Run

This is big water. In most places, the river runs 100 feet wide with plenty of slick rocks and oddly sized boulders making wading a challenge. For those who fished the North Branch or the Savage, wading is not as rough as either of those rivers. As a result of the width, there is no perception of pressure even when other anglers are on the river. The dramatic panorama of forested mountains merging into clean, clear water makes this a "must do" fishing experience. Since the river only drops 300 feet between Hoyes Run and Sang Run, it is low gradient without any exciting drops to produce the deep plunge pools or dramatic waterfalls present at Swallow Falls. In fact, the whitewater kayak crowd skips over this stretch in their description of the river and writes it off as "flat water." Their preference is for the adrenaline producing, human bending, and kayak destroying washing machines that fleck the river from Swallow Falls to the power plant just south of the Hoyes Run access and again from Sang Run down to Friendsville - both include class IV-V rapids.

Since there are no plunge pools, look for channels and pools carved between large boulders. Be alert for random depths that may be over your head since there is no standard size. The river is easily wadeable, just exercise caution and be aware of the surroundings.

Obviously, when the release from the power plant is underway, river levels rise dramatically depending on whether it is a regular or special whitewater release. The water level can go up a foot or two and that brings up a key point of caution. When fishing, do not become so enthralled with what your lure or fly is doing that you ignore what is happening around you. Periodically look upstream and mark the water level against a prominent landmark. As soon as you see that landmark start to disappear, move immediately to the eastern bank since that is where you parked your vehicle. In general, releases occur Monday, Friday and Saturday between 11 AM and 2 PM. Although releases can occur at any time, you should call Deep Creek Hydro at 508-251-7704 for the release schedule. Many anglers use the release schedule to their advantage since the fishing picks up after the churning water stirs up food. To exploit the release, start the day at Sang Run and when the release becomes noticeable, drive to Hoyes Run to fish downstream in its wake.

Sang Run

Sang Run

If you are adventurous, you can follow the trail that connects the two parking lots on the east side of the river to move away from the pressure near the parking lot. There are no other access points off of Oakland Sang Run Road even though it connects Hoyes Run with Sang Run as it runs along the high ridgeline bordering the east bank of the river.

Friendsville (Put and Take)

Approximate Boundary: 39.659165,-79.409101 to 39.664811,-79.407126 (2,322 feet)
DNR Guidance: Upstream side of the MD 42 bridge downstream 0.4 miles to a site 50 yards downstream of Maple Street (at confluence of Minnow Run).

Type: Put and Take

Directions:
From I-68, take exit 4. If eastbound, merge onto MD 42 and turn left onto 1st Avenue and follow it into town. If westbound, turn right on Maple Street and follow it into town.

Access Point:
- Street parking on Chestnut Street (39.662934,-79.406832)
- Under the I-68 bridge on Water Street (39.661148,-79.40886)

There is not much to the put and take section adjacent to Friendsville. This short stretch sits on the west side of town hemmed in by residential property. Access from the east is available by using the trail to the historic town of Kendall adjacent to the intersection of Oak Street and Morris Avenue. The trail runs for two miles along the river as it follows the former Oakland-Confluence narrow gauge railroad bed. Recognize that upstream of the bridge supporting MD 42, no stocking occurs, so anything in that direction is wild. To use this access point, park in town and walk to the start of the trail. If you like to fish using a bike, this is a perfect place to do that. Bike from spot to spot to cover the most river possible. Be sure you are out by sunset since the area closes at that time. No camping! As a side note, the trail provides access to the rough part of the river enjoyed by the kayaking crowd. The rapids have dangerous sounding names like Luke's Final Insult, Double Pencil Sharpener, Wrights Hole, with the Meat Cleaver being about a mile upstream of Kendall. Each of these is associated with dramatic plunges and the associated pools that can produce good fishing. If you venture this far upstream in search of the whitewater, be absolutely sure of your footing and where a PFD.

Trail to Kendall   Downstream towards I-68

Pulling back from the adrenaline associated with Class V rapids to the real world in the designated "put and take" section, options to park are limited. Water Street parallels the western bank of the river, but the shoulder is even more constricted than on the east side. Signs cautioning anglers not to park in this congested area dot the landscape. Continue south on Water Street and park underneath the I-68 bridge.

By the time the river reaches Friendsville, it runs wide and flat. The bottom consists of small to medium sized rocks and boulders. There is a small drop in gradient at the south end of town that creates a set of riffles, but nothing else to attract attention. The east side is usually deeper than the west side, but there are a few deep spots on the west in the short distance between the two bridges.

Friendsville (Delayed Harvest)

Approximate Boundary: 39.664811,-79.407126 to 39.674229,-79.391264 (1.8 miles)
DNR Guidance: Below Friendsville from site 50 yards downstream of Maple Street (at the confluence of Minnow Run) downstream to the gas-line crossing upstream of Youghiogheny Reservoir.

Type: Delayed Harvest

Directions:
East: From I-68, take exit 4. Turn right on Maple Street. Turn left on 2nd Avenue. Turn into the Friendsville Community Park using Old River Road.

South: From I-68, take exit 4 to merge onto MD 42. Turn left onto 1st Avenue. Turn right onto Park Street. Turn left onto 2nd Avenue. Use Old River Road to enter the Friendsville Community Park.

Access Point:
- Friendsville Community Park boat launch (39.66844,-79.398972)
- Various turnouts on the dirt track that parallels the river with the main ones being at 39.67419,-79.39071, 39.67262,-79.39059, 39.66886,-79.39104, 39.66686,-79.39315

In addition to catching trout, you can also pick up walleye and smallmouth bass, making this a year-round fishing destination. Although the delayed harvest section starts north of Maple Street at the west edge of town, private property borders the river until it runs adjacent to the Friendsville Community Park. There is plenty of easy access, to include a canoe launch, from the park. In addition, you can drive east on the dirt road through the South Selbysport Access Area to continue downriver.

The two choices for fishing are driven by the presence of the large island dividing the river at the east end of the park. Unless you are willing to walk or drive another 1,500 feet to the east to rejoin the mainstem of the river, a quick, good option is to begin fishing in either direction from the park itself.

To move downstream, leverage the access the Corps of Engineers granted Maryland and bump down the dirt road all the way to the end. As you drive, observe the river to the left and pick your spot carefully. Initially, the bank is treacherously high, making the descent to the river's edge problematic. Eventually, the road edges closer to the river and access is not an issue. The river continues to offer up ideal fish holding structure. While the amount of sand grows the farther downstream the river runs, there are still plenty of rocks and boulders clogging the riverbed.

The dramatic width of several hundred feet adds to the excitement since it is impossible to feel pressured on a river this large. At normal water levels, the current runs slow. However, the high water marks staining the trees confirm that the river routinely overflows its banks and turns the road into a muddy mess that may be difficult for vehicles without four-wheel-drive to traverse. Those high water marks also scream caution – wear a PFD! If you decide to stop at one of the small turnoffs chipped out of the rocky hill, be sure to leave the road open to allow others to pass. In fact, do not bother to park and fish until you are beyond the tip of the large island (39.66686,-79.39315) that divides the river unless you really want to fish the sideshow instead of the mainstem.

For those who like to fish using a canoe or kayak, there is an informal put-in/take-out at the power line easement that is only about a mile downstream from the canoe launch in the park. If you have a bike, you can do a self shuttle. Leave your bike at the take-out and use it to ride back to your vehicle when done fishing.

Harford County

Deer Creek

Approximate Boundary: 39.623496,-76.400903 to 39.675858,-76.53793 (14.86 miles)
DNR Guidance: Mainstem from one mile south of Rocks State Park upstream to the bridge at MD 23.

Type: Put and Take

Directions:
West: From I-83, take exit 36 onto MD 436 toward Maryland Line/Belair and merge onto MD 439E/Old York Road. Turn left onto MD 23N/Norrisville Road. Turn right on Hartford Creamery Road to enter the upper end of Deer Creek.

South: From I-95, take exit 74 for MD 152 toward Joppatowne/Fallston and turn left onto MD 152N/Mountain Road. Turn right onto US 1N/Belair Road. Exit onto MD 24N/Rock Spring Road. This is the lower end of Deer Creek. The public area starts approximately 600 feet from where the creek abuts the road.

Access Point:
- Rocks State Park:
    - Rocks Chrome Hill Road (39.631289,-76.41546)
    - Rapids parking (39.637623,-76.412522)
    - Small turnout north of the bridge (39.644361,-76.412327)
    - Wilson's Picnic Area (39.642779,-76.413562)
    - Various turnoffs on St Clair Bridge Road (39.63833,-76.41677, 39.63780,-76.42031, 39.637019,-76.424252)
    - Hills Grove Picnic Area (39.638441,-76.424752)
- Eden Mill Nature Center (39.675593,-76.449159) and roadside on Red Bridge Road.
- Hidden Valley Natural Area - Carea and Telegraph Roads (39.680611,-76.492168)

Hold your horses! Even though the DNR map shows Deer Creek consists of almost 15 miles of fishable water. Much of it runs through private property and the DNR only stocks trout in Rocks State Park, Eden Mill, and the Hidden Valley Natural Area. Over the course of the 15 miles, the scenery unwinds from being rocky and trouty downstream to flat and sandy at Eden Mill. Rocks State Park, at the downstream boundary, provides the best fishing experience. The creek does not support any other interesting game fish outside of the season. While smallmouth bass exist in Deer Creek, they are few, small and scarce.

Rocks State Park

Most of the visitors to the 855 acre Rocks State Park come to hike and visit the "King and Queen Seat" that sits on a 190 foot cliff providing dramatic views of the surrounding countryside. There are far more scenery tourists than anglers, so do not be put off by a thickly packed parking lot. In fact, the main challenge to fishing Deer Creek is to find a wide spot in the road where you can safely park. In the initial run up to the intersection of Rocks Chrome Hill Road, there is one turnoff on the left that provides access to the rapids area. If you are willing to walk, there is another parking area (39.631289,-76.41546) on Rocks Chrome Hill Road approximately 1,200 feet west of its intersection with MD 24. Most anglers park at the Rapids Area parking (39.637623,-76.412522) and fish up or downstream from there. The most scenic and compelling trout water is between the southern boundary and this parking lot. There are tall, dramatic boulders along with whitewater and plunge pools making this a fascinating and productive place to fish. Above the parking lot, the creek changes character - becoming flat, sandy and comparatively uninteresting.

| Rapids area | Upstream of Rapids area |

Continuing north, the creek takes a left to detour around the Wilson's Picnic Area and its associated fee-based parking area. To avoid the fee, one choice is to continue across the bridge to the small turnout on the left (39.644361,-76.412327) and follow the trail along the north side of the creek. The better choice is to turn left on St. Clair Bridge Road since the creek eventually reconnects and runs parallel to the roadway. "No parking" signs guard the slender shoulder until the first small turnoff where the road begins to run west around the corner (39.63833,-76.41677). There is a deep channel adjacent to the turnoff bounded on the upstream side by several large boulders that finally provide a welcome break to the sandy monotony of the creek. The creek continues to be 40 to 50 feet wide with a flat bottom until the next turnout at 39.63780,-76.42031. At the corner, where the creek turns sharply north, there is a small turnout at 39.637019,-76.424252 that offers the last free parking prior to reaching the Hills Grove Picnic Area where a day use fee applies. The bend is a prime fishing location featuring a deep hole with additional rocks providing holding structure. Beyond the corner, the road veers away from the creek, grinding up a steep hill to eventually rejoin the river at the edge of the public property.

Luckily, the "posted" signs at the intersection with Holy Cross Road at the bridge clearly indicate that fishing remains legal even though private property surrounds the creek (as of 2011). That may change without notice. However, according to the DNR website, trout are only stocked in the park. Therefore, trout fishing would be sketchy between this point and the next public property upstream, Eden Mill. I have seen other, albeit dated, discussions that advocate entering the creek on Federal Hill Road (MD 165). I believe the world has changed and this spot is not fishable since MD 165 is a major highway with the only parking available on the side of the road. In addition, there was no DNR signage in 2011 providing reassurance that fishing was permitted. While I did not see any "posted" signs, fishing there did not "feel right." Stick to the park.

Eden Mill Nature Center

The focal point of the Eden Mill Nature Center is a gristmill that dates from the 18th century. The park includes a comprehensive nature center highlighting Native American history along with information about local wildlife. When you visit the Center to fish, do not park in front of the building since that lot is for nature center and gristmill museum visitors only. Park in the lower lot next to the pavilion or the turnoff on Red Bridge Road.

From a fishing perspective, the water is not compelling. This section contains flat water with a few rocks, fallen trees and gravel riffles. The center is popular with canoeists and kayakers who make the 4.6 mile run to the take-out in Rocks State Park. According to the DNR, do not attempt to canoe or kayak unless the Deer Creek gage reads at least 2.5 feet or you could find yourself pulling your boat on a long, wet hike.

Hidden Valley Natural Area

Above Eden Mill, the creek roams exclusively through private property. The next public access point is the small parking area at the intersection of Carea and Telegraph Roads (39.680611,-76.492168) in the Hidden Valley Natural Area with a few turnoffs on Telegraph Road to the east. The property upstream from the bridge for the next 5,000 feet is public and is typically the domain of wild trout except for the few stocked fish who defy the normal downstream migration pattern and move in that direction. A well-defined trail runs up the northern bank. The natural area is closer to the headwaters and, as you would expect, the stream is skinnier and tighter with a bottom consisting of small rocks and sand. The creek is not accessible from the southern side as a result of the steep mountainside that plunges directly to the water's edge. Even though the Hidden Valley Natural Area is a public park, there are no facilities beyond parking – no picnic tables or restrooms.

Deer Creek is the second most heavily stocked stream in the State.

Forest Hill Pond

Approximate Boundary: 39.58343,-76.383552 to 39.582917,-76.382554 (1.3 acres)

Type: Put and Take

Directions:
From I-95, take exit 74 onto MD 152N/Mountain Road. Turn right onto US 1N/Belair Road. Exit onto MD 24N/Rock Spring Road. Turn right onto E Jarrettsville Road. Turn right to enter the Friends Community Park.

Access Point: Parking lot to the south of the pond (39.582433,-76.383171)

The Forest Hill Pond is perfect for kids given the level path encircling the pond as well as a bridge to the small island in the middle that puts more water within casting range. The bottom of the pond is shallow where it meets the shore and, later in the season, vegetation clogs the last five feet to the bank. There is a pavilion, a playground and benches artfully sited to allow parents to comfortably supervise activity.

Howard County

Cabin Branch

Approximate Boundary: 39.266019,-77.102666 to 39.276733,-77.104651 (4,982 feet)
DNR Guidance: Cabin Branch from its confluence with the Patuxent River upstream to Hipsley Mill Road.

Type: Catch and Return

Directions: From I-270, take exit 9 onto I-370 east. It eventually merges into MD 200. Take exit 9B for MD 97N. Turn north on MD 650/New Hampshire Avenue. New Hampshire eventually becomes Damascus Road. Turn north on Hipsley Mill Road. The upper end of Cabin Branch is at the intersection of Hipsley Mill Road and Annapolis Rock Road. To fish from the junction with the Patuxent, park at the Hipsley Mill Road bridge crossing.

Access Point:
- Hipsley Mill Road and Annapolis Rock Road (39.276795,-77.104743)
- Hipsley Mill Road Patuxent River bridge (39.26552,-77.114693)

At the junction of Hipsley Mill and Annapolis Rock, Cabin Branch follows the road and hints at the challenge farther downstream. It is 15 feet across with an ideal streambed consisting of a mix of large rocks and cobble. Although there is a trail that starts adjacent to the intersection of the two roads, it does not initially parallel the stream and is sometimes hard to find. The stream tends to stay cooler than the Patuxent and, assuming there is adequate water, trout migrate into the stream during the heat of the summer. This is tight water! It is surrounded and protected by thick vegetation and endless pricker bushes. Short casts rule the day, be prepared for highly technical, highly accurate fishing and shredded waders.

Centennial Lake

Approximate Boundary: 39.241195,-76.863595 to 39.24176,-76.852502 (54 acres)

Type: Put and Take

Directions:
From I-95, take exit 38 onto MD 32W towards Columbia. Take exit 16A onto US 29N/Columbia Pike. Take exit 21B onto MD 108W/Old Annapolis Road. Turn right on Ten Mills Road. Take the first right to go to the boat ramp.

Access Point: Boat ramp (39.241359,-76.858649) and various other places in the park

Centennial Lake is only one of the features that make the 334 acre Centennial Park a spectacular place to visit. First stocked in 1985, the intervening 26 years have seen an explosion in the fish population with fish surveys documenting bass exceeding 6.5 pounds and tiger muskies blowing past 36 inches long.

A key reason was the enforcement of catch and return bass regulations during the early years and subsequent management decisions to facilitate growth. Currently, the DNR claims that there is an "overabundance" of bass waiting to be caught. Therefore, this is a year-round destination and not a place to visit only during the trout season.

In addition to a concrete boat launch, there is a well developed network of paths, including a 2.6 mile paved pathway around the lake, and eases access to the shoreline. If adventurous, rent a boat from the concession area and strike out to less pressured water outside of casting range from the bank. If you bring your own boat, you must buy a daily permit at the boathouse.

There is a fishing pier near the boat launch for those who prefer to fish from a stable platform. The only obstacle to fishing from the shoreline is the prevalence of lily pads that extend 10 to 15 feet from the bank. As with most impoundments, the water is deepest near the dam and shallow near the intake. In this case, the shallow end is to the west where the Centennial Branch of the Little Patuxent River enters the lake. The extreme west end of the lake is a wildlife sanctuary; no fishing beyond the buoys marking the boundary. The average depth of the lake is a little over ten feet.

Centennial Lake is an ideal family destination with beautiful pavilions perched high on the hills overlooking the lake. These, coupled with clean, crisp picnic areas, make it a perfect place to spend the day.

Elkhorn Lake

Approximate Boundary: 39.182764,-76.846363 to 39.184668,-76.8354 (37 acres)

Type: Put and Take

Directions:
From I-95, take exit 32 onto MD 32W toward Columbia. Exit onto the Broken Land Parkway and turn right. Turn right onto Cradlerock Way. Turn right onto Dockside Lane.

Access Point:
- Parking lot on north side of the lake near Dockside Lane (39.18498,-76.844927)
- Parking lot on the south side of the lake off Broken Land Parkway (39.180901,-76.847253)

The Columbia Association controls and allows the general public to use the lake. The northern access is close to the water, while the southern approach requires a 600 foot walk on an asphalt path to reach the shore.

Other than fishing from the dam at the western end, the shoreline is mostly inaccessible except in those places where anglers established trails through the bushy vegetation. The path around the lake is two miles long. Effectively fishing this lake requires a kayak or canoe. There is a launch at the northern access, but it is not immediately adjacent to the parking lot and requires a short carry across the wooden pier.

Once the weather warms up, underwater vegetation clogs the entire extent of the lake except for the deep water near the dam. Most of the lake is only 8 feet deep, reaching 15 feet at the deepest point. The Columbia Association recognizes the need to dredge the lake and, as of 2011, was actively pursuing hiring a contractor to complete that work.

Laurel Lake

Approximate Boundary: 39.091633,-76.859411 to 39.090267,-76.867672 (10 acres)

Type: Put and Take

Directions:
From I-95, take exit 33 onto MD 198E/Sandy Spring Road. Turn right onto Van Dusen Road. Turn left onto Cherry Lane. To go to the last two access points, turn right on Laurel Place followed by a right onto Mulberry Street

Access Point:
- Parking lot of Cherry Lane (39.09177,-76.861403)
- Parking lot off Laurel Place (39.089953,-76.860937)
- Entrance off of Mulberry Street (39.088333,-76.862651)

Laurel Lake, part of the city water supply system, creates the northern boundary of the 28 acre Granville Gude Park. The formal entrance to the park is off Mulberry Street, but there is no parking close to the boathouse, playground and other facilities.

Most people park in the commercial parking lots on the north and east end of the lake. There is a 1.25 mile long hiking and biking trail that runs around the circumference. However, as a result of the thick, bushy shoreline vegetation, access is limited to the beaten paths created by anglers. The bottom drops off quickly from the bank and the lake remains mostly free of clogging underwater vegetation during the summer.

Little Patuxent River

Approximate Boundary: 39.134454,-76.816413 to 39.1489,-76.832721 (2.06 miles)
DNR Guidance: Little Patuxent River from US 1 upstream to Vollmerhausen Road.

Type: Two fish per day

Directions:
From I-95, take the exit onto MD 32E. Take exit 12 for US 1 toward Laurel. Stay right to remain on US 1S/Washington Boulevard. Turn right on Gorman Road. Turn right on Foundry Street.

Options include:
- Park near the bridge to access Savage Mill.
- To go to the park, continue across the bridge and turn left on Baltimore Street. Turn right on Fair Street and follow it into the park. Drive around behind the building to the small lot at the trailhead.
- Continue on Foundry across the bridge to turn right on Baltimore Street. Turn left onto Savage Guilford Road. Turn left onto Vollmerhausen Road. From the school parking lot, follow the Patuxent Branch Trail to the stream.

Access Point:
- Savage Mill on Foundry Street (39.134494,-76.824925)
- Savage Park parking lot near trailhead (39.140471,-76.830152)
- Patuxent Valley Middle School on Vollmerhausen Road (39.147265,-76.829429)

The Little Patuxent offers two remarkably different fishing experiences. If you fish near Savage Mill, you will be shoulder to shoulder with hikers, picnickers and far more anglers than you can count. However, if you move upstream to Savage Park, the short walk down to the river provides just enough of a physical obstacle to reduce pressure significantly. Hikers and bikers will still cruise by on the improved trail, but the density of anglers drops dramatically.

At Savage Mill, begin fishing immediately since everything will be crowded from the road north to the confluence with the Middle Patuxent River. As a result of the additional water contributed by the Middle Patuxent, the section from the junction to the Mill is wide, features plenty of gradient drops, glides and deep pools up to five feet deep. The river runs over a rocky bottom with sand and is 30 to 50 feet wide. There are trails on both sides of the river with the most popular one being the Savage Mill Trail along the southern bank.

The stream has a western Maryland appearance with large boulders strewn across the stream framed by tall trees on either side. Above the confluence, there are periodic fallen logs to create additional interesting holding structure. Although the banks are high, they are set back from the edge of the water far enough to avoid being a problem. You can move easily along the shoreline by dancing across the jagged rocks lining both sides of the river. The most heavily fished area is below the small set of waterfalls a few hundred yards upstream from the Mill. If you venture all the way up to the confluence, be sure to fish the good pool adjacent to the concrete panel that lies within the first 100 feet of the Middle Patuxent upstream from the junction.

If you do not mind hiking 150 yards down a steep hill, park at Savage Park and take the trail to the west. Upon reaching the river, you find yourself on a high bank that guards a long calm glide. The path in either direction is level and easy. There is no advantage in moving up or downstream given the pressure the entire river complex experiences, so start fishing right away. However, the 150 yard investment separates you from the worst of the pressure downstream. Since this spot is above the confluence, it does not have the advantage of the additional water contributed by the Middle Patuxent and is lucky to be 20 to 30 feet wide. The same bottom structure as below, with plenty of rocks surrounded by sand, continues up to Vollmerhausen Road.

As a result of the narrow width forced by the steep hills cradling the river, the water pushes through deep channels around boulders with periodic shallow glides where it spreads out. At normal Spring water levels, the river runs around two feet deep and is easy to wade. While the banks are high all the way down to the confluence with the Middle Patuxent, they gradually moderate and blend in with the stream as it moves north toward Vollmerhausen Road. The density of rocks increases upstream, but there is still plenty of sand. The better pools are closer to the northern boundary of the stocked section. However, be aware of private property in that area.

The Little Patuxent is the 13th most heavily stocked stream in the State.

Middle Patuxent River

Approximate Boundary: 39.168177,-76.883233 to 39.159925,-76.852291 (2.83 miles)
DNR Guidance: From US 29 downstream to Murray Hill Road.

Type: Delayed Harvest

Directions:
From US 29, take exit 15 onto Johns Hopkins Road heading east. Options include:
- Old Columbia Road: Make an immediate turn north on Old Columbia Road and follow it to the river.
- Kindler: Continue a short distance east on Johns Hopkins Road and turn left on Kindler Road. Follow it to the dead end at the gate and walk to the river.
- Murray Hill: Continue on Johns Hopkins Road. It becomes Gorman Road. Turn left onto Murray Hill Road and follow it to the river.

Access Point:
- Old Columbia Road: Road shoulder at the stream (39.168177,-76.883233)
- Kindler Road: Dead end at the gate (39.161988,-76.879027)
- Murray Hill Road: Road shoulder at the stream (39.159925,-76.852291)

The Middle Patuxent River delayed harvest area runs for two miles downstream through Gorman Park from US 29 to the bridge at Murray Hill Road approximately a mile east of I-95. On the other side of I-95, it bubbles downstream to merge with the Little Patuxent River just east of the town of Savage.

There are three primary access points to the river. Starting from the west, pull off on Old Columbia Road and follow it to the river crossing. There is a limited amount of parking near the river. The second is at the end of Kindler Road in the heart of Gorman Park. While the map shows the road going all the way, it is gated approximately a quarter mile from the river. This is your best bet and the easiest access point to use. The last, and worst, access is off Murray Hill Road where the only parking is on the narrow shoulder. The boundary of the public area is clearly marked by prominent "No Trespassing" signs on the downstream side of Murray Hill Road. Of course, given what we know about trout migration, the tragedy is that anything stocked at Murray Hill Road will be in the private section a few days later; hit this hard as soon as it is stocked.

Murray Hill Road

Kindler

Despite the fact that the Middle Patuxent is in the center of a heavily populated area with major roads within a short distance on four sides, it is easy to feel isolated walking between the high riverbanks. There are houses in the distance on the northern bank, but the southern borders a heavily wooded area. Those trees are key to trout survival since they throw a considerable amount of shade and serve to keep the water temperature down. Unfortunately, the trout disappear quickly at the conclusion of the season when the water inevitably warms up. Thankfully, there are a few bass inhabiting the deep pools to provide continued fun throughout the summer.

Kindler

Old Columbia

While there are exceptions to every open-ended statement, the river is unremarkable as it drifts lazily downstream through a broad, flat valley with little change in elevation. It is mostly a mixture of rock, gravel and sand with sand pervasive near Kindler Road and rocks increasingly making a statement near Murray Hill Road. Do not be discouraged by its narrow presentation at either end since the river spreads out to over 40 feet in width depending on the terrain. Each bend usually holds a pool that provides the best shelter for the huddled fish. In fact, the best tactic is to ignore the shallow glides that connect the bends and focus on the bends themselves unless you discover a channel in the middle.

In the past, the Potomac–Patuxent Chapter of Trout Unlimited float-stocked the river. Hopefully, that will continue since it is the only way the fish will be evenly distributed across the two mile length.

Patuxent River

Laurel

Approximate Boundary: 39.105921,-76.841773 to 39.115145,-76.873069 (1.9 miles)
DNR Guidance: Mainstem from base of Rocky Gorge Reservoir Dam in Laurel downstream to the B&O Railroad Crossing.

Type: Put and Take

Directions:
From I-95, take exit 35 to merge onto MD 216E toward Laurel. Options include:
- High Ridge Park: Turn right on All Saints Road. Turn right on Old Scaggsville Road followed by an immediate left onto Superior Avenue. Follow it to the end and take the trail south to the river.
- Swimming Pool: Turn north on Main Street. Turn right on 9th Street.
- Post Office Avenue, Avondale and B Street: Turn north off of Main Street.

Access Point:
- High Ridge Park (39.113879,-76.862694)
- Laurel Municipal Swimming Pool (39.110225,-76.857536)
- Post Office Avenue (39.108435,-76.850042)
- End of Avondale Street (39.107145,-76.845472)
- End of B Street (39.106054,-76.843782)

The stocked section traverses the 30 acre Riverfront Park that borders the river from I-95 east to US 1 (although the DNR description of the fishable area extends this another 5,000 feet downstream to the railroad crossing). After looking at a map, your first instinct will be to make a beeline to the Rocky Gorge Reservoir using West Bend Mill Road (39.115484,-76.874069). Unfortunately, the road does not extend all the way to the river. There is a gated fence that blocks travel on the other side of the baseball field. Moving east, there are no roads to the river between the Interstate and the Laurel municipal swimming pool. If the parking lot next to the pool is full, there is additional parking at the dead end of Main Street on the south side of the pool complex. At the pool, pick up the Riverfront Park Heritage and Nature Trail that runs along the southern bank. Another option is to walk in from High Ridge Park on the northern side, but that approach includes traversing steep hills that make for a tough climb on the way back to your vehicle. Therefore, starting at the pool is the better choice - easier and gets you to the same place.

The trail stretches downstream all the way to the end of the stocked section at US 1 with additional access points from several of the streets that extend north from the main drag to the edge of the park. While there is admission at the end of Post Office Avenue via a stairway that leads to the paved path, the entry road is narrow and well papered with "no parking" signs. Instead of risking being towed, move a little farther east and use Avondale Street to cruise into the picnic area, pavilions and two large parking lots adjacent to the trail and the river. A branch of the trail takes you up to B Street at the last access point.

To the east of the swimming pool, there is more rocky structure, riffles and associated pools. To the west, sand predominates with fewer rocks and boulders. The river runs slow and turns muddy after rain. The banks are thick with vegetation and, unless you find a beaten path to the river's edge, count on bushwhacking.

Near High Ridge Park   Near High Ridge Park

Brighton Dam to Mink Hollow

Approximate Boundary: 39.167468,-76.99821 to 39.191753,-77.004819 (3.05 miles)
DNR Guidance: From red bank posts located on both sides of the river, approximately 400 yards below Brighton Dam downstream to Mink Hollow Road.

Type: Fly Fishing Only

Directions:
- Brighton Dam: From I-270, take Exit 9 onto I-370 east (toll). Continue onto MD 200. Take exit 9B for MD 97N. Turn right on Market Street. Market Street becomes Brighton Dam Road.
- Haviland Mill: From I-270, take Exit 9 onto I-370 east (toll). Continue onto MD 200. Take exit 9B for MD 97N. Turn right on MD 108E/Olney Sandy Spring Road. Turn left onto New Hampshire Avenue. Turn right onto Haviland Mill Road
- Mink Hollow: From I-270, take Exit 9 onto I-370 east (toll). Continue onto MD 200. Take exit 9B for MD 97N. Turn right on MD 108E/Olney Sandy Spring Road. Turn left onto Mink Hollow Road.

Access Point:
- Brighton Dam parking lot (39.191808,-77.005924)
- Haviland Mill Road bridge crossing (39.178491,-77.000005)
- Mink Hollow Road bridge crossing (39.167557,-76.998242)

The erratic outflow from Brighton Dam, that can drop as low as 20 cfs in the summer from an average of 70, creates a marginal tailwater fishery... but it is a tailwater fishery nevertheless. It is limited in the sense that, during the summer, the dam does not release enough cold water to keep the water chilled and crisp to optimum levels for trout survival. The good news is that there is a dense canopy of trees that lean into the center of the river, throwing their protective canopy over the water and blocking a significant part of the heat associated with a scorching Maryland summer. In a good year, the trout will survive and actually reproduce.

In general, the stream is low gradient with no significant drop in elevation as it meanders through the forested valley leading to Mink Hollow Road. The river bed is mostly a sand/gravel mix with clay and mud making wading a challenge along the banks. However, there is plenty of good structure bunched along the shore as a result of the fallen trees that complement the natural twists and turns. In addition, some sections feature dramatic rock cliffs that usually mark the location of a deep pool and associated wary fish.

This is not a wide river. It ranges in width between 10 and 40 feet with random spacious spots. The joy of fishing stems from the fact that the Potomac-Patuxent Chapter of Trout Unlimited routinely float stocks the river. Their public service distributes the fish into the best habitat available. That, coupled with the cold water, extends both the trout fishing season and trout survival into the summer months with some holdovers anxious to be caught the following year.

Brighton Dam

The first 400 yards downstream of the dam is adjacent to a manicured park and open to all types of fishing. If you decide to enter the river at the dam, be aware of the hours! The Park Ranger, whose office perches at the edge of the parking lot, manages the gate that provides the only access through the high chain-link fence. Do not stay late or you may be locked in. The

other two access points are associated with turnoffs from the road and do not have that restriction.

At Brighton Dam, there is a small path on the western bank of the river that follows the stream. It leads along the bank and facilitates reasonably easy movement for the first 0.5 miles. The river bed is mostly sand with periodic muck laden segments that make wading difficult. It is deep enough to require chest waders. As you fish, focus on the overhanging trees and thick bushes. In most cases, the root complex associated with that vegetation caused the river to carve out a deep hole, providing a good holding spot.

Havilland Mill

At the Havilland Mill access, walking is easy in either direction from the small parking area. There is a thin trail paralleling the river that offers a good vantage point to peer into the water from the high banks. The initial bends feature high rock walls with calm, still pools that attract plenty of fishing attention. Fair warning! Nature conspired to protect the banks. The banks are either exceedingly steep or densely wrapped in pricker bushes that take great pleasure in peppering your waders with an infinite number of micro-holes. In addition to taking a fly rod, carry a small pair of garden shears to clip your way to the bank.

Mink Hollow

Mink Hollow continues the trend of high bank and deep water with the added attraction of huge carp. The parking area only supports two or three cars on the shoulder on either side of the bridge. There is a narrow trail on the eastern bank that runs between the water and a fence that marks the boundary of private property. The bottom continues to be sandy with even more fallen logs than upstream. The water stays deep, almost unwadeable, until the river splits west at 39.17508,-76.99811. At that point, it runs down a minor gradient and rocks appear with easier wading upstream.

Patuxent River State Park

Approximate Boundary: 39.238569,-77.056575 to 39.336621,-77.185578 (11.37 miles)
DNR Guidance: The mainstem of the Patuxent River from the crossing of MD 97 upstream to the crossing of MD 27.

Type: Catch and Return

Directions:
From I-270, take exit 9 onto I-370 east. It eventually merges into MD 200. Take exit 9B for MD 97N. To go to the MD 97 access point, continue north. To go to all of the other access points, turn north on MD 650/New Hampshire Avenue. New Hampshire eventually becomes Damascus Road. Turn north on the roads associated with the access points below to reach the river.

Access Point:
- MD 97 bridge crossing (39.238452,-77.056626)
- Howard Chapel Road bridge crossing (39.249819,-77.065533)
- Hipsley Mill Road bridge crossing (39.265371,-77.114843)
- Annapolis Rock Road bridge crossing (39.276378,-77.135121)
- Mullinix Mill Road bridge crossing (39.294786,-77.145016)
- Long Corner Road bridge crossing (39.309334,-77.166076)
- Brown Church Road (39.319525,-77.175955)

The 6,700 acre Patuxent River State Park hosts the upper twelve miles of the Patuxent River with fast access at the scattered bridge crossings. There are formal parking areas at Brown Church Road, Long Corner, Mullinix Mill, Annapolis Rock Road, Hipsley Mill, Howard Chapel and MD 97. Even though the map indicates that the stocked section extends all the way up to MD 27, there is either no water or no parking. From a fishing perspective, Long Corner is as far up as you should go despite the available parking at Brown Church Road (used mostly by birdwatchers).

The Patuxent River is wild trout water with fish up to 25 inches reported in the past. The DNR stocks the lower sections while the river above Annapolis Rock Road is typically left to the wild browns . In addition to the DNR, the Potomac-Patuxent Chapter of Trout Unlimited float stocks the river with the goal of inserting approximately 25 trout per hundred yards.

All rivers have to start somewhere. In the case of the Patuxent River, the headwaters are in the vicinity of Mt Airy where it emerges from a series of small cold springs. As the river flows south, additional unnamed tributaries join to create enough volume to make it fishable by the time it crosses Long Corner Road. It is not worth spending time or energy north of that point. Once concentrated, the river wanders through a tight, narrow valley protected by ridgelines clawing almost 200 feet above the streambed. This compresses the water and creates a good, fishable river. It is not until the confluence with Scott Branch above Annapolis Rock that the squashed geography switches to a level, open valley. From there, the river winds its way down to the Hipsley Mill crossing where it compresses again for the next mile south of the junction of the Cabin Branch. In the final 2.25 miles to the endpoint at MD 97, the gradient levels out, only dropping 50 feet. Over its entire course, the river experiences an elevation change of around 300 feet (about 25 - 30 feet per mile), demonstrating that it is not a high gradient, traditional rock-encrusted trout stream. Instead, it is a rural creek wandering its way through the Patuxent Forest with a bend every few feet and trout taking welcome advantage of the shade thrown by the dense tree cover.

MD 97

Howard Chapel

This is not a wide river. In most places it is only 15 to 20 feet wide, although it does broaden when it enters valleys where the gradient levels out and allows the river to spread. There are infrequent rocky sections, most of the river flows over a sand and clay bottom. That said, the Patuxent River is a nice trout stream. The banks are abrupt, but not overly high with plenty of places where it is easy to step directly into the water. Concentrate your efforts on the pools commonly found at bends or under logjams that average four to five feet deep. The shallow glides between these features, unless there happens to be a channel that is a least a foot deep or an undercut bank, will be unproductive. In fact, most of the river is shallow with the deepest areas being above Howard Chapel Road, forcing you to move from point to point.

Hipsley Mill

Mullinix Mill

Anglers who fish on the North Branch of the Potomac or the Savage River will instantly comment on the hazard presented by the slick, ankle twisting, bowling ball sized boulders that form the river bottom on those two rivers. While the boulders are not an issue on the Patuxent, that hazard is replaced by dense thickets of pricker bushes (rosa multiflora). In fact, if you are not careful, you can count on shredding your waders on a single trip.

It is hard to describe how dense these thickets are beyond just saying "it is so." The best way to deal with the thorns is to find a place to enter the river and stay in the streambed. There are trails paralleling the water, but many wind their way perilously close to the anxiously reaching, trout defending prickers. As a result of the obstacle presented by those bushes, my perspective is that the best time to fish is in the Spring immediately after the normal high water floods. The crush of water compresses the bushes, flattening them until they bounce back when the sun coaxes their seasonal growth spurt. Once they pop up and grow, kiss your waders goodbye. Besides, the water gets a low in the summer and fishing during hot weather puts stress on fish struggling to survive the higher temperatures.

Montgomery County

Great Seneca Creek

Approximate Boundary: 39.128429,-77.335854 to 39.139913,-77.270308 (6.35 miles)
DNR Guidance: From MD 28 upstream to MD 355.

Type: Put and Take

Directions:
Riffle Ford Road: From I-270, take exit 10-11 for MD 124/MD 117/Montgomery Village Avenue. Take exit 10 for MD 117W/West Diamond Avenue. Turn left onto MD 124S/Quince Orchard Road. Turn right onto Darnestown Road. Turn right onto Riffle Ford Road.

MD 118: From I-270, take exit 15 onto MD 118S/Germantown Road.

Black Rock Road: From I-270, take exit 15 onto MD 118S/Germantown Road. Turn right onto Black Rock Road.

MD 28/Darnestown Road: From I-270, take exit 10-11 for MD 124/MD 117/Montgomery Village Avenue. Take exit 10 for MD 117W/West Diamond Avenue. Turn left onto MD 124S/Quince Orchard Road. Turn right onto MD 28/Darnestown Road.

Access Point:
- Riffle Ford Road (39.132777,-77.267919)
- MD 118 (39.126654,-77.296495)
- Black Rock Road (39.127066,-77.31448)
- MD 28/Darnestown Road (39.128159,-77.333001)

It is hard to believe that a trout stream this good can exist just outside of Gaithersburg. The stream runs through the Seneca Creek State Park and offers easy access, well-defined trails (Seneca Creek Greenway Trail) and pretty good fishing during the season. While it consists of mostly a sandy bottom winding its way through a level valley, there are a few places where rocks provide more interesting scenery. The stream runs 20 to 30 feet wide and, depending on the location, has high banks overlooking the stream. Although the stocked length promises an extended stretch of fishable water, there are few trout beyond the immediate vicinity of the entry points. Do not walk more than a quarter mile in either direction.

Riffle Ford Road

Park on the north side of the road and fish in either direction. The deep pools adjacent to the bridge will hold most of the trout - with the rock wall on the north side being particularly good.

Moving downstream, the pool extends below a large fallen tree that spans the creek. Although the banks are two to three feet high, many of them slope gradually and allow for an easy climb or jump down to the sandy shoreline. Regardless of direction, the defined path is on the east bank. The best pools are at the bends where the water gouged out holes. All the fish, as well as the anglers, will be within 100 yards of the bridge.

MD 118

At MD 118, there is limited parking on the side of the road near the bridge. The sandy bottom continues with interesting tangles of fallen trees just upstream.

Black Rock Road

Black Rock Road has the best parking and the best water. Even though the old Black Rock Mill is a roofless wreck with a few bits and pieces of machinery still inside, the parking lot is well-maintained and perfectly positioned adjacent to the creek. It is well worth taking a peek inside the old building to see the startling high water marks from earlier floods. The creek compresses as it runs through the upstream section with plenty of blowdowns and deep pools. The trail upstream starts on the west side of the bridge, do not bother to follow the one upstream on the east. Thick vegetation obstructs the banks and you have to choose your entry point into the water carefully. Moving downstream, there are good trails on either bank. After leaving the deep pool underneath the bridge, the creek cuts a deep channel resulting in banks that loom ten feet above the surface of the water. There are plenty of tangled trees and other holding structure downstream to complement the deep water.

MD 28

At the MD 28 bridge crossing, there is a spacious parking area on the north side of the highway that makes the bridge a popular destination during the season. Most of the interest centers on the deep pool underneath the overarching bridge. The water is wadeable upstream where the creek winds its way through level fields, but trout are scarce in that direction. On the downstream side, the Potomac River impacts the water level and it tends to be too deep to wade, but, on the positive side, you may run into a smallmouth bass or two. When combined with the tight vegetation lining the banks, the water level makes fishing downstream problematic. You must select your entry points carefully.

Great Seneca Creek is the 16th most heavily stocked stream in the State.

Izaak Walton Pond

Approximate Boundary: 39.12007,-77.217843 to 39.120332,-77.219945 (2 acres)

Type: Put and Take

Directions:
From I-270, take exit 9 for I-370W/Sam Eig Highway. Turn right onto Diamondback Drive. Turn right onto Muddy Branch Road. After passing the entrance on Conservation Lane, make a U-turn and drive back to the pond.

Access Point: Parking lot at the pond (39.120869,-77.217371)

Also known as Lake Halcyon, the small Izaak Walton Pond sits at the edge of Muddy Branch Road. The hours are erratic, limited and may change without notice. However, the lake is easily accessible along the southern shoreline via the high berm overlooking the water. The rest of the shore contains enough brush and small trees to restrict access. There are minimal facilities, no dogs or alcohol and the lake closes at sunset.

Kings Pond

Approximate Boundary: 39.244639,-77.276841 to 39.245303,-77.276588 (1 acre)

Type: Two fish per day

Directions:
From I-270, take exit 18 onto MD 121N/Clarksburg Road. Turn left onto Gateway Center Drive. Turn right onto Clarksburg Road. The pond is on the right.

Access Point: Parking lot off Clarksburg Road (39.245748,-77.277492)

Kings Pond is a backup stocking location that sits in the 14 acre Kings Park. Do not go here in search of trout unless it appears on the seasonal stocking list. It was last used in 2008 as a substitute for Pine Lake. Facilities are scarce with a single gazebo and a few scattered picnic tables. The pond is shallow with a bottom that drifts gently towards the deeper middle. Vegetation grows with abandon and clogs the shoreline. The deepest part is along the southern shore near the output vent. In short, not a good fishing destination.

Lake Needwood

Approximate Boundary: 39.114422,-77.129481 to 39.129604,-77.132142 (74 acres)

Type: Put and Take

Directions:
From I-270, take exit 9 to merge onto I-370E toward Metro Station. Exit at Shady Grove Road toward MD 355S/Rockville. Turn left onto Shady Grove Road. Turn right on Crabbs Branch Way. Turn left on Redland Road. Turn right on Needwood Road. Turn right on Beach Road.

Access Point:
- Parking lot at the intersection of Beach Drive and Beach Road (39.123628,-77.126374)
- Roadside parking on Beach Road (39.122029,-77.126755)
- Parking lot at the intersection of Beach Drive and Needwood Lake Drive (39.118546,-77.125977)
- Concession area (39.116116,-77.128391)
- Rock Creek Regional Park lot off of Needwood Road (39.122364,-77.134089)

The Montgomery County Park system undertook major renovations in 2011 that included dredging the lake to increase the depth and improve boating, fishing and water quality. The concession area rents boats and the park system allows anglers to launch private boats from the concrete ramp with a permit. Electric motors only.

The hilly, 1,800 acre Rock Creek Regional Park surrounding Lake Needwood is fully developed with a comprehensive range of activities to include a nature center, archery range and golf course that make it a destination for much more than fishing.

The entire shoreline of this large lake is accessible. There are numerous access points with parking lots on the east side of the lake. The west side is accessible from the Westside Hiker-

Biker Trail that starts near the concession area and ends at the parking lot near Needwood Road. There are also numerous hiker only trails providing additional access to the eastern shoreline.

In addition to the trout the DNR stocks in the spring, the lake has largemouth bass, catfish and crappie with 40 inch tiger muskies being hauled out periodically.

Martin Luther King Jr Pond

Approximate Boundary: 39.05622,-76.985033 to 39.056095,-76.983145 (5 acres)

Directions:
From I-495, take Exit 28 north to merge onto MD 650N/New Hampshire Ave toward White Oak. Turn right onto Jackson Road and follow it for a little over 0.5 miles to enter the park. Continue straight (do not turn) until you see the pond on the left.

Access Point: Parking lot next to the pond (39.055487,-76.984754)

The pond sits in the middle of the 95 acre Martin Luther King Junior Park. The park is packed with features including a swim center, ball fields, picnic shelters, tennis, volleyball and basketball courts. In addition, it is the southern terminal point for the Paint Branch Stream Trail that runs through the adjacent Paint Branch Stream Valley Park. A walk of only a few hundred yards to the east puts you on this additional fishable water. The Paint Branch catch and release section, featuring brown trout, is approximately 1.5 miles upstream at the crossing of Fairland Road. As a side note, brown trout were stocked in the Paint Branch in 1929 and became self-sustaining. Like all wildlife in the heart of a heavily urbanized area, their survival is under pressure from surrounding development. Thankfully, the DNR is monitoring this closely and hopes to protect the spawning habitat.

Unlike the Paint Branch, the pond does not feature a self-sustaining population of brown trout. The only browns swimming in this water are stocked. The pond is mere feet from the parking area and stretches from east to west with an open shoreline, speckled with small bushes at the water's edge, mostly on the northern bank. There are a few small groves of trees along the southern bank that limit access, but not to the extent to impact the fishing. The best fishing is on the eastern end along the dam since that is where the bottom drops off quickly from the shoreline. Elsewhere in the lake, the bottom undergoes a gradual transition from dry land to the "deep" water in the center of the pond. During the season, there is not an unreasonable amount of shoreline vegetation to clog your cast. Regardless of the shoreline structure, movement around the perimeter of the lake is easy on the four foot wide asphalt trail.

Northwest Branch

Approximate Boundary: 38.968018,-76.968942 to 39.066514,-77.029624 (10.03 miles)
DNR Guidance: Upstream of MD 410 to Norwood Road.

Type: Put and Take

Directions:
Kemp Mill Road and Glenallan Avenue: From I-495, take exit 31 onto MD 97N/Georgia Avenue. Turn right on Randolph Road. Turn right on Kemp Mill Road.

Springbrook Drive: From I-495, take exit 30 onto MD 650N/New Hampshire Avenue. Turn left onto Warrenton Drive. Take the right fork onto Springbrook. Go to the end.

Kemp Mill Local Park: From I-495, take exit 32 and merge onto US 29N/Colesville Road. Turn right onto University Boulevard E. Make a U-turn and drive north on University Boulevard. Turn right onto Arcola Avenue. Turn right onto Lamberton Drive. Turn right onto Claybrook Drive. Make a left turn into the park at the intersection of Fairoak Drive.

MD 29: From I-495, take exit 32 and merge onto US 29N/Colesville Road. Follow it to the stream.

Oakview Drive: From I-495, take exit 28 to merge onto MD 650S/New Hampshire Avenue. Turn right on Oakview Drive and follow it to the end.

Ruatan Street: From I-495, take exit 28 to merge onto MD 650S/New Hampshire Avenue. Turn left on Metzerott Road. Turn right onto Riggs Road. Turn right onto Ruatan Street. Drive to the end.

Adelphi Mill Recreation Center: From I-495, take exit 28 to merge onto MD 650S/New Hampshire Avenue. Turn left on Metzerott Road. Turn right onto Riggs Road. Follow it to the center on the right.

W Park Drive: From I-495, take exit 29 for MD 193E/University Boulevard E. Turn left onto W Park Drive. Turn right into the parking area where W Park becomes Lyndon Street.

Lane Manor Recreation Center: From I-495, take exit 29 for MD 193E/University Boulevard E. Turn right onto W Park Drive. All remaining access points are adjacent to W Park Drive.

Access Point:

- Kemp Mill Road and Glenallan Avenue (39.061641,-77.026425)
- End of Springbrook Drive (39.056472,-77.009687)
- Kemp Mill Local Park (39.044836,-77.010761)
- MD 29 (39.0307,-77.005937)
- Oakview Drive (39.016116,-76.990032)
- Ruatan Street (38.996841,-76.976841)
- Quebec Street (38.994102,-76.979949)
- Adelphi Mill Recreation Center (38.993172,-76.972651)
- W Park Drive (38.987827,-76.965689)
- Lane Manor Recreation Center (38.981313,-76.96247)

The Anacostia Tributary Trail System provides the "highway" that parallels Northwest Branch for most of its length. Starting in the north at the Kemp Mill Road access point, the Northwest Branch Trail begins and runs south to join with the Rachel Carson Greenway trail. At the southern end of the Rachel Carson Trail, the name flips back to Northwest Branch Trail and then reverts to the more generic Anacostia Tributary Trail System for the final leg to the southern boundary of the stocked section adjacent to MD 410 (East–West Highway). While the trail does not run within feet of the creek throughout its total length, it is close enough to provide good angler access with a minimum of bushwhacking.

With a few small exceptions, the trail system makes for easy walking or biking. In fact, there is only one access point that produces sweaty anglers as a result of the need to hike down a steep hill to reach the stream. Just to be complete, there are a few additional local access points hidden off of the maze of residential streets surrounding the stream that I will not discuss. For a complete listing, visit Montgomeryparks.org and download the trail map.

Kemp Mill Road

Starting at Kemp Mill Road, a crushed rock, natural surface is the basis of the Northwest Branch Trail for its 10.2 mile run to the junction with the Beltway. South of the Beltway, the trail extends another 2.7 miles with an asphalt surface that makes riding a bike a pleasure. There is a bridge that links the Northwest Branch Trail with the Rachel Carson Greenway Trail approximately a quarter mile from the Kemp Mill Road parking area. The Rachel Carson trail runs down the east side of the stream, remaining closer to the water for its entire length. After taking the short walk to the stream from the Kemp Mill Road parking, you discover that the stream is nothing special. It is basically a holding tank for the stocked trout. The stream bottom is mostly sand in the upper reaches with random rocks to provide a little bit of interest. The banks are high and the best approach is to walk down the edge of the stream until you see fish. At that point, find a place to slip into the water and begin fishing. The banks are unobstructed and present no obstacle to fishing with either fly or spin gear. The wading is easy on the sandy bottom with the water being knee to waist deep depending on where you wander.

Springbrook Drive

The road dead ends at a small, three-car parking area that connects with a narrow, two foot wide trail at its southern end. Follow the path through the intersection with the Rachel Carson Trail down to the stream. After following it for 0.1 miles with a vertical drop of only 10 feet, it begins to parallel the water. At this point, the stream runs over a gravel bottom with a few random large rocks and is approximately 20 feet wide. There are several good pools at the junction of the trail with the best place being near a rock wall.

Kemp Mill Local Park

Theoretically, there is a connector to the trail system from the intersection of Apple Grove Road and Quaint Acres Drive. There is no defined parking at this intersection and it appears to be an access point used by the local residents. A better choice if you want to fish this section of the stream is to gain access via the Kemp Mill Local Park on the other side of the stream. The park is at the end of Fairoak Drive with the stream being a short walk from the parking area across the baseball field.

MD 29

This is the major access point adjacent to the old gristmill (Bealle's Mill) with parking on both sides of the highway. There is a dam on the north side of the road (Old Burnt Mills) that creates one of the rare deep water sections on the stream with a massive fallen tree on the west side providing interesting structural scenery. The shoreline vegetation is thick and requires picking access points carefully. The stream is approximately 50 feet wide with the deep section extending approximately 1,500 feet upstream. This is the place to fish for bass during the summer.

Oakview Drive

At the end of Oakview drive, there is room for three or four vehicles to pull off on the right-hand side. Of all the places to access the stream, this spot requires the most strenuous hike. It is a quarter mile walk with a 143 foot drop in elevation to reach the stream. To get there, walk through the gate and proceed down the wide, gravel road that runs up the small ridge to drop precipitously down to the stream. The intense buzz of I-495 to the north is totally incongruous with the perspective provided by the deep woods surrounding the trail.

The stream is impressive. Instead of being mostly nondescript sand, it has transitioned into classic looking trout water running over a rocky bottom with the riffles, cuts and shaded plunge pools you would expect on a mountain stream. The trail becomes rough as it approaches the Beltway, compressing to a rocky path a mere foot in width. Above the set of riffles just upstream of the intersection of trail to the stream, the stream backs up to create two foot deep pools with the stair step pattern of gradient breaks/pools continuing upstream to the Beltway.

MD 29 - Bealle's Mill   Oakview Drive

Ruatan Street

The access point is adjacent to an open field with manicured grass and a 10 foot wide asphalt path leading to, and continuing along, the stream. A walk of 0.1 miles/25 foot vertical drop puts you on the stream. It maintains the rocky characteristic that began upstream at the Beltway with some sand buffering the rocks. The banks are steep and the water runs shallow with widely dispersed gradient breaks creating pools. The best place to get into the water is adjacent to a small gazebo a short distance downstream from the intersection of the access path with the trail. If you fish using a bike, this is a good spot to start since bikes are not permitted on the trail above the Beltway.

There is another access point 1,000 feet farther south on the west side of the stream at the end of Quebec Street (38.994102,-76.979949).

Adelphi Mill Recreation Center

This is a small park on the north side of the stream. The stream has lost its energy and moves lazily through the arched bridge supporting Riggs Road. The stream bottom is mostly sand with thickly forested banks, making access extremely difficult. There is an additional trail access point off Cool Spring Road downstream from the park, but there is no real parking area associated it, requiring your vehicle to cower fearfully on the narrow shoulder as it waits to be rear-ended. The parking lot at Adelphi Mill is a much better choice. Besides, a short distance south of Cool Spring Road, is the extensive park system off West Park Drive that offers universal, easy access.

Ruatan Street   Adelphi Mill

West Park Drive

This spot is the northernmost edge of the extensive recreational area that parallels the stream throughout its remaining stocked distance. Park at the end of the large asphalted parking lot near the north end of the sports fields. The broad trail at the eastern end quickly transitions into a narrow dirt path that intersects the stream 25 yards from the lot. At this point, the stream has completed its metamorphosis. Instead of being rocky as it was at the Beltway, it is now mostly sand and lazily drifts downstream across a 20 to 30 foot width. There is nothing compelling to make this spot a "go to" fishing destination and that holds true for the remainder of the stream down to the stocked terminus at the East-West Highway.

Lane Manor Recreation Center

There are plenty of parking areas on both sides of the stream between the Lane Manor Recreation Center and the University Hills Duck Pond Park. Taking the turn to the east off W Park Drive, with a jog to the right, it eventually leads to a parking area adjacent to the stream. There is a small drop in elevation that gives the stream some velocity to briefly scour the sand from the rocks. There are deep pools at the bends protected by heavily vegetated tall banks. The eastern side consists of mostly tumbled rocks that present an impassable barrier to access from that side. While there is no discernible trail immediately adjacent to the stream, additional feeder trails lead to the creek across entire length of W Park Drive. Park along the road and pick a path.

West Park Drive

Lane Manor

The Northwest Branch is the 20th most heavily stocked stream in the State.

Paint Branch

Approximate Boundary: 39.077642,-76.976495 to 39.10349,-76.972032 (2.71 miles)
DNR Guidance: Paint Branch and tributaries upstream of Fairland Road

Type: Catch and Return

Directions:
From I-95, take exit 29B for MD 212W toward Calverton. Turn right onto Beltsville Road. Turn left onto Calverton Boulevard. Turn right onto Cherry Hill Road. Turn right onto US 29N. Turn left onto Fairland Road. To go to the Briggs Chaney Road access, continue north on US 29 and turn left on Briggs Chaney Road.

Access Point:
- Fairland Road (39.07784,-76.977881)
- Countryside Drive (39.085044,-76.966262)*
- Briggs Chaney Road (39.088385,-76.964466)
- Bradshaw Drive (39.091914,-76.959739)*
- Fairacres Road (39.095118,-76.964299)*
- Peach Orchard Road (39.097765,-76.965319)
- Maydale Nature Center (39.103361,-76.973558)

*Although access is feasible from these locations, it is not practicable. These spots are in residential areas with bushwhacking required to reach the stream. It is much easier, and you get to the same fishing, using Fairland, Briggs Chaney and Maydale.

A wild trout stream just outside the Beltway? Yes. Even though the only formally designated catch and release area is above Fairland Road, there are trout downstream as well that should also enjoy that same level of protection. Although under continued pressure resulting from surrounding low-density development, the Paint Branch has a reproducing population of brown trout. The stream was last stocked in the early 40s and hit the radar of the DNR in the 70s as a watershed needing protection and was formally designated a "special trout management area" in 1980. Thankfully, as a result of the aggressive efforts of the DNR, Montgomery County and local Trout Unlimited chapters, Paint Branch is hanging on as the centerpiece of the 1,032 acre Upper Paint Branch Stream Valley Park. Specifically, the Montgomery County Council is acquiring 248 acres of additional parkland to protect the two main spawning areas (Good Hope and Gum Springs).

As mentioned in the section on Martin Luther King Jr. Pond, the formal Paint Branch Trail starts to the east of the pond and extends up to Fairland Road. Above that point, there are informal trails that lead from local neighborhoods to the stream (a few documented above) as well as along the stream itself.

The Paint Branch is a low gradient stream, only dropping 115 feet over the 2.71 mile length; a mere 42 feet per mile. Between Fairland Road and the headwaters, the stream runs through a forested park whose thick canopy of trees along with cold seeps and springs, keeps the water temperature within bounds for survival. The stream is narrow, ranging between 10 and 15 feet, with plenty of structure provided by fallen trees and undercut banks. The bottom is a mix of gravel and sand.

At Fairland Road, the only parking is on the side of the road to the west of the stream. Follow Paint Branch Trail (it intersects Fairland Road at the turnout) to reach the south side of the creek. The other option is to walk across the street, locate the fire hydrant a little farther west, and bushwhack to the stream from there. The brush is thick on the north side of the road from the turnout to the creek. The two main spawning tributaries join the creek near the Inter-

County Connector. Please avoid fishing during the late fall so you do not disrupt the spawning cycle.

The access to Briggs Chaney is tricky. If you merely drive-by, it will not be obvious how to reach the stream since there is no significant shoulder. Your first instinct will be to turn south through a gated road into the garden lot section. Although it is usually locked, it may be open. Do not turn there, since entry requires a permit and you may be locked in when a permit holding gardener leaves and locks the gate. Instead, turn south on what looks like a private driveway next to the mailbox with "2225" on it. The road leads to a remote lot with an easement through the parkland and runs on the west side of the creek. Public property is on both sides; turn off and park wherever the ground is stable.

Fairland Road

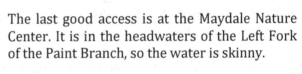
Briggs Chaney Road

The last good access is at the Maydale Nature Center. It is in the headwaters of the Left Fork of the Paint Branch, so the water is skinny.

Remember, the DNR does not stock the stream, so anything here is wild. There is a good-sized parking lot and a trail that runs down the east side of the stream.

Pine Lake

Approximate Boundary: 39.053479,-77.038978 to 39.054879,-77.03842 (5 acres)

Type: Put and Take

Directions:
From I-495, take exit 31 onto MD 97/Georgia Avenue heading north. Turn right onto Arcola Avenue. Turn left onto Orebaugh Avenue. Follow the road to the parking lot at the north end of Wheaton Regional Park. To park at the other side, continue on MD 97 and turn right on Shorefield Road followed by a left onto Shorefield Court.

Access Point:
- North end of Wheaton Regional Park (39.053296,-77.035072)
- Shorefield Court parking lot (39.054515,-77.043311)

Wheaton Regional Park was established in 1960 and includes 536 acres of land. A unique recreational feature is the miniature train as well as an adventure playground designed specifically to accommodate disabled individuals. All of the other normal amenities - playground, restrooms and picnic areas - exist here as well.

Pine Lake tends to become overgrown with aquatic vegetation after the weather warms up, particularly on the western side. In early 2011, the Department of Parks rehabilitated the lake to improve fish habitat and, hopefully, this will reduce the incidence of underwater vegetation. During trout season, it is not a significant issue as a result of the cold weather. Most of the shoreline of the lake is forested with the road on top of the dam at the northern end providing the most universal access. The shoreline adjacent to the dam is also the deepest (up to 8 feet) and will experience the least amount of aquatic growth. Although there are 11 miles of trails in the park, you do not have to walk on all of them to get to the pond. It is an easy, short walk along a gravel trail.

In addition to trout stocked in season, the pond features the normal assortment of largemouth bass and other warm water fish. The lake achieved a brief moment of notoriety in April 2004 when Terry Wintermoyer hauled out a 19 inch northern snakehead. The DNR drained the lake and there have been no reports of this species since. The Regional Park does not allow boats on the pond.

South Germantown Park Pond

Approximate Boundary: 39.150077,-77.311736 to 39.150639,-77.308764 (2 acres)

Type: Put and Take

Directions: From I-270, take exit 15 onto MD 118S/Germantown Road. Turn right on Germantown Park Drive. At the traffic circle, continue onto Central Park Circle.

Access Point: Parking lot on the south side of the lake (39.149915,-77.310969)

The pond is in the middle of the 695 acre South Germantown Recreational Park. Depending on the stocking schedule, this pond may or may not be included. The pond is uniformly shallow with no one area being deeper than any other. Dense, thick cattails pack the shoreline with few beaten paths leading to the water's edge. There is a small wildlife observation pier extending into the pond directly in back of the kiosk. The best access to the shoreline is from the area immediately adjacent to the parking lot, but even that is not optimum and is dependent on the "crop" of cattails.

Prince Georges County

Allens Pond

Approximate Boundary: 38.932699,-76.742175 to 38.934068,-76.738109 (10 acres)

Type: Put and Take

Directions:
From US 50, take exit 11 onto MD 197/Collington Road heading south toward Bowie. Turn right onto Northview Drive and follow it to the park entrance on the right.

Access Point: Parking lot north of the pond (38.935054,-76.73858)

Allens Pond is a typical Maryland lake surrounded by a park. A nice walking path encircles the pond and offers easy access to the open, unobstructed bank. Large trees provide plenty of opportunity for shade. In addition to fishing along the bank, you can leverage the peninsula that sticks into the middle of the lake from the south.

Cosca Lake

Approximate Boundary: 38.735055,-76.915038 to 38.739339,-76.914073 (11 acres)

Type: Put and Take

Directions:
From I-495/95, take exit 7 to merge onto MD 5S/Branch Avenue. Turn right onto Old Branch Avenue (eventually becomes Brandywine Road). Turn right onto Thrift Road and follow it to the park. To reach the lake from the primary parking lot east of the lake, do not make the right-hand turn off Thrift Road into the portion of the park with the baseball field. Continue south and take the next entrance. The road leads to a "T" intersection. Turn left and drive to the west end of the parking area and follow the path to the shoreline.

Access Point:
- Parking lot east of the lake (38.736975,-76.91192)
- Parking lot south of the lake (38.733548,-76.914793)

Cosca Lake is the main geographical feature of the 690 acre Cosca Regional Park. In addition to the lake, the park has a massive playground, four different ball fields, tennis courts, picnic areas and campsites. For those bent on education, the Clearwater Nature Center hosts a wide variety of programs and exhibits.

A path runs along the eastern shore to the boat and concession area. The deepest part of the lake is along the dam in the south. At the northern end, Butler Branch dribbles in and creates a muddy mess. Trees and other vegetation pack the western shoreline and make fishing from that side a challenge. After a strong rain, the lake will be muddy.

Greenbelt Lake

Approximate Boundary: 39.002732,-76.890761 to 39.004863,-76.883956 (23 acres)

Type: Put and Take

Directions:
From I-495, take exit 23 onto MD 201N/Kenilworth Avenue. Turn right on Crescent Road followed by another right into the park.

Access Point: Crescent Road parking lot (39.005067,-76.89061)

The man-made Greenbelt Lake was a depression era construction project completed in 1936. The lake sits in the middle of the Buddy Attick Lake Park (also known as Greenbelt Lake Park). There is a defined, heavily shaded 1.25 mile path encircling the lake providing anglers access to the shore. The easiest fishing is from the dam on the western edge and is also where the DNR stocks the trout. Elsewhere, once the weather warms, underwater vegetation blocks access to deeper water, especially at the eastern end.

Nominally a bass and crappie fishery, the DNR pumps a pretty good number of trout into the lake during the season. The park allows anglers to carry boats to the bank with canoes or kayaks quickly becoming the best way to fish the clogged shoreline. Note that the lake is closed to swimming as a result of high bacteria counts so do not dangle your feet in the water. The lake is a good family destination since the amenities include grills, picnic tables, pavilions, playground and tot lot.

Lake Artemesia

Approximate Boundary: 38.990558,-76.922239 to 38.983737,-76.922089 (38 acres)

Type: Put and Take

Directions:
From I-495, take exit 23 onto MD 201/Kenilworth Avenue south towards Bladensburg. Turn right onto Pontiac Street. Turn left onto 57th Avenue. Turn right on Berwyn Road. Turn left onto 55th Avenue. The parking lot is on the left. Do not drive any farther south.

Access Point: Berwyn Road parking lot (38.993294,-76.92063)

After walking by industrial lots and buildings for the quarter mile between the parking lot and the lake, you might begin to wonder if the scenery and experience at the lake will be decisively urban. Thankfully, the industrial congestion ends at the gate and the vista to the front is of 38 acres of water surrounded by a well developed, 1.35 mile long path with connecting trails linking nearby recreational areas. The lake is an example of aggressive and smart land preservation. The original 10 acres were donated by Artemesia Defs in 1972. The current footprint is a result of the excavation of sand and gravel to support the construction of the Metro Green Line. At the conclusion of the construction, the Metro repaired the damage done by the excavation to create the two lakes and the surrounding park. Beyond the fishing, the Luther Goldman Birding Trail is the key attraction that draws most people to this facility.

That is good because the fishing is not. Lake Artemesia is a tough lake to fish since the shoreline clogs with vegetation and the park does not allow boats. If you get here early in the year, you have a shot from the shoreline, but once it starts to heat up, the vegetation explodes and the quality of fishing goes down. Although the DNR stocks trout during the season, the lake is better known for bass.

There are few places, like the fishing pier, that extend your reach out towards the center of the lake, but mostly it will be an exercise in frustration as you attempt to lob your lure beyond the weed beds to reach any fish that might be cruising in the shallows within range.

Melwood Pond

Approximate Boundary: 38.800373,-76.82543 to 38.801063,-76.824979 (1 acre)

Type: Put and Take

Directions:
From I-495, take exit 11 onto MD 4S/Pennsylvania Avenue. Exit MD 4 onto MD 223/Woodyard Road. Follow Woodyard Road south. Melwood Pond is adjacent to the road.

Access Point: Parking lot next to the pond (38.80045,-76.825695)

Fish early in the season since the entire pond becomes clogged with underwater vegetation as the weather warms. It is the centerpiece of the Melwood Pond Community Park with a small parking area adjacent to Woodyard Road at the southern end of the lake.

As part of a formal park, it has manicured banks that offer universal, easy access with benches spaced periodically for those who enjoy throwing a bobber and waiting for a bite. The pond is shallow with no steep drop-offs from the bank. That said, the northern end is where the water is deepest adjacent to the outflow that feeds a tiny creek.

School House Pond

Approximate Boundary: 38.819342,-76.754299 to 38.820554,-76.750179 (4 acres)

Type: Put and Take

Directions:
From I-495, take exit 12 toward Richie Marlboro Road. Turn left on Old Marlboro Pike. Turn left on Elm Street. Turn left on Governor Oden Bowie Drive. Park on the side of the road.

Access Point: Roadside on Governor Oden Bowie Drive (38.818556,-76.751016)

Despite being in the center of Upper Marlboro across the street from the county administration building, School House Pond is a well developed fishing site. Twelve acres of parkland surround the pond and includes an extensive network of piers allowing anglers to walk far beyond the shore to fish the edges of the dense vegetation that grows thick from the northern bank. The piers extend for 0.75 miles along both the east and west shoreline. Outside of the piers, shoreline access is restricted to the south. While parkland borders the northern edge of the lake, dense underwater vegetation destroys the possibility of fishing from the shore.

In addition to the stocked trout, the lake holds a good population of largemouth bass and redear sunfish. For those who demand a bit of culture along with fishing, visit the Darnall's Chance House Museum adjacent to the pond. The museum provides insights into 18th-century life as seen through the eyes and property of Lettice Wardrop Thomson Sim who lived in the home prior to the American Revolution.

Tucker Pond

Approximate Boundary: 38.787832,-76.975838 to 38.78787,-76.97433 (1.7 acres)

Type: Put and Take

Directions:
From I-495, take exit 4A onto MD 414/St Barnabas Road heading south. Turn left onto Tucker Road and follow it for just under a mile. The park is on the left. Follow the Henson Creek Trail to the pond.

Access Point:
- Small lot on the south side of Bock Road east of Henson Creek (38.789982,-76.97146)
- Tucker Road Community Park (38.786218,-76.976953)

Whether you park on the east or the west, the Henson Creek Bike Trail will take you to the southern edge of the large pond. Like most stocked ponds in the State, it has a well manicured bank for easy access to the fishing. There are plenty of benches and picnic tables scattered around the perimeter that allow you to add picnicking to the day's activities. The west edge of the pond has a small fishing pier that juts into the lake.

Washington County

Antietam Creek

Approximate Boundary: 39.529922,-77.707041 to 39.534647,-77.709564 (1.16 miles)
DNR Guidance: Mainstem from upstream boundary of Devil's Backbone Park to the mouth of Beaver Creek.

Type: Put and Take

Directions:
North: From I-70, take exit 29 for MD 65S/Sharpsburg Pike. Turn left onto MD 68E/Lappans Road. Follow it to all the access points.

South: From I-270, take exit 32 to merge onto I-70W. Take exit 49 for US 40 Alt toward Middletown. Turn left onto MD 68W/Lappans Road. Follow it to all the access points.

Access Point:
- North Lot - Devils Backbone Park (39.538519,-77.710339)
- South Lot - Devils Backbone Park (39.540916,-77.712332)
- Turnoff on Lappans Road near mouth of Beaver Creek (39.535035,-77.709401)

Although Antietam Creek is not the most heavily stocked stream in Maryland, it probably has more stocked fish per mile than any other stream in the State. The DNR guarantees a continual supply of the fish by stocking weekly during the season. The nine acre Devils Backbone Park holds down the northern end and offers a superb facility full of picnic tables, manicured banks with paths and plenty of grass for the kids to roll around on.

The dam divides the park into two sections and backs up a wide, deep lake. With a robust flow plunging over the spillway, the stream carves a few deep channels through the lower park to terminate at a dark hole immediately above the bridge. There is no wading in Devils Backbone Park although, as you can see from the picture, it is not always enforced. Actually, the "no wading" rule is fine since access from the bank is universal and the stream is narrow enough to eliminate any need to get in the water. There is no similar restriction on wading downstream of the Lappans Road bridge.

Once the creek churns through the picturesque arches of the bridge to parallel Lappans Road, it widens to over 80 feet, running over a rocky bottom with plenty of riffles and a few gradient breaks to add interest. For anglers looking for a more solitary experience, it is an alternative to lining up shoulder to shoulder with everyone else in the heavily pressured park. That said, you will share the stream with other anglers during the season, but given the width of the creek, it will not feel as pressured. Resign yourself to moving in the creek since both banks are densely forested and wading is easier than negotiating the narrow, almost indistinguishable, trail on the eastern bank. At normal levels, the creek runs about three feet deep. In addition to the access point noted above, there are one or two small turnoffs between the bridge and the junction of Beaver Creek that may or may not be legal by the time you read this – be alert for any newly erected "no parking" signs.

Beaver Creek

Approximate Boundary:
- Top Section: 39.583341,-77.645007 to 39.587699,-77.640544 (2,169 feet)
- Fly Fishing Only Section: 39.580803,-77.653133 to 39.583341,-77.645007 (1.07 miles)
- Middle Section: 39.573385,-77.654201 to 39.578726,-77.655309 (1,843 feet)
- Lower Section:
  - 39.549953,-77.681667 to 39.551078,-77.67994 (1,039 feet)
  - 39.554511,-77.675101 to 39.558953,-77.672902 (2,700 feet)

DNR Guidance:
- Top Section: From the downstream side of the bridge on the farm lane located below the Albert Powell Trout Hatchery fence downstream to Black Rock Creek.
- Fly Fishing Only Section: From the confluence with Black Rock Creek downstream approximately one mile to a red post located 0.1 mile above Beaver Creek Road.
- Middle and Lower Section: Beaver Creek Road downstream to the confluence with Antietam Creek (sections of this creek are not accessible to the public).

Type: Put and Take/Fly Fishing Only

Directions:

Top Section:
- Take exit 35 from I-70. Turn south on MD 96 and take the first left onto Black Rock Road. Turn left on Country Store Lane. The parking lot is on the left. Walk between the houses to get to the creek.

Fly Fishing Only Section:
- Option 1: Take exit 35 from I-70. Turn south on MD 96 and take the first left onto Black Rock Road. Turn left on Country Store Lane. The parking lot is on the left. Walk between the houses to get to the creek.
- Option 2: Continue south on Mapleville. Turn right on Beaver Creek Road. Turn right on Beaver Creek Church Road. Go across the bridge and turn left. The parking area is on the right. Go through the gate (please latch) to access the creek.
- Option 3: Instead of turning right on Beaver Creek Church Road, continue. There is a fenced area on the right with a gap that opens into a spacious, grass covered parking area. Follow the trail (0.5 miles) to the creek. Fish upstream.

Middle Section:
- Option 1: Continue on Beaver Creek Road to the bridge. There is a two-car small turnout on Cool Hollow Road.
- Option 2: Follow Cool Hollow Road south to the junction with US 40. Turn east (left) and drive 100 yards. There is a wide shoulder and a gated dirt road on the right. Park and follow the road to the creek.

Lower Section:
- Option 1: From Boonsboro, drive north on US 40 (Old National Pike). North of Benevoia, turn left on Roxbury Road. There is a small turnout on the south side of the bridge
- Option 2: Continue on Old National Pike. Turn right on Toms Road. Make another right when it reaches the intersection (if you go straight, you will be on Lemuel Lane). Follow Toms Road to the bridge and park in the small turnout.

Access Point:
- Top Section: Parking lot on Country Store Lane (39.58294,-77.642764)
- Fly Fishing Only Section:
    o Parking lot on Country Store Lane (39.58294,-77.642764)
    o Parking lot on Beaver Creek Church Road (39.585907,-77.646352)
    o Parking lot on Beaver Creek Road (39.57794,-77.652872)
- Middle Section:
    o At the bridge on Beaver Creek Road (39.578764,-77.655464)
    o Shoulder of the road on the south side of US 40 (39.576926,-77.654539)
- Lower Section:
    o Toms Road bridge (39.554784,-77.675167)
    o Roxbury Road at bridge (39.551154,-77.682015)

In addition to offering plenty of put and take water, Beaver Creek is one of Maryland's premier fly fishing destinations as a result of 3,000 gallons of 52° alkaline water that emerges naturally each minute from Maryland's largest limestone spring. That flow supports year-round trout fishing for the biggest "hogs" east of Garrett County and west of the Gunpowder. The stream runs through farmland with minimal drop in elevation – there are no violent rapids or plunge pools to add sparkle and character to the creek. Instead, it meanders adjacent to open fields shaded by thick, tall trees. The streambed is a mix of rocks and silt with the silt becoming more prevalent farther downstream. A problem with Beaver Creek is inconsistent public access that requires anglers to be constantly alert for "posted" signs. If you have any questions about where to go or how to get there, check in at the Beaver Creek Fly Shop. They are consistently helpful and will know any current developments that impact accessibility to the stream.

Top Section

Fishing the top section is straightforward. The put and take area starts at the hatchery and runs down to a spot south of the I-70 bridge. Starting at the Beaver Creek Fly Shop, the good channel is initially on the right-hand bank with the deep water flipping to the left bank at the end of the row of houses. By the time the creek gets underneath the bridge, it widens and shallows. There are no access issues with the put and take section as long as you pay careful attention to where you walk and do not stomp on trees or other vegetation planted by the creek side landowners. As always, it is up to every angler to protect our permission to cross private land by being exceptionally respectful of property owners' rights.

Fly Fishing Only

The fly fishing only section begins downstream from the Beaver Creek Fly Shop and extends to within 700 feet of Beaver Creek Road. Fishing downstream into the fly fishing only section, there are no property issues until reaching the western bend in the river approximately 50 yards west of the Beaver Creek Church Road parking area (39.586211,-77.648183). The landowner has several "posted" signs dotting the landscape making the section immediately above a small bridge off-limits. From that bridge down to the start of the fly fishing only section, there are no other restrictions as of 2011. The low gradient translates to easy access, walking is effortless.

If you choose to park at the southern access point, there is a wide, manicured trail leading to an open field and the stream. There are plenty of signs to direct you around the private property. Once at the stream, another trail leads up the east bank for effortless walking to points upstream. One of the most popular spots is the deep pool at the sharp elbowed corner (39.583623,-77.651878). Once beyond the corner, move to the northern bank since there is a steep hillside on the southern bank that blocks passage (39.583176,-77.650103 to 39.584226,-77.646841).

Middle Section

Moving to the middle section below US 40, fishing becomes more difficult, especially for fly anglers. The banks are tall, gradually sloping and tightly hemmed in by packed vegetation. The combination of these characteristics make it difficult for a fly angler to launch an effective backcast. For them, fishing this section requires a well-developed roll cast. Spin and bait anglers will have no problem attacking the numerous deep holes near fallen structure along the bank. Given the thick vegetation, access to the creek is limited to the beaten trails made by generations of anglers pushing the vegetation aside. There are a few wide spots that offer salvation to those who find it difficult to fish when hemmed in by nature. These are obvious and easy to find along the perimeter of the field next to the stream.

This situation persists until reaching a gradient break marked by a island and a collapsed tree at 39.57303,-77.65394. Note this spot because the creek deepens on the other side. Shortly after, it goes through a sharp turn to dump into the deepest pool and also marks the end of public access. On the other side of the pool, "posted" signs appear – ending your downstream hike.

As a side comment, the DNR guidance states that the fishable area in the middle and lower sections include "Beaver Creek Road downstream to the confluence with Antietam Creek (*sections of this creek are not accessible to the public*)." While this is completely true, it implies that there are miles and miles of fishable creek. Instead, the "middle section" runs a short distance from US 40 and the property is private all the way to the lower section above Benevoia. Below the town, in the lower section, private property reoccurs all the way to the junction with Antietam Creek. In short, there is far more private property between the start point below the I-70 bridge and the junction than there is fishable water. Years ago, the fishable water included everything upstream from Newcomer Road. Not anymore. Given that, each angler must accept responsibility for being alert for "posted" property.

Lower Section

There are only two good access points to the lower section. The one off Roxbury Road has the best parking. The creek is narrow and rocky with a good, deep pool underneath the bridge. Below the bridge, heavily vegetated banks are the rule. Upstream, the public section ends at the US 40 bridge and at the southeast corner of the field downstream from the bridge.

The other access point is at the Toms Road bridge. The bridge runs over deep water that is a popular holding place for fish and even more popular destination for anglers. During the season, lures, flies and associated strands of monofilament decorate the bridge structure, confirming that this is one of the most heavily pressured sections of Beaver Creek.

Downstream is private property - no access - and is a sad story of inconsiderate anglers ruining a good thing. The landowner used to permit fishing until some anglers blocked the road into his dairy farm and, when the landowner asked the anglers to move their vehicles, they were rude to him. *Absolutely, spectacularly stupid!* Thanks to those jerks, we cannot fish below the bridge any longer. Above the bridge, the creek narrows with long portions being 6 inches deep. The fish will hide in the scattered locations that offer deeper water.

I am grateful to Mike, blogger at www.mikescatchreport.com, for providing some additional information I used to write this chapter.

Beaver Creek is the 21st most heavily stocked stream in the State.

Blairs Valley Lake

Approximate Boundary: 39.696081,-77.942423 to 39.702124,-77.942294 (32 acres)

Type: Put and Take

Directions:
From I-70, take exit 18 to merge onto MD 68W/Clear Spring Road. Turn left onto US 40W. Turn right onto Broadfording Road. Turn left onto Blairs Valley Road. Veer right to stay on Blairs Valley Road when the road forks. The left fork is Hanging Rock Road - do not take that fork.

Blairs Valley Road runs up the east side of the lake.

Access Point:
- Parking area below the dam (39.695839,-77.941144)
- Boat launch parking (39.697424,-77.940951)
- Northern marsh parking (39.701795,-77.941062)

Fed by the Conococheague Creek, the DNR constructed the 32 acre Blairs Valley Lake to provide habitat for waterfowl between 1967 and 1968, making an additional investment to complete needed repair work in 1997. In the process of making the repairs, most of the lake was drained with only five acres of water remaining. Since then, the DNR invested in the fishery, causing it to rebound and become a worthwhile destination.

Even though the lake is 18 feet deep near the dam, the DNR reports most fish can be found above 8 feet because of the excessive growth of phytoplankton depleting oxygen farther down. Despite that, in addition to stocked trout, the lake's vibrant warm water fishery includes bass, muskie and crappie, making it a popular spot mere feet from the border with Pennsylvania. The DNR permits boats with electric motors to use the free boat launch. Most of the shoreline is accessible except in the northern reaches where the lake merges into a marshland. As a result of the positioning of the lake inside the Indian Springs Wildlife Management Area, visitors can also take advantage of several trails leading to good birding locations. The area is also a popular hunting destination, so anglers should exercise caution and wear blaze orange during hunting season.

Blairs Valley Lake is the 24th most heavily stocked location in the State.

Greenbrier Lake

Approximate Boundary: 39.535611,-77.620622 to 39.541387,-77.616888 (42 acres)

Type: Put and Take

Directions:
East: From I-70, take exit 42 for MD 17N/Myersville Road. Myersville Road becomes Main Street. Turn right on Ellerton Road to make a left onto US 40W. Once past I-70, look for the entrance to the Greenbrier State Park on the left.

South: From I-70, take exit 35 for MD 66S/Mapleville Road. Resist the temptation to divert to Beaver Creek and continue on Mapleville Road to the intersection with US 40. Turn left and follow US 40 to the entrance to the Greenbrier State Park on the right.

Access Point:
- North end of the lake at the boat ramp (39.540998,-77.615834)
- Parking lot adjacent to the southern beach area (39.535915,-77.618614)

There is a fee to use the park, but the combination of a beach and fishing make it worth the price of admission. For those who would like to claim to have walked on the Appalachian Trail, they can do that here since the trail winds its way through the park, crossing Boonsboro Mountain Road to crawl along the ridgeline defined by Bartman's Hill (39.53496,-77.60791) and Pine Knob (39.5 4263,-77.59679) on the northern side of US 40.

In addition to being stocked with trout, the lake is a good summer fishing destination for those whose passion is bass. If you have a boat, the ramp is at the northern end of the lake on a short pipe stem inset to the east from the main body of water. The entire northern section, until you reach the main lake, is shallow with plenty of underwater vegetation. By the time you drift down to the boat rental at the upper end of the beach (39.539709,-77.617703) most of the vegetation disappears. There is no fishing off the beach, so to fish from the shoreline, you must follow the trail to the west side of the lake where the path winds between the trees and offers welcome shade on hot days.

Greenbrier Lake is the 18th most heavily stocked location in the State.

Indian Springs Pond

Approximate Boundary: 39.692684,-78.031271 to 39.693588,-78.030573 (1.3 acres)

Type: Put and Take

Directions:
East: From I-70, take exit 12 toward Indian Springs and merge onto MD 56W/Big Pool Road. Turn right on US 40E and go a short distance to turn left on Mooresville Road. Follow Mooresville Road to the pond on the right.

West: From I-70, take exit 9 (left exit) for US 40W. Follow US 40W (left turn after exiting) and turn right on Pectonville Road. Follow Pectonville Road to Mooresville Road. Turn right onto Mooresville and follow it to the pond on the left.

Access Point: Parking lot next to the pond off of Mooresville Road (39.693262,-78.029994)

The Indian Springs Pond is a small speck within the 6,400 acre Indian Springs Wildlife Management Area and is the second pond in the area, along with Greenbrier Lake, the DNR stocks with trout. There is a well defined path encircling the pond that frames the sharply sloping bank.

There is shallow water on the eastern and western sides with deep water all along the northern edge. The pond remains relatively clear even after a heavy rain. The greatest barrier to fishing is the thin ribbon of cattails growing adjacent to the shallow areas on the east and the west. Use them to determine where the shallower spots are. According to the information posted near the parking lot, gourmet cooks scour the landscape in this part of the wildlife management area for fresh, edible wild mushrooms.

Israel Creek

Approximate Boundary:
- Lower Section: 39.349407,-77.685626 to 39.353232,-77.685154 (1,419 feet)
- Upper Section: 39.357645,-77.683985 to 39.361129,-77.678116 (2,480 feet)

Type: Put and Take

Directions:
East: From Frederick, drive south on US 15. Merge onto US 340W and follow it past Brunswick to take the exit onto MD 67. Access the creek via Garretts Mill Road or Frog Eye Road.

South: From Leesburg, drive west on VA 7, turning onto VA 9 towards Harpers Ferry. In Mechanicsville, turn right on SR 671/Harpers Ferry Road and follow it to the junction with US 340. Go across the river and take the exit onto MD 67. Access the creek via Garretts Mill Road or Frog Eye Road.

Access Point:
- Valley Road bridge (39.349418,-77.685648)
- Garretts Mill Road bridge (39.352523,-77.685424)
- Frog Eye Road bridge (39.360835,-77.678665)

Israel Creek is a nondescript, small stream that runs through a rural setting. The fact that it is broken into two sections gives me the opportunity, once again, to emphasize that anglers must be aware of private property. This used to be a single unified stretch. Not that it matters much since the topography will keep the trout close to the road crossings that comprise the three access points. From Garretts Mill Road, turn left on Valley Road to reach the southernmost access point (fish upstream). There is enough parking for three or four vehicles on the west side of the bridge. Garretts Mill Road crosses the creek near a "residential" area with room for one vehicle to pull off the narrow shoulder on the east side of the creek (posted property begins 300 feet upstream of the bridge). The northernmost access point, Frog Eye Road, has limited parking next to the creek, but there is a shoulder a short distance to the west next to the cemetery (fish downstream since posted property begins 200 feet upstream of the road).

The creek is narrow and shallow, roaming 15 feet wide across a freestone bottom that is a mix of rocks and sand. The banks are congested and tight with vegetation that will make casting a challenge. There is no discernible trail on either side of the creek, bushwhacking required. Each of the access points features a pool near the crossing that will be the primary repository of the stocked fish. In general, the creek is easiest to fish from Valley Road moving upstream since the banks are not steep and the vegetation does not overlap the water. Frog Eye Road, on the other hand, is the most demanding section with dense bushes and branches stretching across and throwing shade onto the water below.

| Valley Road | Frog Eye Road |

Licking Creek

Approximate Boundary:
- Northern Section: 39.675902,-78.042759 to 39.67582,-78.039476 (1,253 ft)
- Southern Section: 39.669185,-78.043357 to 39.669376,-78.040364 (997 ft)

Type: Put and Take

Directions:
East: From I-70, take exit 12 onto MD 56/Big Pool Road heading north. Turn left onto US 40W. Turn right onto Pectonville Road immediately before US 40 merges into I-70. Follow Pectonville Road north to the Camp Harding Park. Go through the gate to the parking lots. Continue on Pectonville Road to the bridge to fish the northern section. Go across the bridge and turn right on the small dirt road to park along the creek.

West: From I-70, take exit 9 for US 40 toward Indian Springs (this exit is only available to eastbound traffic). Turn left onto US 40W. Turn right onto Pectonville Road immediately before US 40 merges into I-70. Follow Pectonville Road north to the Camp Harding Park. Go through the gate to the parking lot. Continue on Pectonville Road to the bridge to fish the northern section. Go across the bridge and turn right on the small dirt road to park along the creek.

Access Point:
- Bridge crossing for the northern section (39.675902,-78.042759)
- Camp Harding Park parking lot (39.669185,-78.043357)

Licking Creek is a broad, fast running stream with a rock and cobble bottom that starts above the Pectonville Road bridge, takes a break for posted property in the middle, and picks back up adjacent to the western boundary of the Camp Harding Park.

In the northern section, there is a small two car turnout on the south side of the bridge with better parking on the other side using the small dirt road that extends along most of the compressed public section. The road is narrow with limited ability to turn around at the end near the bridge. Be prepared to back your vehicle out if there are other cars blocking the turnaround. The only access to the creek is from the northern bank since the southern shore is a steep cliff face comprised of solid rock. There are two additional turnouts off Pectonville Road prior to reaching the "posted" sign that marks the end of the public section where the road turns north and moves away from the creek.

Downstream from bridge

Dirt access road

In the southern section, the creek forms the southern boundary of the Camp Harding Park. Fishing can be problematic given the steep bank. At the western end, it is precipitous with no opportunity to climb down safely to the water's edge. Thankfully, the distance between the water and the top of the bank drops moving east. There is easy access to fish from the manicured lawn, shaded by the tall trees that line the shoreline, once you move away from the western boundary. At the eastern end, there is a small trail leading to the end of the public section.

Downstream in park   Upstream in park

The park is open from the first Saturday in May through the last Sunday in October from 9 AM until sunset. Outside of the open season, the County permits walk-in access, but there is limited parking on the side of the road outside of the gate. The park includes pavilions, a playground, restrooms, picnic tables and everything else one would expect in a well developed and maintained public park. Of historical note is that the County named the park to commemorate the fact that President Warren G. Harding camped here in July 1921 with Thomas Edison, Henry Ford and Harvey Firestone.

Little Antietam Creek

Approximate Boundary: 39.483991,-77.70482 to 39.486259,-77.701462 (1,718 feet)
DNR Guidance: At Keedysville, from Coffman Farms Road downstream to MD 34.

Type: Youth and Blind

Directions:
East: From Frederick, take US 40 Alt W. Turn left onto MD 34W/Potomac Street. Once past the Fairview Cemetery, turn left on Coffman Farm Road.

West: From Hagerstown, take I-70 to exit 32A to merge onto US 40E. Turn right onto MD 66S/Mapleville Road. MD 66 joins US 40 in Boonsboro. Turn left onto US 40 followed by a right onto MD 34W/Potomac Street. Once past the Fairview Cemetery, turn left on Coffman Farm Road.

Access Point: East side of the Coffman Farm Road bridge (39.486259,-77.701462)

Probably best known for its proximity to the only publicly viewable cave complex in Maryland, Crystal Grottoes Caverns, the small town of Keedysville straddles Little Antietam Creek. Just to finish the story, the cavern complex was discovered by accident in 1920 when crews were mining limestone for road construction. According to the owners, the high and narrow limestone cave complex "has more formations per square foot than any cave known to man." Sadly, the limestone has not influenced the ability of Little Antietam Creek to maintain a trout population year-round farther downstream. There is, however, a sustaining population of wild trout to the north, near Smithsburg, where the DNR estimated the presence of 421 adult trout per kilometer in 2005.

The landowner, who graciously permits fishing, has a field that snugs up to the west side of the creek. This makes for easy walking to reach the edge of the water. Standing at the edge of the creek, all looks good. The creek runs 20 feet wide over a rocky bottom that offers up superb trout holding structure. There are plenty of deep holes between the rocky outcrops where some sand will collect along with the fish.

Since this is a youth and blind fishing area, be advised that banks are steep with a precipitous five to seven foot drop to the water. The eastern bank abuts a residential area; no access from that side. The easiest place to fish the stream is the pool on either side of the bridge. Although the northern side is not explicitly stocked, the fish will not be able to figure that out. Since the stream runs adjacent to a public park above the bridge that is the upper boundary of the restricted area, others can join in the fun on the park side of the bridge.

Rough banks midway down   View back to bridge

The Caverns? They are two miles north of town on MD 34.

Little Tonoloway Creek

Approximate Boundary: 39.707984,-78.199657 to 39.70592,-78.195602 (1,915 feet)

Type: Two trout per day

Directions:
East: From I-70 westbound out of Hagerstown, take exit 1B onto US 522S toward Hancock. Turn onto MD 144/Hancock followed by a right toward Limestone Road. At the "T" intersection, turn left on Limestone followed by an immediate right onto Creek Road. Turn left on Kirk Farm Road and drive into the park.

West: From I-68 eastbound, take exit 77 onto MD 144E/Western Pike. Turn left onto Sandy Mile Road. Immediately after crossing over I-68, turn right on Creek Road. Turn right on Kirk Farm Road and drive into the park.

Park at the bridge over the creek or continue across to the baseball field.

Access Point: Kirk Farm Road in the park (39.707868,-78.199764)

The stocked section starts downstream of the bridge. The best way to attack the water is to drive across the bridge and park near the ball field. Walk around the field to the downstream border of the park and fish upstream. The southern bank, the one next to the ball field, is accessible although there can be sharp drops from the bank to the water level. The northern side backs up on a steep, red dirt hill that prevents all approach from the north until the stream runs through "left field." Shortly after the creek takes a sharp turn to the west, it bisects two open fields that offer lateral access ending at the small footbridge connecting the two halves of the park. West of the footbridge, fish from the northern bank as a result of the heavy vegetation and rock cliffs.

The creek is a typical western Maryland freestone stream with a rocky bottom that features small, unobtrusive boulders and mixed cobble. Although mostly level, there are a few riffles to provide interest as the stream drops slightly in elevation, about 15 feet, from west to east. Typically, the bends hold deep water and fish.

Since it will not take long to fish the stream, you may want to build in a visit to the Fort Frederick State Park and its well-known lake called "big pool." It is a 14 mile drive from the creek south to the 585 acre park. The park provides a unique venue that allows visitors to gain a perspective on colonial history - made even better by the opportunity to chase bass in the lake or in the nearby Potomac River. Beyond fishing, the park offers plenty of historical programs to include an 18th Century Market Fair in late April, artillery demonstrations as well as other educational, *yet still interesting*, activities.

Little Tonoloway Creek (Widmyer Park)

Approximate Boundary: 39.701461,-78.188819 to 39.700057,-78.18707 (1,200 feet)
DNR Guidance: Within Widmyer Park in Hancock.

Type: Youth and Blind

Directions:
East: From I-70 westbound out of Hagerstown, take exit 1B onto US 522S toward Hancock. Turn onto MD 144/Hancock followed by a right toward Limestone Road. At the "T" intersection, turn left on Limestone followed by an immediate right onto Creek Road. Turn left on Park Road. The park entrance is on the south side of the creek.

West: From I-68 eastbound, take exit 77 onto MD 144E/Western Pike. Turn left onto Sandy Mile Road. Immediately after crossing over I-68, turn right on Creek Road. Turn right on Park Road. The park entrance is on the south side of the creek.

Access Point: Parking areas in Widmyer Park (39.701604,-78.189049)

According to the DNR written description, the youth and blind fishing area runs from one end of the park to the other. If you go to the DNR website (as of 2011) to view the limits, there is an error since the drawn eastern boundary ends at Park Road instead of extending all the way to the eastern end of the park (W Main Street). Therefore, do not rely on the boundary displayed on Google Maps and obey the signs posted throughout the park.

At the western end, the stocked area starts at the dam that creates a deep backwater adjacent to the baseball field. The grass is mowed all the way up to the edge, permitting easy access for even the smallest children. After flowing over the dam, the water runs through a small drop in elevation, increasing velocity and providing some small scenic interest mitigated by the built-up area looming over the southern bank. The stream moves at a good pace under Park Road to slow down into a deep pool starting where the creek takes an abrupt turn to the south next to a picnic pavilion.

The southern bank is packed with picnic equipment, a public swimming pool and other kid friendly recreational activities that amplify the experience of taking a young child fishing. If they get bored with the on-stream action, pop them onto the playground equipment so they can burn out excess energy.

Pangborn Pond

Approximate Boundary: 39.649371,-77.701849 to 39.650247,-77.701573 (0.8 acres)

Type: Youth, Senior or Blind

Directions:
North: from I-81, take exit 6 onto US 40E toward Hagerstown. Turn left onto N Locust Street. Turn right onto Fairground Avenue. Turn left onto N Mulberry Street. Turn right on Manila Avenue. Manila turns into View Street. Turn right on Pangborn Boulevard and follow it to the park and the pond.

South: From I-70, take exit 32 onto US 40W toward Hagerstown. Turn right on Eastern Boulevard. Turn left on MD 64W/Jefferson Boulevard. Turn right onto Pangborn Boulevard and follow it the park and the pond.

Access Point: Park along Pangborn Boulevard (39.650149,-77.700188)

If any pond in the State has perfect accessibility, it is this one. It is surrounded by an asphalt path separated by a thin strip of manicured grass from the concreted shoreline. Beyond the shallow northern edge, the depth is uniform and vegetation free. Once the kids get tired of fishing, they can take advantage of the children's playground and picnic area adjacent to the water.

Sharpsburg Pond

Approximate Boundary: 39.456488,-77.743453 to 39.455885,-77.742399 (1 acre)

Type: Put and Take

Directions:
North: From I-70, take exit 29 for MD 65S towards Sharpsburg. It becomes S Church Street in the town. Turn left onto E High Street and follow it to the parking area at the north end of the pond.

From Frederick, go west on US 40. Turn left onto MD 34W/Potomac Street in Boonsboro and head towards Sharpsburg. Turn left onto S Church Street. Turn left onto E High Street and follow it to the parking area at the north end of the pond.

South: From Northern Virginia, head toward Shepherdstown, WV on WV 230. Continue onto W Washington Street in the town and turn right onto WV 480N/S Duke Street. Go across the river into Maryland where the road becomes MD 34E. Turn right onto S Church Street. Turn left onto E High Street and follow it to the parking area at the north end of the pond.

Access Point: Parking lot north of the pond off E High Street (39.456667,-77.743556)

The elongated Sharpsburg pond huddles on the western side of the Antietam Battlefield. On a misty morning, one can almost hear the ghostly staccato roar of musket fire and the pulsing shockwaves of artillery still echoing off the gentle hills - remnants of the brutal day on September 17, 1862 when 450 Georgia sharpshooters held off 12,000 Union troops at the Burnside Bridge just east of the pond. Thankfully, the 150 years since have dimmed the passion that was at the root of the battle, leaving us to enjoy our peaceful pastime.

Identical to many of the other small ponds in the State, it features a manicured bank that surrounds a shallow pond whose perimeter is sprinkled with picnic tables and benches. During the season, there is usually a portable toilet plopped at the left edge of the parking lot. As the season progresses, so does the growth of underwater vegetation. Since the east and west ends of the pond experience the most significant growth, focus your attention on the center.

Do not let the small size dissuade you from throwing a lure in the summer if you happen to be passing by. Bass up to five pounds have been caught from here as recently as 2009. Another option is to exploit three miles of Antietam Creek as it winds through the battlefield. It is open to anglers, offering plenty of opportunity to catch smallmouth bass. The only restriction is that the park prohibits fishing within 500 feet of the Burnside Bridge. Below the bridge, there is a mile long foot trail providing good access.

Sideling Hill Creek

Approximate Boundary: 39.648668,-78.345873 to 39.708451,-78.330209 (11.22 miles)

Type: Put and Take

Directions:
From I-68, take exit 72.

High Germany Road: At the exit, drive a short distance north on High Germany Road and turn right into the Nature Conservancy parking area on the north side of the bridge.

The following directions assume you are at the intersection of High Germany Road and US 40 on the south side of I-68.

McFarland Road: Turn left to drive east on US 40. US 40 becomes McFarland Road. Follow it to the bridge over the creek. There are small parking areas on the right on either side of the bridge.

Whitfield Road NE: Turn left on US 40 followed by an immediate right onto Swain Road. Turn left onto Whitfield Road NE and follow it to a fork in the road. Take the right fork onto the dirt track. You have an opportunity to make a wrong turn to the right when the dirt road forks at 39.68647,-78.32402. Stay to the left, heading east.

Harry Norris Road: Turn left on US 40 followed by an immediate right onto Swain Road. Turn right on Swain Hollow Road NE. Turn right again on Harry Norris Road. There are several turnoffs as well as a Nature Conservancy parking area at the end of the road.

Cliff Road: Turn left on US 40 followed by an immediate right onto Swain Road. Turn right on Swain Hollow Road NE. At the junction with Harry Norris Road, continue to drive straight with the name of the road changing to Stotlemeyer Road. Eventually the road comes to a fork with Hoop Hole Road on the right and Cliff Road on the left. The parking is where Cliff Road rejoins the creek.

Allegany Line Road: Turn right on US 40. The road eventually changes its name to Turkey Farm Road NE. Follow Turkey Farm Road. Turn left on Orleans Road NE. Turn left on High Germany Road SE. Turn left on Ziegler Road. After crossing the bridge over the creek, turn left on Allegheny Line Road. There are several turnoffs on the left side of the road after it rejoins the creek.

Access Point:
- High Germany Road Bridge (39.708694,-78.331107)
- McFarland Road Bridge (39.700275,-78.317076)
- WMA off of Whitfield Road NE (39.685362,-78.31793)
- Harry Norris Road (39.67416,-78.34252)
- Cliff Road at creek (39.66111,-78.36264)
- Allegany Line Road turnouts (39.65338,-78.34123 to 39.653526,-78.342778)

Sideling Hill Creek winds its way through the 3,100 acre Sideling Hill Wildlife Management Area for most of its fishable distance.

High Germany/McFarland Road

The creek runs adjacent to Nature Conservancy property that holds down the north bank of the stream and is off limits to fishing for the first 1,600 feet downstream from the New Germany Road bridge. The better approach is to go to the defined parking area off McFarland Road and fish upstream or downstream from there to avoid violating the Nature Conservancy restriction. Interestingly enough, the sign posted in the Nature Conservancy parking area indicates that the 400 feet upstream from the bridge has public access for fishing even though the DNR map indicates that the stocked stretch ends downstream of the High Germany Road bridge. As of 2011, there was a DNR sign above the bridge reinforcing that message. Accessible private property borders both sides of the river at the McFarland Road access point.

The section between the New Germany Road bridge and McFarlane Road features steep banks. Remember, no fishing from the northern bank. At the first McFarlane Road parking lot, there is a faint fisherman's trail that moves in both directions on the western bank. Even if you park in the larger lot on the eastern side, the better access is from the west since a steep cliff begins just downstream that closes out progress in that direction.

Wildlife Management Area

The next spot downstream is in the Wildlife Management Area at the end of the dirt road that branches to the right off of Whitfield Road. Unless it has been graded and improved, this is a rugged, rough road. Do not be deceived by the fact that it looks gentle as it makes the initial right into the Wildlife Management Area. Conditions change quickly and it becomes deeply rutted. At the end of the dirt road, there is a spacious parking lot that will accommodate approximately 10 vehicles. Walk through the yellow gate restricting vehicular access to the creek and stay to the right along the faint road to avoid the "posted" property on the left. The road defines the general boundary of the Wildlife Management Area. The creek is a quarter-mile walk, with a gentle 30 foot vertical drop, away from the parking area. Like it was upstream, wading access continues to be restricted to the western shore. The vertical Sideling Hill Ridge rises dramatically on the eastern side. These pictures were taken at high water.

Harry Norris Road

At Harry Norris Road, access is easier from the turnoffs adjacent to the creek. After turning onto the road, it leads to a hillside overlooking the creek. Do not stop there, instead, drive past an old gate and begin fishing where there are some wooden posts on the left-hand side of the road. Alternatively, continue down to the Nature Conservancy parking lot adjacent to the old Riser Road ford. The banks are steep above and below Harry Norris Road, so be prepared to wade unless you want to fish from the bank next to your vehicle. After disappearing in the immediate area of the road, steep cliffs continue a few hundred yards downstream on the eastern bank and create some dramatic fast water around a rocky bend. After that burst of excitement, the creek levels out, becomes 50 feet wide and runs smoothly into the distance. Rocks predominate as the subsurface structure. Private property borders each side of the road until the creek turns to the east at 39.667297,-78.335248. There is a small game trail on the western bank that leads to a shallow spot where you can wade across. A four-wheel-drive vehicle is not required on this dirt road. Even though I discuss two additional access points below, I do not believe they are actively stocked.

Cliff Road

The Cliff Road access point is at the western side of the Green Ridge State Park. There is a small turnout next to an old concrete slab. Here, the general typography reverses itself with steep cliffs being on the west bank heading upstream. Downstream from the concrete pad, Green Ridge Park property continues on the western side with easy access via gentle banks. A word of caution for those who do not have four-wheel-drive. Farther south, Cliff Road moves up a narrow, slick track next to a steep cliff that may be a tough climb in a normal vehicle.

Allegheny Line Road

The final area of the creek to explore is off of Allegheny Line Road on the east bank of the stream inside of the Sideling Hill Wildlife Management Area proper. The road is rough, but negotiable without a four-wheel-drive. After driving along a high ridgeline that makes access to the creek impossible, the road eventually drops back down to parallel the water. There is a 700 foot section that offers turnouts and easy access via a low bank. There are several campsites marked by fire rings as well. Even though the Wildlife Management Area extends in all directions to the east, do not drive any farther since the dirt road does not return to the water.

Sideling Hill Creek is the 23rd most heavily stocked stream in the State.

CPSIA information can be obtained
at www.ICGtesting.com
Printed in the USA
LVHW061819180222
711491LV00008B/273

9 780982 396285